INTERIORS

INTERIORS

THE HOME SINCE 1700

STEVEN PARISSIEN

LAURENCE KING PUBLISHING

CONTENTS

INTRODUCTION

Interiors and the Designer

Best age, when all men may procure
The title of a connoisseur...

(Robert Lloyd, 1759)

Opposite. A reproduced floorcloth is glimpsed through the doorway of this well-to-do early eighteenth-century house (Pallant House in Chichester, Sussex), painted in imitation of tessellated marble. The walls are appropriately painted in shades of that ubiquitous Georgian finish, 'stone'. Floorcloths were popular in all but the grandest houses until the mid-nineteenth century.

Right. Early electric fittings borrowed existing lighting terminology to lend an aura of reliability and familiarity. This example, from the 1890s, cites both the candle and the well-known Argand oil lamp.

W hat is interior design? Is it to do with the mere design and placement of objects? Or is it more about us than the elements we are buying and arranging; interior design as either, in the words of pioneer decorator Elsie de Wolfe, a mirror to our individual 'temperaments, habits [and] inclinations' or, as rephrased by two modern design critics, 'a tangible record of values, technology, economics, regionalism and genius of ... evolving culture'?[1]

Interiors can, as historian Stephen Calloway has noted, be intended 'variously to shock or reassure, strike an avant-garde note or underline the establishment values and social position of the owner, or simply be comfortable and pleasing'.[2] No one denies that domestic interiors have always been a way of demonstrating the social position and aspiration of the home's adult inhabitants: 'As domestic environments have come to be regarded as signs of the occupants' characters, people have gone to great lengths to present a satisfactory account of themselves.'[3] The principal goal in determining how the home was ordered and decorated was, at least until the middle of the twentieth century, comfort. This was seamlessly blended with the love of display, both for the sake of aesthetics and to impress others, and the perceived need to demonstrate an appreciation of novelty and innovation. The householder-consumer has always shown that he or she is effortlessly familiar with the latest styles and technologies: no one likes to be laughed at as out of date.

The balance between the supposed aims of interior design has always been skewed in different ways across the globe. The pursuit of comfort has, for example, always been regarded as an especially Anglo-Saxon trait, while the quest for fashionability has often, rightly or wrongly, been identified with France, Italy and the Scandinavian countries. And comfort and display have not always sat easily together, a disparity particularly evident in the radical Modernist interiors of the 1920s and 1930s. Yet for most homes, even in the supposed heyday of Modernism, very few technological innovations made their way into 'domestic spaces where comfort and display were uppermost'.[4]

For far too long, 'design' in general, and 'interior design' in particular, has been associated only with the later nineteenth and twentieth centuries. As David Lowenthal observed, historical perspective is vital if we are not to indulge in an understandable, if unhelpful, over-emphasis on the achievements and advances of our own time: 'Have television, computers, nuclear power, and space flights altered life more in our time,' he asked, 'than ... the railroads, gaslights, steamships, telegraph, factory-made clothing, and household goods that transformed the Western world between 1800 and 1860?'[5]

As one recent commentator has noted, the history of design 'used to start with the Great Exhibition and William Morris in the 1850s', with anything prior to the 1850s (and, indeed, anything that was not deemed 'forward-looking') being wholly ignored.[6] Nikolaus Pevsner's hugely influential *Pioneers of Modern Design*, originally published in the thrilling Modernist dawn of 1936,

The Egyptian Drawing Room at Thomas Hope's home at Duchess Street, London, drawn in Hope's characteristically spare, ascetic style. In 1807 Hope coined the term 'Interior Decoration'.

is perhaps the best-known example of this tendency. Pevsner blamed the machine for stamping out taste and for 'irremediably poisoning the surviving craftsmen', something that even William Morris had been careful not to do. In historian Adrian Forty's opinion, 'It has long been the convention to see mid-Victorian design as degenerate and to blame this on the introduction of machine manufacture', together with 'the British workman's ignorance and lack of artistic ability'. It is also revealing that, of the professionals singled out for praise in Pevsner's Pioneers, almost all of them were male architects.[7]

The history of interior design has for decades been seen much as Pevsner painted it in the 1930s, through the Modernist end of the telescope. Today, as we are able to enjoy and exploit the celebration of global eclecticism and technological autonomy of the twenty-first century – giving us the freedom 'to be innovative as well as to copy, to play with styles rather than to imitate them in a pedantic or slavish manner, and to mix together the old and the new' – the impact of Modernism has receded. Christopher Wilk's stunning Victoria and Albert Museum exhibition of 2006 on the subject rightly emphasised the style's immense influence. At the same time, it carefully avoided the undue hagiography of the movement's progenitors and demonstrated that its pioneers had feet of clay, just like any other artists. Perhaps the greatest lesson from the exhibition, however, was simply how dated both the theories and the products of Modernism look today. One might even agree with Calloway's justifiably provocative view that 'now that we view the Modern movement more historically and in the light of a greater range of alternatives which now flourish, we may well come to see *Modernismus* to some degree as just another historic style'.[8]

Most of the studies written on the subject of interior design history have followed the same path as Pevsner's. Far too much attention has been given to the great and the good, and the handful of properties they helped to create. And this has invariably been at the expense of the homes, the furniture and the fittings that the majority of homeowners were buying – purchases which were rarely, for reasons of both cost and aesthetics, able to be included in the progressive canon. As Paul Greenhalgh has argued, 'the history of design can be seen as one of recurring tension between historical eclecticism and those ideologies which sought to replace it'.[9] A textbook of 1966 claimed that 'Until the modern era of mass-communication, fashions began among a small and influential minority ... From this point fashions filtered downwards, first to the bourgeoisie, denigrating in

the process, and finally to the poorest stratum of society, where they were crudely imitated in cheap materials,' the Regency and Victorian periods being subsequently (and very briefly) covered in a chapter labelled 'The Nineteenth-Century Debacle'.[10] (More recently, the same period has been written off as an era of 'mindless revivalism' – and this from a professed Victorian specialist.[11]) To one design historian writing in the 1980s, the 'horrors' of mid-nineteenth-century taste were entirely due to the middle classes' 'vulgarisation' of what the rich bourgeois and upper classes had achieved in previous decades: 'The machine now generalized, driving through the morass of ill-understood motifs and forms inherited from the past. The result was a vulgarity without precedent, and its impact was made even worse by mass-production.' The writer's remarkable, class-ridden conclusion was that industrial advance had 'resulted not in the better provision of better quality for all, but in generally poorer standards for the many'.[12] As always, it was mass-production, and the mass-consumer, who got the blame.

This is a different sort of book. It is not yet another retelling of the familiar gospel 'of the genesis, emergence and triumph of the Modern movement'.[13] It is about how the middle classes of the West were deciding to dispose and decorate their homes. The impact of industrialisation is crucial to the development of the average interior over the last three centuries, and is consequently the principal theme of this book. In this tale of the impact of technology on everyday interiors, the crisis comes neatly in the middle of our 300-year period: the Great Exhibition of 1851, focusing as it did on new technologies and the potential of manufacturing industry, represented a watershed in society's celebration of the machine. The next 150 years have been largely about how we have dealt with that dichotomy: how to establish a precarious balance between craftsmanship, 'taste' and the benefits of mass-manufacture.

The effect of mechanisation on the home cannot be underestimated. Mass-production robbed the craftsman of individual decision and input; once the process had begun, he or she could not alter the product. Thus it was the initial design that went into the manufacturing process, rather than how that process was developed, that became of key importance. This is a concept with which we are still wrestling.

The book is also about upward mobility, and about homeowners being able to enjoy the fruits of the industrial revolution without guilt, and without condescension from others. Technological advance meant that what was seen by most householders at the beginning of the eighteenth century as an inaccessible luxury was, a hundred (or even fifty) years later, wholly attainable. An English writer of 1835, for example, reported that a typical peasant cottage was now as well furnished as that of a respectable tradesman had been in 1775.[14] Such observations were indeed common throughout the nineteenth century.

Industrial advance also helped to liberate women, providing them with a specific arena – the home environment – that they could control and dispose. In late nineteenth-century Paris, for example, middle-class women were already recognised as a distinct consumer group, 'with the leisure time to visit the great Parisian shopping arcades and stores and the means to indulge their whims in purchases'.[15] Nevertheless, as we will see, the battle is far from won. Even a recent history of the subject has remarked that 'Traditional decorators may say, "Just leave out all the architects and tell us what the decorators did" – by which they mean women and traditionalism.'[16] It seems that the equating of women with the traditional and the unchallenging, first posited by the male design reformers of the 1860s, is still with us. Undoubtedly, in the 1980s historians and critics began to pay more attention to twentieth-century designers such as Eileen Gray, Ray Eames and Marion Dorn. However, such inclusions smacked distinctly of tokenism: were these female designers cited merely because they 'extended the modernist canon'?[17]

Since the dawn of the Arts and Crafts and Design Reform movements, the history of interior design has invariably been portrayed as a desperately serious, and intrinsically moral, battle between modernisers and home decorators – the latter being implicitly allied with unthinking superficiality or, on occasion, with cheats and fakers. Yet this image of an epic struggle between the forces of light and darkness hardly provides us with a representative picture of how the average home developed. Homeowners have, for a start, rarely adhered to what design historians have declared they should be buying. Few middle-class homeowners in the 1920s or 1930s wanted, or indeed could afford, a Breuer or Mies chair. (As one history has dared to ask: 'Why have the designs of innovators often been so uncomfortable?'[18]) The triumphant emergence of Art Deco after the 1925 Paris Exposition, contrasted with the lukewarm reception for the early products of the Modern Movement (see below, Chapter 10), is one example of the public going one way while the headlines of design history have gone another. It is time to reconcile the two.

This is not a tale of big-name male designers, nor of the styles propagated by the great mansions and palaces. Many of the architects who traditionally feature in histories of interior decoration are barely mentioned. Nor are studios or groups that have contributed little to the development of the average home. This is a story of what you and I might have done, had we been there.

Opposite. The average eclectic twentieth-century interior generally flew in the face of design historians' paeans to the virtues of unadulterated Modernism. Here a well-stuffed, Victorian-style armchair sits comfortably in a refurbished nineteenth-century terraced house which combines a Modernist preference for bare, white surfaces and Art Deco touches. The location is London's highly fashionable Notting Hill. (Apartment by Kallosturin Architects; 'Burnt Chair' by Marcel Wanders and Cappellini.)

1. Quoted in Joanna Banham, Sally McDonald and Julia Porter, *Victorian Interior Design* (1991), 12; Allen Tate and C. Ray Smith, *Interior Design in the Twentieth Century* (1986), xx. 2. Stephen Calloway, *Twentieth-Century Decoration* (1988), 13. 3. Penny Sparke, *An Introduction to Design and Culture* (2004), 58; Adrian Forty, *Objects of Desire* (1986), 106. 4. Penny Sparke, *As Long As It's Pink – The Sexual Politics of Taste* (1995), 47. 5. David Lowenthal, *The Heritage Crusade and the Spoils of History* (1998), 8. 6. Charles Newton, *Victorian Designs for the Home* (1999), 2. 7. Forty, *Objects of Desire*, 42, 60. 8. Calloway, *Twentieth-Century Decoration*, 27, 158. 9. Paul Greenhalgh, *Ephemeral Vistas* (1988), 160. 10. George Savage, *A Concise History of Interior Decoration* (1966), 11, 225. 11. Jeremy Cooper, *Victorian and Edwardian Furniture and Interiors* (1987), 24. 12. Charles McCorquodale, *The History of Interior Decoration* (1983), 181. 13. Calloway, *Twentieth-Century Decoration*, 27. 14. Mary Schoeser and Celia Rufey, *English and American Textiles from 1790 to the Present* (1989), 73. 15. Calloway, *Twentieth-Century Decoration*, 33. 16. Tate and Smith, *Interior Design in the Twentieth Century*, xxi. 17. Brenda Martin and Penny Sparke (eds.), *Women's Places: Architecture and Design 1860–1960* (2002), xi. 18. Tate and Smith, *Interior Design in the Twentieth Century*, 558.

THE WIND OF CHANGE

The European Home in 1700

By looking at the exterior of a building, one should be able to see how it is distributed inside.

(Nicolas Le Camus de Mezières)

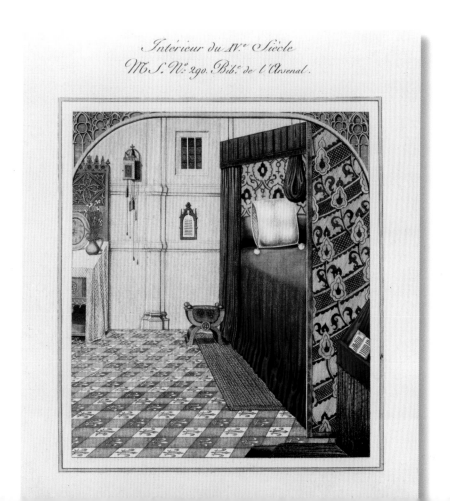

Intérieur du IV.ᵉ Siècle
M.S. N.º 290. Bib.ᵉ de l'Arsenal.

Opposite. A Dutch interior of *c.*1662: *Boy Bringing Pomegranates* (oil on canvas; Wallace Collection, London) by Peter de Hooch (1629–84). Notwithstanding the plain plastered walls, hard-wearing marble floors would have been a symbol of wealth and status.

Left. A recreated 'fifteenth-century' French interior from Amedée Perée's *Monuments Français* of 1839 (colour lithograph). Perée's colourful work remained an important source book for the Gothic Revival in France for decades. A fitted carpet, a fashionable X-frame stool and the bright fabrics used for the bed all suggest a well-to-do household.

Our media-driven image of the Late Renaissance and Baroque periods is one of graceful homes, impeccable manners and social inflexibility. It is also one of unchanging habits and primitive environments. But in reality, the benefits of the industrial revolution began to be enjoyed well before the nineteenth century, with which it is popularly associated. Even in the age of Louis XIV, the average house was a crucible of industrial advance and social aspiration.

Technology had indeed exerted a critical influence on the seventeenth-century home. New materials introduced during the sixteenth and seventeenth centuries substantially changed how the average interior was used and disposed. The increasing use of internal brick house partitions and external brick

or stone walls in Northern Europe, for example, allowed for better structural strength, improved insulation, greater and more elaborate use of interior plasterwork and more effective protection against fire.

The fear of fire was understandably endemic in the homes of 1700. The Great Fire of London of 1666 was by no means the only conflagration of its time: houses, streets, towns and cities, comprised largely of wood-faced houses and lit only by naked rushlights or candles, burnt down with depressing regularity. By 1700 the penny had finally dropped, and across Northern European towns most newbuild of any pretension was being executed, or at least faced, in fire-resistant brick or stone rather than inflammable wood. The London building acts of 1667–1709 explicitly forbade the construction of wooden eaves and cornices, and demanded that wooden windows be recessed at least four and a half inches behind the face of masonry walls. By 1698 the indefatigable traveller and diarist Celia Fiennes was observing that even the city of Nottingham was 'built of stone and delicate and are long Streetes much like London and the houses lofty and well built', and that it possessed two avenues of masonry-faced homes 'much like Holborn'. Even in the sleepy Welsh town of Hawarden she found 'a very fine new built house of brick and in the exact form of the London architecture'.[1]

This shift in attitudes was apparent inside, too. The increasing use of coal in Northern Europe in the seventeenth century prompted numerous innovations in fireplace technology.

Left. A simple iron rushlight of the type common throughout the Western world by 1700. This would have held a rush taper dipped in wax.

Above. Candle-making in Early Modern France. From volume 1 of Denis Diderot's invaluable *Encyclopédie, ou dictionnaire raisonné des sciences, des arts et des métiers*, published in 28 volumes from 1751.

Below. A wood-panelled, middle-class living room of *c.*1710 in Holland House, Barnstaple, Devon. Note the flat chimney surround: chimneypieces only thrust forward into the room from the 1720s.

There was a growing awareness that size was not, after all, everything: the bigger the chimneypiece opening, it was gradually being realised, the more heat was wasted up the flue. The fireplace aperture was thus diminished, and the chimneypiece thrust into the room as a decorative as well as a highly functional wall fitting, a development which significantly altered the orientation and decoration of principal rooms.

Coal was the engine of the technological revolution, its increasing use allowing for all manner of home improvements. In the early seventeenth century, James I of England (and VI of Scotland) ordered that coal be used for industrial purposes in place of wood – a measure derived largely, it has to be admitted, not from a messianic vision

of Victorian Britain but from a wish to preserve rapidly diminishing wood stocks in the south-east. Crucially, the use of coal rather than wood fuel produced hotter kiln temperatures; this in turn

Right. A marble chimney surround of the eighteenth century from the Joseph Pitkin House of 1723 in East Hartford, Connecticut (now in the Wadsworth Atheneum Museum of Art, Hartford, Connecticut). Marbling was particularly common in the seventeenth century, but by the mid-eighteenth had fallen temporarily out of favour across America and Europe.

Opposite. A wooden grid of leaded window-lights, typical of the sixteenth and seventeenth centuries (and known locally as 'the Armada Window'), at Sutton House, Hackney. Although out of date in 1700, in that year it was relocated to its current site.

helped foster a number of important breakthroughs in the manufacture of construction materials. Bricks could now be made faster and harder, which meant that they were more resilient to load-bearing stresses and to climate change. Higher temperatures also helped the development of the glass industry: by 1700 domestic glass was no longer a rarity in the windows and on the tables of European homes, while after 1665 Parisian glassmakers excelled at producing ever-larger (if still vastly expensive) wall mirrors.

Perhaps most importantly, the coal-fired furnace also enabled the greater use of iron in the home. Cast iron could increasingly be employed in a load-bearing role, rather than being

seen as a largely ornamental addition, as wrought iron had been. The resulting metamorphosis of the home over the next century was considerable.

Wrought iron – obtained by heating iron ore in a furnace and then hammering the resulting metal – had first appeared about 2000 BC, and had reached Europe around 500 BC. In Belgium in the early thirteenth century a primitive type of blast furnace had been developed, in which 'pigs' of what was effectively 'cast iron' (properly, an alloy of iron and carbon) were produced, by smelting the iron ore with charcoal, and later re-melted and converted to wrought iron by the removal of the carbon. Such archaic, charcoal-fired furnaces were still very common in 1700. In 1709, however,

Facciata del secondo muro della stanza

C. Meyer Inv.

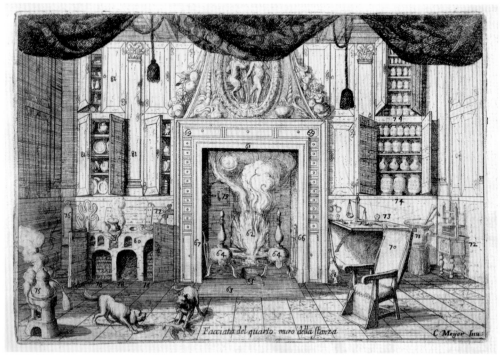

Facciata del quarto muro della stanza

C. Meyer Inv.

the Englishman Abraham Darby established the Coalbrookdale Company in Shropshire, and used coke instead of charcoal to smelt the ore. Modern cast iron was born.

By 1700 wrought iron was still used for gates and railings – a very recent innovation – as well as for door furniture. In 1600 the medieval wrought-iron strap hinge was still extremely common, but during the seventeenth century the classic door latch appeared in Northern Europe – a product (termed a 'Norfolk' or 'Suffolk' latch in Britain and its American colonies) which proved perennially popular and was easily adapted for mass-production in the mid-nineteenth century. The years following Louis XIV's repeal of the Edict of Nantes in 1685 saw a flood of artisans coming to the Protestant capitals of Europe, and the result was a flowering of domestic ironwork and the burgeoning of the metalwork trades – all, as Colbert predicted, at France's expense.

The development of the sash window in Britain, Holland and their American colonies during the late seventeenth century also added a degree of sophisticated climate control to the interior. Single-hung sashes were actually invented by the French in the middle of the century; however, they were, it seems, soon abandoned by their progenitors, and taken up instead by their Protestant neighbours to the north. Britons developed the form into a double-hung sash window, both frames supported by cord-hung lead weights suspended in wooden boxes or, in less urbane contexts, propped up by wooden pegs or blocks. This arrangement

allowed the householder to control the throughflow of air around the home with greater accuracy than had been possible with the all-or-nothing approach of the casement. The result was an instant success – so much so that in 1696 William III's cash-strapped government slapped an iniquitous tax on the growing number of domestic windows.

While the exterior of the 1700 house was increasingly faced in masonry, the interior remained dominated by wood. However, even here there were considerable changes, as families began to think less of the exigencies of daily survival and more about the possibilities of display. Ceiling beams began to be hidden behind plaster; staircase balustrades became bolder and more orotund; wooden floors became less utilitarian – the French fashion for wooden parquet being exported to Britain and Germany in the 1660s. In seventeenth-century France, grander homes began to espouse the new fashion for an 'enfilade' of rooms, whose

Opposite. Plates from Cornelio Meyer's splendid *Nuovi Ritrovamenti divisi in due parti* and, below, his *Book of Knowledge*, both of 1696, showing a kitchen and living room with oversized fireplace, all in marvellous monochromatic detail.

Below. Wooden parquet flooring of *c.*1690 at Ham House in Surrey. Hugely popular in middle-class homes at this time as an indicator of wealth and taste, parquet floors receded as the fitted carpet spread across the floors of the mid-eighteenth century.

doors lined up neatly along a well-fenestrated wall. Difficult to reproduce in the average town house, this mode nevertheless marked another promising step forward for the marriage of convenience and display.

The preceding century had also witnessed a revolution in internal colour. The medieval tradition had been to cover every element of the interior in bright hues. Recent academic research has indicated that medieval interiors were not, as is still often assumed, designed to reveal building materials to their best advantage, but were instead wholly covered in bright, piercing colour. As Eric Mercer has noted of the palaces of the sixteenth century, 'The only reason for leaving things unpainted seems to have been the physical impossibility of reaching it with a brush.'[2] Stone and wood surfaces, as well as plaster finishes, appear to have been treated in this manner. The Renaissance world, it seems, was by no means the pallid environment of exposed brick, unpainted wood and whitewashed plaster of popular myth.[3]

By 1700 this use of bright colour was replaced by a more sophisticated approach, combining the use of off-whites or bursts of colour with a general background of sombre wood colours. Green was, interestingly, the most popular colour for seventeenth-century New England interiors, and was frequently employed alongside red, yellow ochre and grey.[4]

The use of brown relief to complement off-white walls was still prevalent in Northern Europe by the 1650s. In 1659 Thomas Wilsford listed 'red oaker, umber, red and white lead'

as the common pigments of the time. By the 1670s, though, 'stone colour' was being regularly cited as the principal ingredient of any interior of fashion. 'Stone', incidentally, could denote a bewildering variety of shades, but generally signified a 'broken' white – white lead mixed with a little black and a little yellow ochre – designed to suggest the colour of expensive Portland stone. White lead paint itself comprised merely a mixture of white lead (a powder produced by steeping lead sheets in vinegar) and oil, generally nut oil, poppy oil or linseed oil; the latter was a far cheaper substance than the others, but was one which, unfortunately, tended to yellow with age. Whites and stone colours made with boiled linseed oil were even creamier, since the boiled product dried quickly but yellowed faster.

At the beginning of the seventeenth century, the whitewashing or limewashing of internal plaster walls

Opposite. An early eighteenth-century tall-backed chair, with caned seat and back, in the Painted Parlour at Canons Ashby, Northamptonshire. Note the painting of the fluted columns and wall panels: rarely would any Early Modern interior have been left as bare wood, except those executed in the finest oak or (from the 1720s) mahogany.

Left. Vertically operated 'festoon' curtains at Abbot Hall in Kendal, Cumbria. By 1740 these were becoming increasingly common in well-to-do households.

– particularly in poorer households or in servicing areas – was still common, the resulting areas of off-white being relieved by brown or red-brown woodwork. White was, though, soon promoted to a bigger role by those designers or decorators who sought to reflect the Italian classical tradition. In 1613, for example, Inigo Jones stipulated of a brick house of his design that 'all the pillasters, freezes, cornishe, windowes and frames' be 'fairely and cleanely finished white as is accustomed in buildings of a like nature'. Woodwork could still, however, be painted brown – a custom which survived throughout the Western world during the eighteenth and nineteenth centuries. Henti Louw has discovered evidence of windows being painted 'russett coloure' at the Lord Chamberlain's lodgings in Whitehall after 1607, a door of c.1618 at Sir Edward Cecil's house in the Strand being painted red-brown, and the windows at Queen

Henrietta Maria's residence at Oatlands in Surrey being painted 'timber cullor in oyle' in 1637.[5]

Internal timbers were still often daubed with red ochre. Rarely, if at all, were they painted black – the fashion for which appears to have been a late nineteenth-century innovation. Nor were they ever left bare, a modern conceit which derives from the Modern Movement's obsession with the 'honesty' of materials. Warm-toned and organic pigments such as those from the ochre family could be used in combination with simple whiting and red lead to obtain a variety of yellows, browns and reds.

Blues and greens were also available. However, paint colours derived from blue- and green-coloured pigments such as lapis lazuli and verdigris were generally highly expensive to manufacture and, while prevalent in well-funded ecclesiastical interiors, were

Splendid marbled plaster and woodwork of the early eighteenth century at the American Museum in Bath (the 'Perley Parlor', left) and Abbot Hall, Kendal (right).

not widely used in domestic contexts. Only with the technological advances of the late eighteenth century did such powerful pigments become common in humbler households. Lapis lazuli or smalt blue, to say nothing of gold leaf, were clearly not within the financial compass of many households, which had to make do with the simpler, cheaper colours obtained from natural earth pigments (yellows, reds and browns), from particular vegetable pigments (pinks and reds), and from basic animal products such as pig or ox blood. These, when used in combination with a variety of naturally produced ingredients (including animal dung), went to make the russet-brown that must have been such a common colour in humble interiors up until the French Revolution.

By the seventeenth century, a growing concern with display encouraged the painting of timbers in grander houses in imitation of expensive materials. In 1619, for example, Inigo Jones's Banqueting House in Whitehall in London, the first truly classical building to be completed in Britain, incorporated timber columns painted in imitation of marble and stone. The techniques of graining and marbling were indeed particularly widespread by 1700. Most interiors of any pretension were now panelled in deal (planks of fir or pine) or other cheap woods, which were then painted to mimic costly woods such as oak or walnut and subsequently usually varnished. Only the richest families could afford the real thing. Inevitably, however, it is the wealthy houses which have survived relatively intact, and which have provided modern-day decorators with inappropriately grandiose models. *Trompe l'œil* decoration, too, was increasingly employed in the wealthiest homes. Nevertheless, Sir Henry Wotton's *Elements of Architecture* of 1624 – the first down-to-earth building guide in the English

language – advocated simplicity, and denounced excessive ornament such as *trompe l'œil* painting in language which anticipates the Arts and Crafts prophets of 250 years later.

The 1700 house was still a predominantly brown environment. In that year the architect William Winde recommended painting closets, anterooms and bedchambers 'light walnut colour', specifying darker graining (with 'a glossey varnishe') for the larger rooms, which were invariably better lit. Wood panelling could also be painted white and 'marbled' – overpainted with a second and even a third colour, applied with a thin brush, to resemble foreign or native marbles. However, Winde denounced the practice of painting wainscots white alone. This finish would, he alleged, 'groe darke and in spotts'. He recommended instead 'wainscot colour', which presumably replicated the colour of walnut or oak.[6]

The brown nature of the average home was underlined by its furniture. Seat upholstery was for the wealthy; most could afford only simple wooden chairs, which could on occasion be cane- or rush-seated. Colourful upholstery, of leather or fabric, was reserved for the best dining room or living room seat furniture. Elsewhere, the family had to make do with simple, utilitarian designs such as the ubiquitous Dutch ladderback chair, later adapted by the British into the classic Windsor chair. Cupboards, wardrobes, chests, commodes and the like remained heavy and looming; they had to wait for the eighteenth-century cabinet-makers to elevate them to a starring

Left. Turned staircase balusters mirrored in paint on the corresponding wall at the Merchant's House in Marlborough, Wiltshire, of c.1660.

Below. The dining room at Packwood House, Warwickshire: a well-to-do interior of the mid-seventeenth century, showing a Cromwellian refectory table, Charles II chairs, window with seventeenth-century Flemish glass, and part of a large panel of Bargello needlework.

part in the standard room display.

Paints provided much of the colour relief in the average home. Curtains, where they existed, were exceedingly simple and strictly utilitarian. And luxury carpets were rarely found outside the great houses. By 1600 Turkish imports were being augmented by newer Persian designs; at the same time, the first attempts were being made to replicate Middle Eastern carpets in Europe. (Boughton House in Northamptonshire, for example, has four carpets of 1584–5, made in Britain but in a Turkish style.) Those who were fortunate enough to be able to afford imported Near Eastern carpets – there was as yet only negligible European manufacture of grander floorcoverings – used them principally as symbols of their wealth and status, and placed them more on dining tables and walls than on floors, where the muddy boots of the ignorant would soon reduce their value. As Pamela Clabburn has noted, as late as 1727 *Chambers' Cyclopaedia* defined the word 'carpet' as 'a sort of covering to be spread on a table, trunk, an astrade [dais]' and only, as a last resort, on a 'passage or floor'.[7]

Wallpaper, too, was rarely found in Europe or its colonies. Decorative papers appear to have originated in China around 400 AD; the earliest surviving European wallpapers, however, date only from the beginning of the sixteenth century. The oldest wallpaper yet discovered *in situ* in Britain dates from *c.*1509 and was found at the Master's Lodge at Christ's College, Cambridge. (The pattern of this Cambridge paper typifies the imitative

Right. The new fashions of the eighteenth century: floorcloth and stone colours at Pallant House in Chichester, Sussex.

character which wallpapers have always possessed: the stylised flower pattern is highly reminiscent of both Italian damasks and Spanish stamped leather hangings of the fifteenth century.) The earliest reference to a wallpaper in America has been found in the 1700 inventory of a Boston stationer.[8]

Most of the early European papers were based on simple black-and-white designs, featuring flowers, coats of arms and strapwork. Coloured papers do seem to have been used, but evidence for them is rare. Many of the black-and-white papers were given a colour wash after printing, the result being termed 'domino' paper.

Opposite. The common site for a carpet in the seventeenth century was on the table, not on the floor. Given that it had been imported from Persia or Turkey at great cost, such exquisite flatweave creations were status symbols to be afforded a prominent position in the room, not to be subjected to visitors' muddy boots. This Dutch view, *Woman Drinking with Soldiers* (oil on canvas; Louvre, Paris) by Peter de Hooch, is of 1658.

Even by 1700, wallpaper was still reasonably scarce and expensive. Thus papers were often printed on to the backs of book proof sheets or leaves of condemned titles, or even on to printed pages – the latter being usually used to line boxes or drawers. Lining spaces with inferior wallpaper is certainly not a new practice.

Patterns were either hand-painted, stencilled or, most frequently, printed using carved wood blocks. In block printing, the initial drawn pattern was committed to paper, which was then cut into small squares and the pattern transferred to pearwood blocks of the same size. The blocks were then hammered into place on the paper or set between two rollers fixed in a frame. To ensure that the pattern repeated correctly, successive blocks would be lined up with pin marks left by their predecessors on the paper. In 1691 William Bayley received government assistance for his invention of brass (as opposed to wood) printing blocks. However, little was subsequently heard of his invention, and metal pressing was not, as we will see, widely introduced until the second quarter of the nineteenth century.

After sunset it would, anyway, have been very difficult to see patterned papers. Simple dipped rushlights, or wax and tallow candles – the former for best, the latter far more widely used – were used sparingly to illuminate the average interior of 1700. (The price differential can be seen in a British statute of 1709, which taxed tallow at one-eighth the rate of wax.) All but the great houses of the period were very dimly lit by modern standards: the multi-branched candelabra beloved of modern TV period serials would, in most homes, have used up a month's worth of candles in one go. Generally, only one or two candles were used per room. Wax, too, was generally used only for grander public occasions. Its humbler relative, tallow, was unreliable, being prone to guttering and smoking, and smelt strongly of the sheep from which it had originated. Technology had come far in the past century, but had yet to revolutionise what could be done after dark.

---

1. C. Morris (ed.), *The Journeys of Celia Fiennes* (1947), 22 and *passim*. 2. Eric Mercer, *English Vernacular Houses* (1975), 36. 3. As the Victorians discovered to their delight, at the (now demolished) Deanery at Worcester, for example, the beams and much of the rest of the internal woodwork were apparently originally in bright blues and reds, with additional gilding to heighten the rich effect. More recently, evidence came to light suggesting that each panel of the 'Tudor' room at Sutton House in Hackney, East London, was decorated in a rich scheme of 'mahogany' red-brown, gold stars, cream and dark green – a vivid palette which, when applied to each of the linenfold panels which stretched from cornice to floor, must have been visually stunning. 4. Edgar de N. Mayhew and Minor Meyes, *A Documentary History of American Interiors* (1980), 10. 5. Henti Louw, 'Colour Combinations', in *The Architect's Journal*, 4 July 1990. 6. D.C. Barre and R.A. Chaplin (eds.), *William Winde: Advice on Fashionable Interior Decoration* (1983), 22. 7. Pamela Clabburn, *The National Trust Book of Furnishing Textiles* (1988), 37. 8. See Steven Parissien, *Palladian Style* (1994), 178.

Doors, windows are condemned by passing fools,

Who know not that they condemn Palladio's rules...

(John Gay, *Epistle to Paul Methuen*, 1720)

Opposite. By 1720 the chimneypiece was established as the visual centre of any sizeable public room in Northern Europe or North America. This fine example, from Peckover House in Wisbech, features elaborate moulded decoration. It does terminate uncomfortably near to the cornice, however, suggesting that it was not designed expressly for this room.

Right. Design for a tessellated marble floor from John Carwitham's highly original manual, *Various Kinds of Floor Decoration*, of 1739.

The proportional 'Palladian' interior that formed the basis for what is now generically known as the 'Georgian' or, in America, the 'Colonial' style was a peculiarly Anglo-Saxon phenomenon. As France and its imitators in Continental Europe persisted with the ever more excessive and lubricious forms of High Baroque and Rococo, Britons and Americans developed a restrained and formalised approach to architecture which deliberately eschewed the Rococo's flaunting of structure and expressed order, much in the way that Britain's Perpendicular Gothic style had reacted to the Flamboyant Gothic of the Continent three centuries before.

It is not hard to ascribe the appearance of Palladianism to the growth of national self-confidence and wealth. No longer did Britain have to rely on mimicking the forms of its traditional enemy, France. It could now go its own way, developing a style which celebrated the average villa or terraced home as much as the great house or royal palace. The Palladian revolution, effected when Lord Burlington and his disciples took over the royal Office of Works following the accession of George I in 1714, was part political accident – Burlington and his fellow Whigs were able to seize power in the wake of the accession, whose required general election witnessed the demolition of the Tories – and part expression of a wish to change the parameters of style and patronage after sixty years of Wrenian Baroque. But it is surely no accident that this coup was enacted only a year after the Treaty of Utrecht of 1713, which had ended the long and harrowing War of the Spanish Succession definitively in Britain's favour. The British were now firmly established in America, in the West Indies and in the Mediterranean. The trading benefits that resulted were soon felt in every British and colonial home.

The proportional system that dictated the Palladian or Georgian style was based on concepts of Order and Perfection, ideas central to the social structure and cultural aspirations of the eighteenth-century world. They also to some extent reflected the emerging national character of (to use de Gaulle's misleading but useful shorthand) the Anglo-Saxons. As Mario Praz has noted, Georgian interiors were characterised by 'affability... humanity and classic restraint', and governed by 'reason, the sense of proportion and elegance'. In contrast with the mellifluous excesses of French Rococo, Georgian chairs, for

example, 'imparted a lesson of sanity and balance'.[1]

The basis for Palladian or Georgian proportion was simple. It derived from the classical world's identification of mathematical rules which governed the earth and its universe. Apply these to architecture, the theory went, and you arrived at 'perfect' buildings. The Ancient Roman architect M. Vitruvius Pollio had written that 'Architecture depends on Order' which gave 'symmetrical agreement to the proportions of the whole'.[2] He looked to Nature for his inspiration; from the perfection of Nature he divined three fundamental criteria which all structures should meet, inside and outside: Utility, Strength and Beauty. Vitruvius's message was revived by the Renaissance and embodied by Italian architect Andrea Palladio (1508–80) in his *Quattro Libri dell' architettura* of 1570. Every constituent of every building, Palladio reasoned, was governed by one supreme set of proportions, which derived from the proportions of the human body and, ultimately, from God himself.

To translate these human proportions to the dimensions of an elevation or a room, Renaissance architects like Palladio needed a standard module, which they devised in the form of the Roman foot (of twelve or fourteen inches) and then applied to every architectural element. From this module they also recreated what they believed were the seven basic proportions of nature, all of which were based on combinations of elementary geometry: circles, squares and half-squares. When expressed in three dimensions, as a

One of the earliest surviving fanlights: a wooden example of *c.*1725 at Marble Hill House, Twickenham.

A

B

C

D

The Measures Invented proportioned and affixed
By Batty Langley 1739.

Plate LXVIII.

Tho. Langley Sculp.

Designs for chimneypieces by the astonishingly prolific pattern-book author Batty Langley, from his *The City and Country Builder's and Workman's Treasury of Designs* of 1739.

grand façade couched in one of the five ancient orders or as a living room in a humble cottage, these proportions were always implicit. Even the humblest Georgian wall was regarded as a direct analogy of the classical column, with the skirting corresponding to the base of the column, the dado with the pedestal, the wall space with the column shaft, the frieze with the capital, and the wall cornice with the entablature cornice. It was only with the nineteenth century that such distinctions began to evaporate, as designers disregarded the classical rules of proportion, removed the dado rail and installed picture rails below the cornice.

To attain this goal of perfect proportionality, British and colonial Palladians of the first half of the eighteenth century used Palladio's seven basic proportions (which he himself had derived from the seven-number Platonic ratio) as the building blocks for a wide variety of mathematical solutions, which they believed would solve all manner of design problems. Eighteenth-century authors noted the close analogies with music: Palladian theorist Robert Morris noted that, in order to realise the 'Harmonick Proportions of Rooms', as 'in Music there are only seven distinct Notes, in Architecture likewise are only seven distinct Proportions'.[3] But, as in music, things rapidly got more complicated.

From the mid-1720s a flood of pattern-books appeared, aimed not at the architect or the grand patron but at the average householder and, more particularly, at his or her builder, surveyor or craftsman. The primary purpose of these volumes was to ensure that Palladian detailing was executed with professional exactness, and to help local builders master a new style whose proportional discipline often proved more technically demanding than the relative freedom of the vernacular or Baroque styles with which they were familiar. Thus it was important that the new philosophy was not cloaked in over-complex jargon or masked by elaborate historical explanations. And to aid the builder to get the interior just right, each book inevitably contained a different table of proportions, guiding the tradesman as to how high to place

the cornice or dispose the chimneypiece.

British pattern-books were very helpful in guiding colonial householders and builders who wished to evoke the fashionable Palladianism of the British metropolis. The most frequently used volumes were William Salmon's highly successful *Palladio Londinensis* of 1734, which remained the standard builder's manual for forty years, and the copious works produced by Batty Langley, whose vast if repetitive oeuvre helped him to sustain his family of fourteen children. While most householders could not afford the services of an architect like William Kent or Henry Flitcroft, they could afford the pattern-books of Batty Langley or William Salmon. The vast majority of homeowners adhered to the basic principle of maximising perceived value and status for a socially and fiscally justifiable, and attainable, price. For both public and private interiors, fashionable

A mid-eighteenth century depiction of a cabinet-maker and client in earnest discussion (English school, *A Cabinet-maker's Office*, c.1770; Victoria and Albert Museum, London): the cabinet-maker points to a coloured design for a bookcase and commode, for presentation to a client. The simple panelled room contains a plain bookcase, stool and desk for housing his business records. Grey-painted walls were typical of the period in both Europe and America.

currency was always an issue, whether the patron, owner or designer was familiar with stylistic benchmarks or not. No one ever likes to be laughed at as out of date. Thus the popular pattern-books that began to appear with increasing frequency during the 1730s and 1740s, and which were aimed at both owners and building professionals, were intended not to propagate style, but to promulgate and promote a short-cut to 'taste' as a goal theoretically accessible to all. In effect, then, 'style' was not the key determinant of the average Georgian interior. Accessible advice, and the widening availability of materials and luxury goods, was far more important. Technological advance during the Georgian period made choices possible for the middle-class householder, choices that were the prerequisite of 'taste'.

Palladian 'taste' was simple to the point of puritanism. Plainness and simplicity of form represented the basis of the style on both sides of the Atlantic; the term 'plain', for example, recurs with Shaker-like emphasis throughout the books of Robert Morris. Mouldings of the 1720s, 30s and 40s were accordingly basic, heavy and pronounced, frequently involving the family of 'ovolo' mouldings based on the quadrant or quarter circle. There was a conscious move away from 'the Baroque concern for parade and progression': the growth of women's influence on the interior was 'paralleled by a growth of interest in comfort, intimacy and privacy, light and informality in houses'. Room use became more specific, with areas allocated to public and private functions. Thus the parlour originated in the Early Georgian

period as an everyday living room, 'in which people sat as well as ate', but by the 1740s it had become exclusively a sitting room. The term 'dining room' – first identified by historian John Cornforth at Ham House in 1670s – was also being commonly used by the 1730s.[4]

While the owners of new Palladian homes did not seek to mimic the virtuoso interiors of the Italian Renaissance, though, they did happily borrow one aspect of Italian style: the lightness of their interiors. After proportionality, perhaps the most significant legacy of the Palladian style to the average home was the increasing use of pale hues in place of the wood colours so prevalent in 1700. Graining and marbling now fell out of fashion, sacrificed to the Italian-inspired trend towards light, white interiors. Seventeenth-century browns often survived only as decoration for skirtings, doors and other framing woodwork. Instead, off-white, cream or 'stone' colours, or other light hues, predominated internally in even the humblest Palladian interior. These new tones were invariably applied uniformly between skirting and ceiling. Indeed, the general application of a single colour on internal walls is an important feature of Early Georgian interiors. Architectural elements such as friezes or cornices were never painted the same colour as the adjoining ceiling – which, in all but the grandest homes, was invariably white. Only the skirting was painted a different colour: usually chocolate-brown or blue-black, a finish which both provided a visual termination to the wall and, more

Opposite. Sinuous acanthus buds and generous wave ornament (or 'Vitruvian scroll') adorn this splendid closed stair string of the 1720s at Peckover House, Wisbech.

practically, hid scuff marks made by shoes or boots. And by the 1750s, even skirtings and doors were being painted white.

White and pale tints appeared all over the house. They were embraced not just because they were fashionable, but also because they could be made inexpensively. Halls, staircases and circulation spaces tended to be painted in stone colour 'because it was hard-wearing and cheap'.[5] Plaster walls, particularly those in kitchens, laundries or other service areas, could be painted with white finishes as cheap and simple as unbound whitening or limewash, while plaster ceilings and wall mouldings were invariably painted with size-bound distemper.

Oil paints, the least porous of internally applied house paints, began to be used for woodwork and metalwork. To achieve the flat, matt tone so popular in

British oil paints after *c.*1740, turpentine was either added to the oil or applied to the topmost painted surface. Yet, contrary to current decorating practice, mouldings and decorative motifs in the cornice (or ceiling) were never picked out in another colour. Gold leaf was used to highlight decorative mouldings in the grander houses, which from the 1760s onwards were sometimes provided with the bold colourings pioneered by the Adam brothers. However, middle-class and working-class households relied on the effects of light and shade conjured by candlelight to give their mouldings a more three-dimensional aspect.

By the 1730s a number of oil and distemper colours were available as alternatives to the whites and stone colours for interior paintwork. Those that could be cheaply manufactured from easily available pigments were termed 'common colours'. In 1734 William

Salmon's bestselling *Palladio Londinensis* listed 'pearl colour, lead colour, cream colour, stone colour, wainscot colour or oak colour' as the most basic and frequently encountered common colours. A little more expensive were the family of greens, which included pale olive and pea green (probably a fresh, bright green: the colour of uncooked, not dried, peas), the chocolate brown commonly used for skirtings and internal doors, and the sandy colours which went under the name of 'straw'. Colours such as deep blues and greens remained difficult to produce, and were accordingly beyond the reach of most households. Red had the grandest connotations, and was used for all royal state apartments during the eighteenth century; in the average home, cheaper, madder-derived red dyes were increasingly used for furnishing fabrics, but red paint finishes were rare. Greens were far easier to obtain cheaply (although in Salmon's gazetteer, the 'fine deep green' derived from verdigris was by far the most expensive colour on the market); hence the popularity of olive colour in the early decades of the century.

The increasing popularity of blue was largely due to the introduction, and subsequent fall in price, of the pigment known as 'Prussian blue'. Strong Prussian blue (potassium ferric ferrocyanide) was invented in 1702 from a number of seemingly unlikely organic materials, including animal bones and pig's blood. It was first advertised in Britain in 1710 and first used by William Kent in Kensington Palace in the early 1720s. Previously, the only way to arrive at a strong mid-blue – which traditional indigo dyes were never able to realise – was by strewing 'smalt', crushed blue glass, over white paint. This, however, was both costly and time-consuming. Unsurprisingly, after the appearance of Prussian blue, smalt died out. Used sparingly, Prussian blue could create a wide variety of delicate pale blues; these, though, tended to turn grey-green with age, largely a result of prolonged interaction with the linseed oil used as a dryer.

Lighter paint colours on the walls helped candles to light dark rooms. Most households still relied on transporting candles from room to room via candlesticks, rather than installing expensive, fixed sconces or girandoles. Wax candles were usually white (although the American colonies made use of a natural green wax), but could now be found dyed. As the price of wax fell, tallow dips became rarer, and were

Fashionable blue paint, derived from the new pigment Prussian blue, in evidence in the hall at the Cupola House, Edenton, North Carolina (now in the Brooklyn Museum of Art). Use of Prussian blue in the 1720s signified an awareness of the latest fashions in interior decoration – as well as a deep purse.

Typical 'common colours' of the Palladian era – off-white, dark stone and straw yellow – are complemented by the more vivid tones of the seat upholstery and imported carpets in these Colonial American interiors, now in the American Museum at Claverton Manor near Bath. The low-relief chimney surround and flat overmantel, below, were somewhat old-fashioned by the mid-eighteenth century.

generally used to illuminate servants' and children's rooms.

Furniture and fittings increasingly mirrored the proportional architectural shell, rather than the mere originality of the cabinetmaker, and took both their scale and their stylistic cue from the walls. In the American colonies, simple, battened internal doors were replaced with more sophisticated and properly proportioned panelled designs. Chimneypieces decreased in size while becoming more of an architectural feature, erupting further into the room. Grates were invariably of iron, although cast brass was being employed by 1750; gradually the simple, freestanding iron basket grate, with two or three bars at the front and a grid at the bottom to dispose of the ash, metamorphosed into the 'hob' or 'stove' grate, equipped with iron cheeks, decorated front bars and permanent or moveable plates or hobs at each side to warm kettles and pots.

The arrangement of fireplaces was one aspect of the interior in which the colonies departed from accepted practice in the mother country. Britons now generally burned coal in open fires, whereas Central and Northern Europeans burned logs in iron stoves. America's tradition of preferring stoves comes from examples taken there by emigrants from the early eighteenth century onwards, a development which famously prompted Benjamin Franklin to invent the 'open' stove – a double-skin metal stove fitted with an integral grate – in 1742. By 1760 Franklin stoves, called 'Philadelphia stoves' in Britain, were being manufactured in British foundries for export back to America.

Britons were never sluggish in devising new ways to fit and furnish the home. The pace of change quickened with the passing years: John Kay's flying shuttle of 1733 allowed cloths wider than three feet to be woven by one person; the world's first cotton mill was opened in Birmingham in 1741; this was followed by Richard Arkwright's water-frame mill of 1769, whose progeny were soon to be seen dotted all over Lancashire, Derbyshire and Scotland; and as early as 1740, Manchester was recognised as the world's centre for the manufacture of printed cottons. In the 1750s Francis Nixon developed copperplate printing in Ireland, using copper sheets three feet square. He sold the process to a Surrey printer, in whose activities the astonishingly fertile polymath Benjamin Franklin took a great interest.[6]

A finely proportioned Early Georgian chimneypiece, with Sienna marble inset, at Peckover House in Cambridgeshire.

The result of these technical innovations was that colours grew brighter and more durable, patterns bolder, and furnishing fabrics immensely cheaper. Curtains were also becoming more common. By the 1730s even grand houses possessed simple draw curtains in the bedroom; these either matched the bed upholstery, or were simply dyed white. Elsewhere in the home, printed fabrics were beginning to appear. In 1708 Daniel Defoe was already writing how chintz had 'crept into our houses, our closets and bedchambers, curtains, cushions, chairs, and at last beds themselves'.[7] Chintz slip or case covers, to protect expensive upholstery from direct light and mucky clothes, were being referred to by 1740.[8]

The European silk industry was thriving, too, although as early as 1696 Spitalfields silk weavers in London had rioted against cheap Indian imports. In 1700 Parliament forbade the importing or wearing of Indian or Persian silks or calicoes, while a further Act of 1720 prohibited all wearing of printed or dyed Indian calicoes; in 1722 this was extended to their use as furnishing fabrics. This was finally repealed only in 1774. Even English-printed calicoes were targeted in 1721; fifteen years later this nonsensical piece of legislation was supplemented by a ban on all home-produced cottons except 'fustian', a very cheap fabric with a linen warp and cotton weft.

Growing trade with the Eastern Mediterranean additionally enabled imported luxury carpets to become less expensive and thus more widely available during the early decades of the eighteenth century. In 1749 John Wood famously observed that, during the past two decades, 'as the new Building advanced, Carpets were introduced to cover the floors'. For everyday use, though, good deal or oak floorboards were generally left bare, though often limewashed. This valuable protective coating allowed moisture to pass in and out of the wood, and also produced an attractive silvery sheen much imitated today. In 1772 an American visitor noted that English deal floors 'are washed and rubbed almost daily' with lime water, which resulted in 'a whitish appearance, and an air of freshness and cleanliness'.

Opposite. Detail of the chimneypiece mouldings, with vine leaf and egg-and-dart patterns, at Peckover House. Note the anchors and chains embellishing the latter, indicating the naval connections of the owner.

Right. A design for geometrically laid marble floor from Batty Langley's *Treasury of Designs* (1740).

A similar white patina was achieved by the widespread practice of cleaning wooden floors by scrubbing them with dry sand, sometimes mixed with fresh herbs. Alternatively, aromatic herbs such as mint or tansy could be rubbed into the grain to give the boards a fresh smell and a dark stain.

During the seventeenth century, the principal woods used in furniture construction had been oak and walnut. Oak, however, was also needed for shipbuilding, and in time of foreign war good oak was scarce. In grander homes, walnut had been used for wall panelling in place of oak; in the majority of homes, cheaper 'deal' (that is, pine or fir) was used instead, and always painted. Now wood panelling, unless of oak or another high-quality wood, was invariably painted.

A high-quality substitute for oak was ultimately found in mahogany, imported from the Caribbean colonies of Britain, Spain and France after the peace of 1713. Jamaican mahogany was first introduced into England soon after the Treaty of Utrecht, and within a few years was being supplemented by dark mahogany from Santa Domingo (termed 'Spanish mahogany', which when aged seemed virtually black) together with reddish-brown varieties from Cuba and, later, from the British colony of Honduras. At the same time, cheaper native woods such as elm or (painted) pine remained perennially popular for items designed for provincial households. By 1760 mahogany furniture was commonly found in homes of any reasonable wealth or pretension, although other West Indian imports (most notably straw-coloured satinwood) also found favour with designers. By the 1780s it had caught on in France, too.

Along with new woods came new types of furniture. Chests of drawers began to appear, as did large mirrors, for those who could afford the costly (and invariably Parisian) mirror glass. Wealthier households increasingly turned to the upholsterer for advice; the cabinetmaker, though, was now of lesser importance, his advice on design matters eclipsed by the readily available books of printed designs for furniture.[9]

Left. Blue Delft tiles in the lavatory at The Admiral's House in Chatham Dockyard, Kent, of 1708. Once commonplace, such tiled walls are now extremely rare.

Opposite. Mirror-making from Diderot's hugely informative *Dictionary of Sciences* of c.1770. Paris was then the centre of Western mirror manufacture, and the possession of a large glass the unmistakable sign of sophistication and wealth.

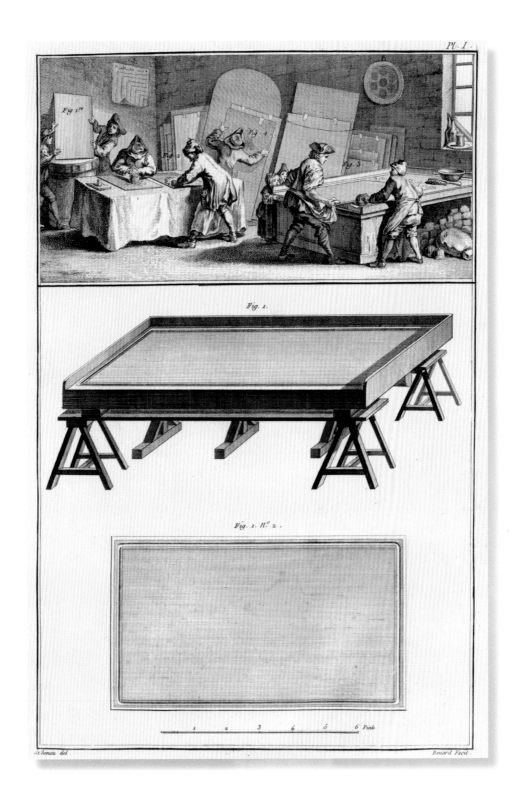

Pl. I.

Fig. 1.

Fig. 1. N.º 2.

1   2   3   4   5   6 Pieds

Se Renau. del.   Benard Fecit.

Left. A plate from Diderot's *Encyclopédie* (c.1770) showing the manufacture of crown glass. Panes of window glass made in this way were cut from a large disc.

Opposite. A refined interior (the 'Readbourne Parlour') of the late 1740s, now at the Winterthur Museum in Delaware. Note the fine tiled fireplace inset and the imported Persian rug – now daringly placed on the floor. The curtains are of a later pattern.

The age of the expert decorator had faded: thanks to the availability of accessible pattern-books, consumers were now able to make complex design decisions for themselves. The liberation of the householder had begun.

1. Mario Praz, *An Illustrated History of Interior Decoration* (1962), 56, 59, 60. **2.** Vitruvius, *Ten Books of Architecture*, quoted in Steven Parissien, *Palladian Style* (1994), 38. **3.** Robert Morris, *Lectures on Architecture* (1734), quoted in Parissien, *Palladian Style*, 86. **4.** John Cornforth, *Early Georgian Interiors* (2004), 209, 34. **5.** Ibid., 116. **6.** Florence Montgomery, *Printed Textiles* (1970), 29. **7.** *The Weekly Review*, 31 January 1708, quoted in Charles Saumarez Smith, *The Rise of Design* (2000), 46. **8.** Cornforth, *Early Georgian Interiors*, 105. **9.** Ibid., 212.

EXPANDING HORIZONS
Rococo and Chinoiserie

We have freed ourselves from the slavery
of squares and circles to which tradition
had formerly bonded us.

(Jacques-François Blondel, 1737)

Opposite. Chinese
wallpaper in an early
eighteenth-century room at
the Château de Talcy in
France's Loire region.

Right. A 'Chinese'
scene from Jean-Baptiste
Pillement's *The Ladies
Amusement; or, Whole
Art of Japanning Made
Easy* (1760).

While Britain and its American colonies turned towards the ordered sobriety of Palladian proportion, Catholic Europe indulged in the non-structural fantasies of the Rococo and the East.

The Rococo style appears to have originated in France around 1700, but it was not until the 1720s – exactly the time that the Palladian doctrine was taking hold in the English-speaking world – that it began to dominate French interiors. In contrast to Palladianism, Rococo (a derogatory term not used until the late eighteenth century, and originally applied to paintings) was very much an aristocratic creed, pioneered by the noble hotel-owners of Paris. Its influence, however, permeated every aspect of the Western interior. Even in the mid-twentieth century, ranges of Rococo ('Louis XV') chimney surrounds were still proving profitable lines for manufacturers, while the asymmetrical Rococo mirror and bowed Rococo chest of drawers have, similarly, never gone out of fashion.

In French Rococo, decorative motifs hid or displaced the architectural framework of a room. The style was characterised by everything that Palladianism had rejected: 'bold opulence, plasticity and, above all, a rigid distinction between the dominant architectural structure and the surface decoration'. If any entablature remained, it was reduced down to a single moulding 'with little resemblance to an acknowledged "order"'; in the more extreme cases, the division between wall and ceiling 'disappeared altogether in a gentle curve'.[1]

More depth could be achieved with carved wood than with applied plasterwork: thus most elegant French houses kept at least one wood-panelled room until the Revolution. Where the decoration was painted, white and pastel shades were preferred; ceilings – decorated with delicate pre-cast ornament – were also invariably white or gently tinted. Ornament, not proportion, was the key element in Rococo rooms. Grotesque decoration finally came into its own. And, again in contrast to the rigid symmetry of Palladianism, Rococo was emphatically asymmetrical. Flowing 'S' and 'C' curves dominated compositions, and naturalistic plant life – growing not in conformity with architectural order but in an unbalanced manner, as in nature – adorned items as disparate as chairs and candelabras.

The architect-designer Juste-Aurèle Meissonier (1695–1750) has been termed the godfather of Rococo. Certainly his books, notably his *Livre d'ornament* and *Oeuvre* of collected engravings of 1750, were crucial in disseminating the style beyond the borders of France. It was partly thanks to his prints that the style became popular in the German states of Central Europe: Austria, Swabia, Saxony and particularly Bavaria. In the Bavarian capital of Munich, the French architect François de Cuvilliés (1695–1768) created stunning Rococo rooms in the palaces of the ruling Wittelsbach dynasty. From Central Germany the idiom spread to Northern Italy – especially Venice – and northwards to Prussia, Sweden and the Austrian Netherlands (present-day Belgium). Aside from the largely French

Above. An eccentric French Rococo design for a chimney surround of 1745 by Giles-Marie Oppenord. His marine exuberance would clearly not have left any room for any ornaments on the mantelshelf.

Below. Rococo overmantel decoration at Peckover House of the 1720s. Britain and America took to the Rococo style very warily, and rarely used this lascivious idiom for entire interiors.

designs for the Swedish court, however, the Rococo manner made little headway in Protestant Europe. It is not hard to see why: the almost irrational licentiousness of form and line, the submergence of structural narrative and the ostentatious love of display that were all central to the Rococo style were not designed to appeal to the strait-laced peoples of Northern Europe or North America, who saw the style as morally degenerate and as a mirror of the corrupting material values of Catholic Europe. Rococo generally only appeared in those regions in the form of single items of furniture, light fittings or plaster ceiling decoration, and only very rarely in the form of holistic decorative schemes.

Rococo was particularly suited to wood and porcelain, which could be easily carved or modelled. Commodes and chests bowed out on spindly legs; painted wooden chandeliers sprouted arms of asymmetrical foliage; clock cases became overrun with twisted ornament. The royal-owned Sèvres factory in Paris and the Meissen factory in Saxony both produced a huge range of porcelain wall-lights, candlesticks and even mirror frames in the Rococo idiom. Perhaps the style's most long-lasting influence, however, was on seat furniture. In the hands of the great Rococo designers, armchairs and sofas swelled and expanded. Provided with increasingly generous, rounded upholstery, they possessed few if any flat surfaces. They may have been less than elegant, but they were certainly comfortable. As a result, Rococo armchairs continued to be made well into the twentieth century.

Much Rococo furniture was,

by the 1740s, lacquered, or painted red or black in imitation of lacquer. Genuine oriental lacquer was a shiny, hardwearing varnish made from the sap of the tree *Rhus vernificera*. Imitation lacquer had been made in Paris by the Gobelins factory from 1672. By the 1750s lacquered tin, known as 'tole', provided a cheap substitute for genuine oriental lacquer or Sèvres porcelain and was commonly used for table-tops and trays.

Enthusiasm for the Rococo spilled over into a fascination for all things 'Eastern'. The West's obsession with Chinese and Japanese porcelain from the late seventeenth century onwards in turn encouraged manufacturers to graft Asian forms or motifs on to Western models. As trade links with Asia improved during

the seventeenth century, even middle-class Europeans became more familiar with household luxuries brought from the East. Notionally, the fruits of these commercial connections also bred familiarity with Eastern landscapes and lifestyles. Ceramics, wallpaper, screens and printed textiles imported into Europe frequently bore painted or printed scenes of what purported to be everyday life in both Near and Far East. The burgeoning fashion for the East was satisfied not only by these imports but also by locally made pieces inspired by them. This style, known as 'chinoiserie', found its most elaborate manifestations in the early eighteenth century, when

Chinoiserie decorative panels in a French room of c.1725–50, showing door, wall and window designs.

prominent European dynasties indulged in their own fanciful recreations of what approximated to Eastern environments.

However, such constructions never ventured beyond the realm of fantasy. While blue-and-white porcelain from China was a familiar sight on mantelshelves by 1700 – shown to its best advantage against the predominantly brown-wood wall colours of the time – its owners rarely evinced any knowledge of, or indeed any genuine interest in, the realities of life in the Far East. Similarly, while incursions into the Indian subcontinent by European powers increased in number and ambition during the eighteenth century, for the

most part these did not prompt a greater appreciation of South or East Asian culture beyond a narrowly mercantile understanding of trading opportunities. The Asians responsible for the exotic imports remained an unknown quantity to most in the West, their homelands faraway countries about which most Europeans preferred to know nothing.

For most Europeans in the seventeenth and eighteenth centuries, the Orient remained very much, to use Edward Said's term, 'a Western projection'.[2] It was a fantasy principally conjured by the Northern Europeans who constituted the principal foreign powers in the East after 1600. And its

lure became particularly strong at the end of the seventeenth century. By 1700 the craze for Indian objects (particularly in Britain and France), for all things Siamese (in France) and the Sinomania which enveloped much of Northern and Central Europe proved a marked influence on the development of the aristocratic domestic interior. Yet this interest was never particularly academic in its expression. (In truth, Louis XIV's interest in Siam only derived from his interest in using the country as a commercial and military springboard for French expansion in China. Following the failure of the embassies of the 1680s, his roving eye turned westwards once more.) Goods from all these oriental sources 'were assigned random attributions in a spirit of topographical indifference', with differing pieces and contrasting colours being displayed 'towering and clustering on cabinets and chimneypieces [in] quite un-eastern fashion'.[3]

The sudden explosion of interest in the East was fuelled by the ambitions of the British, French and Dutch East India companies, and the expanding commercial horizons of the European maritime nations from which they sprang. And it was a fashion that became

Interior of a French 'Emporium' shop of the mid-eighteenth century. This type of outlet imported porcelain and other decorative objects from the Far East for European collectors.

The Chinese wallpaper at Middleton Park, Oxfordshire. The room was redecorated in 1810 as a late example of chinoiserie, but this watercolour was executed almost thirty years later by William Alfred Delamotte, in 1839.

particularly noticeable by 1700, by which time the import of hand-painted Chinese wallpapers, Chinese porcelain and Indian fabrics into Western Europe had increased significantly. This in turn inspired the Dutch to begin the manufacture of imitative blue-and-white Delftware tiles and bowls, directly inspired by Imari wares from both Japan and China.

Predictably, this flood of imports caused consternation for many European businesses. Thus the explosion in the import of Indian textiles during the 1680s encouraged the French in 1686 – followed, as we have seen, by the British

in 1701 – to prohibit the import of Indian chintz in order to protect their native silk industries. These attempts only succeeded in the short term, and they could not suppress the rising interest in Eastern-styled goods. By 1719 the silk weavers of Spitalfields in the East End of London were rioting in protest against Indian textile imports, and ripping the dresses from any women they encountered wearing Indian calicoes.

In the ensuing decades, ground-breaking works such as Engelbert Kaempfer's *History of Japan* (first published in English in 1727, and subsequently translated into French and

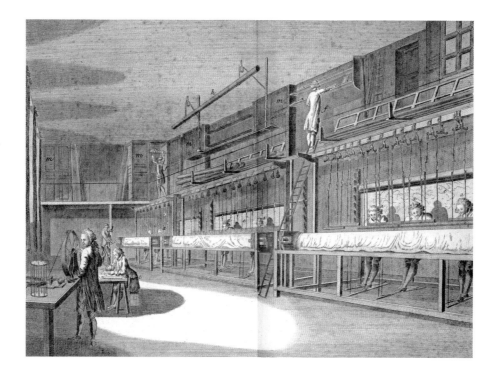

Dutch) helped to inspire the emerging porcelain works of Meissen and Chantilly, the wallpaper manufacturers of London and Paris, and the tapestry works of Gobelins and Beauvais. And by the 1720s the French were beginning to publish formulas which could supposedly guarantee the authentic manufacture of Eastern-style lacquer and porcelain.

The sudden increase in enthusiasm for the Orient during this period can of course be attributed to factors other than Europe's mercantile avarice. The spread of Huguenot craftsmen (many of whom were pioneering the use of Eastern motifs) across Protestant Europe in the wake of the repeal of the Edict of Nantes in 1685 is one obvious factor, as is Queen Mary II's introduction into the English court of her passion for collecting Chinese and Japanese blue-and-white after 1688.[4] The demand for Eastern luxury goods or their home-grown imitations, however, can be at least partly traced to an important psychological factor: the perceived diminution and neutering of the East as a military threat, and its consequent repackaging as a passive, indolent and benign artistic influence.

The Ottoman Empire had for centuries represented that part of the East with which Europe was most familiar – and by which it was most terrified. Until the late seventeenth century, Europeans constantly believed themselves to be under threat from the Turks' territorial ambitions, with the Ottoman Empire being cast as merely the latest in a centuries-old series of brutal Eastern invaders. The failure of the Turks' siege of Vienna in 1683, however,

was followed by a complete collapse of Ottoman power in Eastern Europe. This was, coincidentally, paralleled by the crumbling of Mughal hegemony in India. While the latter did not have the psychological impact on the West that the revelation of Ottoman dotage had prompted, they both nevertheless helped to raise European confidence regarding commercial and military prospects in the East. Far from posing a threat to Western trading aspirations, India in the eighteenth century became a battleground for the European powers themselves. Thus Britain and France were engaged in three protracted bouts over the mastery of the subcontinent after 1740, with the Mughal Emperor relegated to the position of an irrelevant doge.

Apparently politically neutered, the East was now considered by Europeans as a subject suitable for adapting as a decorative motif for domestic interiors. In these contexts the Orient was pictured as a harmless, picturesque and sometimes magical idyll whose inhabitants were invariably languid, melancholic and indolent, and governed largely by primitive religious obsessions and the excessive consumption of hallucinogens. Despite the imputation of cultural decadence, however, Eastern figures as portrayed in Western chinoiseries were often strangely androgynous, indicating a European apathy towards individual identities. China became, in Western eyes, 'a haven of leisure and luxury, peopled by the gay Chinese of the porcelains who lived in beautiful gardens filled with rounded bridges, temples with curved eaves from which hung

tinkling bells, and pagodas stretching skywards'. The Orientals portrayed in the designs of François Boucher (1703–70) were invariably 'charming and faintly erotic', while in many of his scenes 'the activities of its inhabitants involved nothing more arduous than the playing of weird musical instruments, carrying birds in bamboo cages, and dallying among their fishing tackle or tea-trays'.[5] For Boucher and his contemporaries, stereotypical images of the Chinese – with their long queues, their voluminous sleeves and their strange hats – 'were only reproduced to make people laugh or smile'. What these designers sought to create was a light-hearted fiction, using Asia as an exotic backdrop which encouraged spectators to suspend disbelief at the drop of a conical hat.

Significantly, the fishing party – a simple, passive and emphatically un-warlike activity – became a favourite theme for chinoiserie designers in the West. Alternatively, Eastern landscapes were simply emptied of people and filled with birds and animals – preferably monkeys: diminished, comic semi-humans whose exoticism connoted a wider and geographically vaguer sense of overseas 'other'. Thus was the East tamed and domesticated into an idiom of 'meandering informality' ideally suited to Western Rococo design.

Regarding the East as something remote and easily dismissed relieved designers and craftsmen of the need to be 'authentic' in their reinterpretation of the exotic. Invariably, then, Eastern motifs and messages became deliberately jumbled in the hands of their Western interpreters, and were cited with little care or concern about social or pictorial realities. Some no longer necessarily held an automatic Eastern connotation at all; they were there simply to represent 'exotica' and an impression of 'otherness'. Thus the French Chantilly porcelain of the 1730s combined sculpted representations of 'Chinese' figures with images from Indian textiles and Rococo modelling after Meisonnier. London wallpaper manufacturers who were advertising 'Japan' papers by the 1750s were in truth marketing a mélange of Chinese, Indian and Western designs. Chinese wallpaper manufacturers in their turn were cannily flexible in adapting their product for Western uses, often supplying extra papers from which 'birds and branches could be cut... and pasted over damaged or discoloured areas, used to fill awkward corners, or simply to embellish the overall effect'.[6] Meanwhile, the new British chinoiserie papers of the mid-eighteenth century – based on comfortingly repetitive, hand-blocked patterns – confined and reduced Chinese compositions for the average British or Colonial home, making Eastern conventions far more easily digestible for Western walls. At the same time, the cabinetmaker Thomas Chippendale (1718–79) happily mixed 'Chinese' with Rococo and Gothick in the pages of his *Gentleman and Cabinet-Maker's Directory* of 1754.

Craftsmen and designers working in the oriental idiom, whatever the notional geographical inspiration for the piece, were happy to fill any spare space available with Asian stereotypes garnered from all over the continent – elephants, palm trees, monkeys, and so on. Even

Jean-Antoine Fraisse, whose influential *Livre de desseins chinois* of 1735 tried far harder than its contemporaries to reflect actual Eastern idioms and conventions, was still happy to combine Mughal and other Islamic motifs with Chinese and Japanese forms. Fraisse never went to the East himself, and even the opening of his book gave away his intrinsic lack of interest in stylistic accuracy – the title page revealing that his images were inspired by material from Persia, India, China and Japan. As a recent historian has noted, French chinoiserie of this nature was appreciated only when it was

Right. Italian chinoiserie wallpaper of *c*.1755: the Orient fused with the West. The design is block printed in black, with stencil colouring.

Detail of a 'Chinese' console mirror frame and matching porcelain figure by Oppenord of 1736, from Brühl, Germany.

'integrated into French surroundings, adding some strange seasoning' – an adaptation which, she argues, constitutes 'the very definition of exoticism'.[7]

Eurocentric imagery was particularly evident in the works of the greatest exponents and popularisers of chinoiserie in mid-eighteenth century France: François Boucher and Jean-Baptiste Pillement (1728–1808). Boucher happily presided over 'a sort of Cloud-Cuckoo China, with palm trees, doll-like people, feathery hats, and a mass of properties such as fans, parasols, guitars – suggesting a generalised, amusing exoticism'; although his inspiration came from genuine Chinese woodblock engravings, his finished designs still represented an assimilation of Chinese imagery for the French market.[8] Pillement's

designs, though they quoted directly from genuine oriental sources such as Chinese and Japanese porcelain, were also significantly removed from the reality of the East. Pillement's fairyland imagery, including graphic images such as Chinamen wearing upside-down flowers instead of hats, transmuted what had, a century before, been popularly regarded as a warlike race into a set of harmless cartoon characters.

Only at the very end of the eighteenth century did European cultural attitudes to the East begin to change. Edward Said has defined this development as a move away from the 'appreciation' which characterised the seventeenth and eighteenth centuries towards the 'definition' of the nineteenth century, when 'there

A 'Chinese' drawing room from William Chambers's influential *Designs of Chinese Buildings* of 1757. Note the stools stacked along the dado in approved Western manner.

emerged a complex Orient suitable for study in the museum, or reconstruction in the colonial office'. William Jones's brave declaration of 1787, that 'it is my ambition to know India better than any other European ever knew it',[9] prefigured a new era of genuine interest in the culture and intellectual potential of the East. Yet Jones (1746–94) and his German contemporary Johann Gottfried Herder (1744–1803) were very much ahead of their time. Their Indophilia was only usefully developed during the nineteenth century, initially by a generation born in the heady, pre-revolutionary days of the 1770s and 1780s.

Oriental escapism reached its zenith in the fabulous Indo-Chinese interiors of the Brighton Pavilion, refurbished after 1815. Yet the Pavilion's bravura interiors, however glitteringly executed, proved a negligible influence on the average interiors of the day. Instead, they merely provided a fitting coda for a century of domestic fantasy.

Opposite. A delightful detail from an illustration in Jean-Baptiste Pillement's *Art of Japanning.*

1. Christine Riding, 'Rococo', in Joanna Banham (ed.), *Encyclopaedia of Interior Design* (1997), vol. 2, 1069. 2. Edward Said, *Orientalism* (1978), 95. 3. Danielle Elisseeff-Poisle, 'Chinese Influence in France', in Thomas C.H. Lee (ed.), *China and Europe: Images and Influences in the Sixteenth to Eighteenth Centuries* (1991), 154; Dawn Jacobsen, *Chinoiserie* (1993), 31–2. 4. Unfortunately, this bold patronage ended with Mary's death in 1694; her husband, William III, subsequently sold or dispersed much of her collection. Interestingly, the first Chinaman to set foot in England appeared at James II's court in 1685. See Jonathan D. Spence, *The Chan's Great Continent: China in Western Minds* (1998), 65. 5. Donald F. Lach, *Asia in the Eyes of Europe* (1991), 14; Jacobsen, *Chinoiserie*, 73. 6. Gill Saunders, 'The China Trade: Oriental Painted Panels', in Lesley Hoskins (ed.), *The Papered Wall* (1994), 49. 7. Elisseeff-Poisle, 160. 8. Michael Levey, *Painting and Sculpture in France 1700–1789* (1972), 164. 9. Said, *Orientalism*, 7, 78–9.

If this be Grecian, give me Chinese, give me Gothick! Anything is better than this!

(Lord de la Warr, 1764)

Opposite. Robert Adam rooms of the 1770s at 20 St James's Square, London.

Right. Printed colour samples from George Smith's *The Cabinet Maker's and Upholsterer's Guide* of 1826 – one of the first instances of an author and publisher attempting to provide consumers with a guide to paint choice.

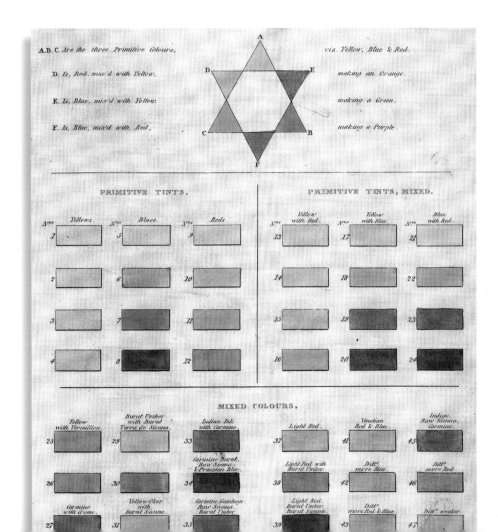

The middle years of the eighteenth century saw a sea-change in attitudes to the ancient world. Rather than continue to view classical civilisation through the prism of the Renaissance, as the Palladians had done, historians and designers sought to learn directly from the antique monuments that survived in Italy and, particularly, in Greece, 'the Place where the most beautiful Edifices were erected, and where the purest and most elegant Examples of ancient Architecture are to be discovered'. In the view of a new generation of architects, the works of Palladio and his Renaissance contemporaries were a poor substitute for the real thing: 'Descriptions are so confused, and their Measures so inaccurate,' declared one of the first Neoclassical guides, that they 'cannot be said to afford a sufficient variety of Examples for restoring even the three Orders of Columns'.[1]

Intrepid Germans, French and Britons began to visit Greece and Southern Italy to analyse and draw the ancient ruins there in the 1740s. The buried sites of Pompeii and Herculaneum were rediscovered, and the first tentative attempts at excavation begun. In 1751 the French architect Jacques-Germain Soufflot (1713–80) visited the ancient Greek ruins at Paestum, near Naples, with Mme de Pompadour's brother, the Marquis de Marigny. (His drawings of the temple were published in 1764–5.) He was to be the first of many.

The public dissemination of all this study began in 1755, with the publication of Robert Wood's esoteric *Ruins of Palmyra* and Winckelmann's

art-historical *Reflections on the Imitation of Greek Works in Painting and Sculpture*. Johann Joachim Winckelmann (1717–68), the Rome-based Prussian art historian now regarded as the 'Father of Archaeology', followed this with more architectural studies – *Observations on the Architecture of the Ancients* (1762), which included a study of Paestum, and two analyses of the latest finds at the Herculaneum site, of 1762 and 1764 – before publishing his encyclopedic masterwork, *A History of Ancient Art*, in 1764, four years before his grisly murder in a sordid inn bedchamber.

By that time, James Stuart (1713–88) and Nicholas Revett (1720–1804) had provided a similar service for the English-speaking world. (Winckelmann's *Reflections* were translated into English by Henry Fuseli in 1772, but his *Observations* – although translated into French in 1783 – have never appeared in English at all.) Their seminal first volume of *The Antiquities of Athens*, published in 1762,

The second half of the eighteenth century was, in Britain and America, the great age of the fanlight. This is a typical example of the 1770s in London's Bedford Square, Bloomsbury, executed in iron and lead.

was the fruit of five years' exploration of Greek sites, braving pirate attacks, palace coups and shipwrecks. Their original idea, they declared, had been that 'if accurate Representations of these [Greek] originals were published, the World would be enabled to form, not only more extensive, but juster Ideas than have hitherto been obtained'.[1] Important though *The Antiquities of Athens* was, however – and it went through numerous editions in Britain and America, remaining in print until the 1880s – it was not directly aimed at the average homeowner or builder. It was left to works such as Stephen Riou's *The Grecian Orders* of 1768 to reinterpret the new, Neoclassical message for the building and decorating trades, much as the works of Salmon and Langley had done for Palladianism thirty years before.

Stuart and Revett designed relatively few buildings, and all were for the wealthy. (The notoriously indolent Stuart allegedly 'ended his days playing skittles in the afternoon, and drinking in public houses in the evening'.[2]) The key figure in ensuring that the new Neoclassical fashion did not remain merely of antiquarian and archaeological interest, but exerted a fundamental influence on all classes of building in the English-speaking world, was the architect Robert Adam (1728–92). Adam had exactly the right credentials: the son of a Scots Palladian architect, he had visited ancient sites in Italy and the Adriatic in the 1750s (some of the results of which he published in 1764). His achievement was to synthesise what he and others had found in the ruins of the ancient world and combine it with Palladian practice – Georgian proportions still governed the shape and disposition of each interior – and contemporary French and Italian influences. He made use of recent discoveries about the antique not in a slavishly academic way (as the subsequent generation of European architects was to do), but in a highly personal and, at times, light-hearted fashion. Heavy Palladian motifs were reduced in scale and given movement and vivacity, while the excesses of French Rococo were tamed and made more overtly architectural. The result was, in Sir John Summerson's words,

A tasteful late eighteenth-century living room at Seabrook Plantation, Charleston, South Carolina. While the chimneypiece is restrained, the wallpaper is demonstrative.

'a personal revision and reconstruction of the antique into which many threads from a variety of sources were drawn and interwoven'.[3]

Adam's own practice was largely confined to country houses. However, his influence on average interiors was profound. By the end of the 1760s, the heavy and at times overly academic style of the Palladians had disappeared in Britain and America, replaced by busy, low-relief decoration, which enabled the chimneypiece to dominate the room as never before. Unsurprisingly, this rather camp, Continental style was not to everyone's taste. Adam's great rival William Chambers dismissed his competitor's decorative approach as 'filigrane toy work', while Horace Walpole later famously dismissed his work as 'sippets of embroidery'. Even a hundred years later, Edith Wharton and Ogden Codman still judged that there had been 'a certain timidity about the decorative compositions of the school of Adam and Sheraton'.[4] Nevertheless, it was to Adam's bravura style, and not to the more plodding, academic Neoclassicism of the next generation, that homeowners in Britain and America looked for inspiration until well into the twentieth century. In the US, the Federal style was based soundly on Adam's personal Neoclassical style, and almost lasted long enough to greet the Adam Revival of the 1860s. Today, 'Adam' chimney surrounds and wall mouldings are still perennial favourites for old homes and newbuild alike.

Adam was always a great supporter of the latest building advance, taking a personal financial interest in

Opposite. An internal fanlight and side lights from the fine Federal house of Homewood in Baltimore, Maryland, of 1801

Above. By 1800 advances in glazing technology allowed windows to be extended down to floor level. The tripartite sash window of c.1805 here, at Thomas Jefferson's home of Monticello, Virginia, can as a result also be used as a means of escape to the garden.

Left. Improvements in cast iron technology enabled the builders and architects of the later eighteenth century to use the resulting lightness of construction to attain more space, as in this room with cantilevered stair and carved walnut balustrade at Shirley Plantation, Virginia.

the development of stucco and cast iron in the 1770s. Indeed, while the homes of the later eighteenth century looked backwards for their stylistic inspiration, they were rarely backward in their embrace of the latest technologies. The notional 'style' in which they were couched may have ostensibly looked to antique precedent and spatial philosophy. But however academic their style, their technology was always forward-looking. Industrial advance made the inaccessible accessible, and the luxury item a generic. By the 1780s the rapidly expanding canal system in Britain was able to transport ceramics from Josiah Wedgwood's Etruria factory, metalware from Matthew Boulton's Soho factory and papier-mâché goods from Henry Clay's Birmingham factory all over

the country. These objects also helped spread the Neoclassical taste popularised by Robert Adam; Wedgwood's middle-class market was, in the words of one eminent design historian, 'randy for antique' by the end of the century.[5]

Advances in all areas of home construction and decoration could liberate both architect and householder, and by 1800 enabled the middle classes to take a lead in evolving the definition of 'taste', in sharp contrast to the days of Burlington and Kent. Technology had thus made 'style' affordable and socially inclusive. Kitchen ranges were redesigned and reduced in size – and price – following Count Rumford's influential patent stove of 1796. While in Burlington's day iron smelting was still in its infancy, by 1800 iron balusters,

Opposite. Neoclassical mouldings of 1801 at Homewood, Baltimore.

Left. Adam-designed door furniture of 1777 at Home House, London. The Adam brothers designed every element of their grander interiors themselves.

glazing bars, balconies, verandas and cantilevers were widely available to middle-class households from firms such as Coalbrookdale and Carron. In 1774 Robert Adam designed the famous 'Heart and Honeysuckle' anthemion pattern for 7 Adam Street, at the heart of his Adelphi development. Adam's design synthesis, in which an anthemion or palmette was used with interwoven tracery and small lead medallions at the intersections of the struts, was reproduced in all manner of homes over the next seventy years. By the 1800s whole staircases, and not just the balusters, were being made from cast rather than wrought iron. In Germany the vogue spread for fixing japanned iron or tin sheets to the walls or ceiling, a fashion which was later exported by German immigrants to the US. Other new materials appeared in the home. Increasingly, papier-mâché – often called 'paper stucco' – was used

for light ceiling or wall ornament, being both lighter and cheaper than pre-cast or moulded plaster ornament. In 1780 George Jackson, who had made his name creating papier-mâché mouldings for Robert Adam, founded his own company to mass-produce the material. By this time the manufacturing base of papier-mâché had moved from London's Spitalfields to Birmingham and Wolverhampton, and the quality and durability of the material had greatly improved. Henry Clay's 1772 patent specified a 'plaster' made from rag paper pasted together, dried on a stove, soaked in oil and then, if a long length was required, wrapped around greased wooden planks. The finished product, painted or gilded, was much used for complex wall and ceiling decoration before the advent of embossed and moulded papers in the second half of the nineteenth century. It also remained highly popular for mirror and picture frames, when it was either gilded or 'japanned' with black lacquer or varnished black paint. By 1800, papier-mâché – together with its superior French relative *carton pierre*, made from pulped paper, whiting and glue – was much sought after as a lighter, cheaper and hard-wearing substitute for wood for furniture and household objects of all kinds. The manufacturing process was further improved by mechanisation in the 1830s, when steam-pressing and the use of pulped paper resulted in a far denser and more durable product.

That homeowners were increasingly able to exercise choice was partly the result of the growing mechanisation of manufacturing

Right. Designs for cornices by William Pain of 1788. The Greek anthemion motif, based on the honeysuckle flower, is very much in evidence.

practices and the increasing availability of luxury goods, and partly due to the continuing proliferation of printed advice. By 1770 pattern-book authors were arguing in print over the respective merits of Neoclassical mouldings, and still disputing who had the best guide to the mathematical proportions of a room. In 1767 John Crunden's *Convenient and Ornamental Architecture* – 'the most successful book of ... designs of the period, indeed of the century'[6] – declared with astonishing certainty that a room ten feet square in size should have a chimneypiece that was precisely two feet five inches wide and two feet eleven-and-a-half inches high, with a four-inch cornice. William Chambers's magisterial (if less financially successful) *Treatise on Civil Architecture* of 1759 sensibly confined its advice to the precept that 'the size of the chimneypiece must depend of the dimensions of the room wherein it is placed'.

In exercising choice, the average homeowner increasingly opted for comfort over style. In the living room, sofas and armchairs became more stuffed, and were often covered with loose covers except when in polite use. In the bedroom, spiral springs were inserted into mattresses from the 1790s, although this did not preclude more eccentric experiments such as air-filled oilskins, first used in Paris in 1774, or rubber air cushions, patented in Berlin. Daybeds were now common in the living room, often taking the form of single-ended chaises longues. Sofas – made by chairmakers, and always regarded as part of the decoration of the room, their backs mimicking the design of

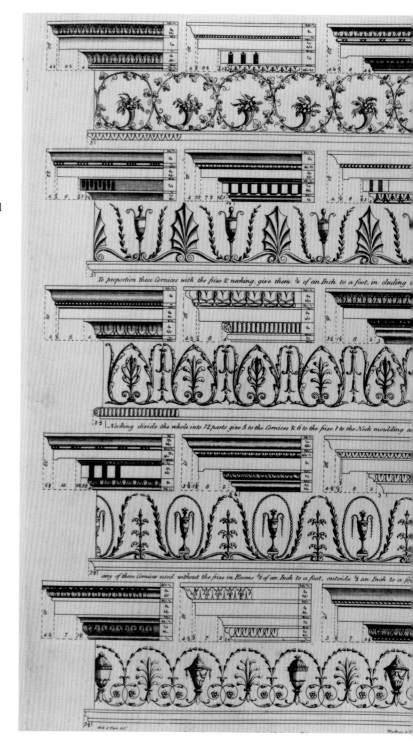

the dado rail and adjacent panelling – were upholstered with increasing generosity. Even the most rectilinear, architecturally derived chairs of Sheraton and Hepplewhite were provided with a degree of padded or caned comfort unheard of fifty years before.

Comfortable and washable furnishing fabrics could also now be had relatively cheaply. Indeed, the progress of the British cotton fabric industry in the late eighteenth century was revelatory: by the outbreak of the French Revolution in 1789, washable, light and inexpensive plain and printed cottons had flooded the market and displaced the majority of the heavy, dull and expensive products prevalent fifty years before. Woodblock and copperplate printing techniques developed rapidly during the 1750s: by 1758, six years after Francis Nixon had invented the printing of cotton by copper plates, copper-printed cottons were already widely available in London.[7] The colours preferred by printers were, nevertheless, limited by technology:

mostly indigo blues, rich browns and madder-derived reds (most of which have since faded to sepia).

The rapid expansion of British cotton manufacture, and the consequent revolution in furnishing fabrics, created exciting new possibilities for the householder and decorator across the whole of Europe and America. Prior to the mid-eighteenth century, as we have seen, most European cotton goods were imported from India or other foreign markets, with locally made furnishing fabrics depending largely on wool or silk. By the 1780s, however, cotton mills processing cotton from the Eastern Mediterranean and, increasingly, from the southern states of the new United States had sprung up all over Britain and had become a major feature of the Lancashire landscape. Hargreaves's spinning jenny of 1770, Crompton's 'mule' of 1779, James Watt's development of steam power in the early 1780s, the cylinder printing of fabrics (first patented by Thomas Bell in 1783) and Cartwright's power loom of 1787 ensured that the manufacture of cotton fabrics was quickly able to overtake and eclipse that of other traditional furnishing materials. Cotton chintzes and calicoes of all grades were quickly available, and chintzes and other cotton fabrics of greater sophistication soon displaced the more expensive silks and heavier woollen goods as essential fabrics for the interior.

Cotton fabrics particularly helped satisfy the new demand for lighter, washable furnishing materials and were widely used in every room in the house. Curtains, which had been a rare luxury before the 1760s, were now widespread. Sometimes, indeed, they were too profuse, 'smothering rooms with muslin veils and turning beds into veritable Niagras of textiles'.[8] Nevertheless, the French 'Empire' fashion for tumbling drapery in living rooms and bedrooms soon spread to the rest of Europe and to North America. By 1800 divided 'French rod' curtains were replacing the older 'festoon' variety, with pelmets being made to mask the curtain rods and rings and tasselled tie-backs being introduced to keep the heavier fabrics at the window's architrave.

In the bedroom, heavy traditional fabrics used for bed and window curtains, such as moreen ('apt to harbour moths and other vermin', noted J.C. Loudon in passing), were being discarded by the 1780s in favour of washable cotton chintzes. The materials on the mattress itself, though, were still of wool, and invariably white or undyed. Robert Southey's fictional Spanish tourist remarked in 1807 that British

blankets were 'of the natural colour of the wool, quite plain; the sheets plain also. I have never seen them flounced nor laced, nor ever seen a striped or coloured blanket.' Southey also reported that 'damask curtains which were used in the last generation have given place to linens' which were more easily washable – silks or satin failing, he added, to give 'that clean appearance which the English always require'. For households of limited means, plain white, washable cotton dimity was invariably chosen for curtains and bed hangings. And even the more exotic fabrics were now within easy reach of most purses. Merino was a popular new material made from the superb wool of the Spanish Merino sheep – introduced into Britain by George III himself in 1786. Its relative cheapness soon prompted Regency entrepreneurs such as Rudolf Ackermann to recommend it as a substitute for dearer silks or superfine cloths. Even cheaper were the new 'Manchester velvets', cottons with small diaper patterns

A fashionable Parisian drawing room design published in the 1777 volume of Jacques-Francois Blondel's *Cours d'Architecture*. French Neoclassicism eschewed the rectilinear rigidity of its Anglo-Saxon cousin.

stamped by machine, and machine-pressed 'watered' fabrics which imitated the highly expensive watered silks of the Early Georgian period.

Chintz, however, remained the most successful of all the new cottons. Glazed or unglazed, it could be used for bed hangings or window curtains, for loose covers or upholstery. It was cheap and it was washable. As the enterprising publisher Rudolf Ackermann noted in 1809, as the novelty of the early, brightly coloured British chintzes faded, so 'the gaudy colours of the chintz and calico furniture' gave way 'to a more chaste style, in which two colours only are employed to produce that appearance of damask'.

Not all advances in the cotton industry were of British origin, however. The opening in 1760 of Christophe-Philippe Oberkampf's textile factory at Jouy-en-Josas (near Versailles, and to the west of Paris) has been heralded as 'the

beginning of the age of chintz'.[9] By the 1780s cotton chintzes, with their large and colourful designs and proven washability, were hugely popular for seat covering in most homes. Furniture was now being permanently brought out from the side walls (see below). With the consequent prominence of furniture backs, the most important motifs of these fabrics were invariably placed on the rear, where they could be more easily admired, rather than on the seat. In France, the fashion even in middle-class households was to change seat upholstery every season, although by 1800 this often meant just changing and washing the loose covers rather than the upholstery itself.

Although the later eighteenth century is generally associated with Austenesque calm and politeness, much of the period was actually set against the background of war in Western Europe and North America. This had a fundamental effect on every aspect of life. Thus when France entered the American War of Independence on the colonists' side in 1778, this closed French fabric and wallpaper markets and had a disastrous effect on the native silk industry, already suffering through the spread of cottons. Despite the ravages of war, however, keen British manufacturers were able to leap into the gap; thus by 1795 North America accounted for half of British cotton exports.[10]

With cheaper cottons now available, the middle classes could comfortably afford curtains. 'Festoon' curtains were common by 1760, either divided or drawn horizontally, when they were confusingly called in both Britain

Left. A late eighteenth century engraving of a 'spinning jenny' loom. Invented by Englishman James Hargreaves in 1770, the spinning jenny revolutionised the production of cotton goods – and made them far more widely available.

Opposite. Three fine French printed silks of 1785 demonstrate what heights French workmanship could achieve in the years immediately before the Revolution.

and France 'Italian curtains'. 'Venetian' fabric blinds were regularly in use in Britain and France by 1770, too.

Elsewhere on the wall, the repertoire of colours was escalating. Increasingly, richer colours based on antique Roman precedents appeared alone or in combination with paler, complementary tints. However, Neoclassical designers and decorators did not, as is often alleged, rely on washed-out pastel hues. Bright blues, greens, browns, lilacs and even strong yellows were becoming increasingly popular and, owing to technological advances, increasingly cheap. Many of these bright colours were used as the background for newly fashionable print rooms, where engraved prints were arranged above the dado (often itself merely a *trompe-l'œil* print) between elaborate paper borders.

Nowhere were the new, richer

colours seen to better effect than in the ceilings of Robert Adam, with their strongly coloured panels and details picked out in white. It must be emphasised that these strong Late Georgian colours were not simply the result of purely decorative whim: many had a firm grounding in antique practice. Thus 'Pompeian red' – a dusty, brownish terracotta colour – was originally taken by John Soane and others directly from the hues found on the walls of long-buried Pompeii itself. (Soane himself actually carried a lump of red-painted Pompeian wall back to London to serve as the model for the colour of his new drawing room.) C.R. Cockerell's publication in 1819 of the archaeological discoveries recently made at Aegina in Greece, which had revealed that the walls of ancient Greek buildings had not been left as bare stone but had been highly coloured, gave the widening range of contemporary colours a timely academic sanction.

Britain led the way in wallpaper technology in the late eighteenth century. At the beginning of the century wallpaper colours were largely distempers, heavy and pasty with glue. John Baptist Jackson (1701–77) was the first to use oil-based colours rather than distempers, which enabled him to achieve more intense colours and greater accuracy in printing than ever before. His oil-printed papers did not get damp, were not darkened by smoke, and could, for the first time, be washed. The British also developed upmarket flock paper: in the 1750s King George II was actually replacing his silk wall hangings at Kensington Palace with flocked paper, and even Louis XV's mistress Madame de Pompadour had British flock papers hung in her home. But, in the opinion of one design historian, by the 1770s 'the level of design was generally poor', and not a patch on that of French printed cottons.[11] Nevertheless, in technological terms, the British were way ahead: the French were creating single-sheet wallpapers well into the 1770s, whereas by 1750 British firms had already begun joining sheets together to make the now familiar wallpaper roll. Distemper colours were introduced: these dried more quickly than oil colours, and looked more solid when printed. In

Chiaroscuro print from an English architectural wood-blocked wallpaper of 1769. Such products could give households the illusion of living in a Neoclassical idyll.

1753 Edward Dighton began printing from etched or engraved plates using a rolling mill. And from the 1760s onwards cylinder printing, in which hand-operated cylinders replaced the customary wood blocks or metal plates, began to be adopted. Yet while the printing of two or three colours on one paper became commonplace in Britain, the seventeenth-century practice of colour-washing a background by hand continued well into the next century. It was not until the 1830s that mechanised cylinders were substituted for blocks on a large scale.

Both British and French wallpaper manufacturers were, by 1760, making paper borders and ribbons to adorn the new fad for print rooms. Indeed, British wallpapers were regularly imported into France until the advent of the Seven Years War in 1756. Following the war, French wallpaper manufacturer Jean-Baptiste Réveillon (1725–1811) initiated a quantum leap forward in wallpaper design. His high-quality, expensive products, often lauded as the high point of wallpaper design, could mimic woven silks from Lyon, toiles de Jouy, Indian cottons or hand-painted Chinese designs. In 1773 Réveillon and other French papers were finally permitted to be imported into Britain and its colonies. (Interestingly, the enthusiasm for wallpaper during this period remained confined largely to Britain and France and their respective colonies: Germany, Austria and Italy remained impervious to the allure of paper until the post-Napoleonic period.) Fifteen years later, however, the Réveillon factory, possibly because

A floral printed silk from Lyon of c.1780, exported to Pavlovsk in Russia. The rich colours and dense composition could date from sixty years later.

of the exclusive, upmarket nature of its papers (or simply because it was one of the largest businesses in the French capital), became the first target of the Parisian revolutionaries. On 28 April 1789 the factory was looted by the mob – who were swiftly joined by factory staff – in response to a rumour that Réveillon was planning to cut wages. The uprising was put down with great savagery, resulting in 'the bloodiest day of the French Revolution' prior to 1792; soon afterwards, Réveillon retired.[12]

The European carpet industry had been, like regional wallpaper manufacture, almost non-existent in 1700; a hundred years later, its products could be seen on middle-class floors all over Britain, America and Northern

Europe. The first truly commercial carpet workshop in Britain had been founded in 1735 in Kidderminster, Worcestershire, to make both pile and flat carpets. In 1740 the 9th Earl of Pembroke established a factory at Wilton in Wiltshire which, like Kidderminster, specialised in 'Brussels'-style looped-pile carpets as well as their cut-pile cousins. In 1750 a factory was established at Fulham in London by French émigrés to produce Turkish-style knotted carpets. This rapidly failed, but other factories making knotted carpets were soon founded at Moorfields in London, at Exeter and, most famously, at Axminster in Dorset in 1755. Axminster knotted carpets were soon known for the quality of their design, which relied on both Turkish and Persian influences and on more topical Neoclassical patterning. Such carpets were clearly cheaper than their Levantine models; nevertheless, they were still beyond the reach of many households. Brussels and Wilton carpets were made in British factories, as were more utilitarian double-weave, reversible 'Scotch' flat carpets (made in Edinburgh, Kilmarnock and Kidderminster, and often termed 'Kidderminster carpets') and the even more basic 'list carpets', made from single-coloured fabric strips sewn together.[13]

Close carpeting, fitted right up to the edge of the skirting, was prevalent in Western homes by 1800. The poet Robert Southey also remarked on the British practice of using small Wilton cut-pile carpets as hearthrugs on top of the fitted carpets – 'a fashion of late years', he remarked in 1807, 'which has become universal because it is at once ornamental, comfortable and useful'.

Left. An anonymous French wallpaper design of *c.*1800.

Opposite. The fashionable French interior shown in this engraving by I.S. Helman of 1781, after Jean-Michel Moreau's painting *The Fine Supper*, combines Neoclassical wall divisions with Baroque detail and a Rococo lamp.

Opposite. A recreated floorcloth at Homewood, Baltimore, in a pattern called 'tumbling block'. Floorcloths were generally printed in imitation of hard flooring, particularly marble.

By the 1830s, though, J.C. Loudon was advocating leaving a small border of floorboarding of between one-and-a-half and two feet in width between carpet and skirting. The resulting border was then grained or covered in some similar fashion. By Loudon's day, too, carpet specialists were available to measure and fit the carpet, chalking the design out on the floor before proceeding. The middle-class householder had certainly come a long way in barely a century.

1. James Stuart and Nicholas Revett, *The Antiquities of Athens*, vol. 1 (1762), Preface. The second volume did not appear until 1789, a year after Stuart's death. The later three volumes, of 1794, 1814 and 1830, were by other hands. 2. J. Mordaunt Crook, *The Greek Revival* (1972), 75. 3. Quoted in Steven Parissien, *Adam Style* (1992), 49. 4. Edith Wharton and Ogden Codman, *The Decoration of Houses* (1897/1978), 129. 5. Charles Saumarez Smith, *The Rise of Design* (2000), 46. 6. Eileen Harris, *British Architectural Books and Writers 1556–1785* (1990), 171. 7. John Cornforth, *Early Georgian Interiors* (2004), 195 8. Peter Thornton, *Authentic Decor* (1984), 154. 9. Elsie de Wolfe, *The House in Good Taste* (1913), 197. 10. Mary Schoeser and Celia Rufey, *English and American Textiles from 1790 to the Present* (1989), 30. 11. Peter Thornton, *Form and Decoration: Innovation in the Decorative Arts 1470–1870* (1998), 166. 12. Bernard Jacqué, 'Réveillon', in Joanna Banham (ed.), *Encyclopaedia of Interior Design*, vol. 2, 1057. 13. Thornton, *Authentic Decor*, 101. Thornton notes that list carpets were still being used in Sweden in the early twentieth century.

THE DEMOCRATIC INTERIOR

Celebrating the Middle-class Home in the Early Nineteenth Century

5

Dark, handsome new carpets and curtains, an arrangement of some carefully selected antique ornaments in porcelain and bronze, new coverings, and mirrors, and dressing-cases for the toilet tables, answered the end: they looked fresh without being glaring.

(Charlotte Brontë, *Jane Eyre*, 1847)

Vibrant French chintz designs of the 1830s show just what could be achieved by the latest looms and pigments. French craftsmen of the period were expert in dyeing and in producing intricately complex patterns, which here derive from Indian antecedents.

The increasing pace of industrial-isation had a fundamental effect on the average Western home of the early nineteenth century. Technology democratised taste, allowing the middle classes real choice for the first time in history. Deciding how to decorate interiors became pleasurable, congenial – even amusing – for the first time, liberated as homeowners now were from the dictates of the rich by the freedoms conferred by mass-production and by the spread of printed material. Homeowners shrugged off the patrician dictates of Palladianism and Neoclassicism and instead bought what they liked, indulging in an orgy of tongue-in-cheek revivalism that embraced all periods and all styles. Even the more mainstream classical and Gothic styles were adapted to incorporate an increasing variety of stylistic approaches.

If you had to point to one factor which, more than any other, changed the way homes were decorated and disposed during this period, it would be the rapid industrialisation of textile production. By the 1840s most middle-class households in Europe and North America could afford mass-produced woven and printed cloths. These textiles in turn helped effect a sea-change in taste: comfort and informality were now established as the prime goals even in the most public of middle-class rooms, in place of the rigid, correct formality which had so characterised polite society in eighteenth-century Europe.

The wealth of mass-produced textiles, though, was not the only basis of this new-found confidence. The large number of published guides on interior decoration available from the early 1800s onwards helped to liberate homeowners, putting them – rather than, as before, established architects, writers or scholars – in the driving seat of fashion and taste. This development helped to quicken the turn-round of room redecoration, 'the pace of which accelerated from about a thirty-year lifespan in the late seventeenth century to about seven two centuries later',[1] which in turn helped stimulate the market for decoration manuals. It was onwards and upwards for the ambitious middle-class decorator.

The standard late eighteenth-century furniture manuals by Chippendale, Hepplewhite and Sheraton had long served the furniture-makers. What was different about the manuals and periodicals published after 1800 was that most of them were aimed not at the trade but at average homeowners, thus

Opposite. A 'before and after' contrast from one of Humphry Repton's celebrated Red Books, this example – the 'Old Cedar Parlour and the Modern Living Room' from *Fragments on the Theory and Practice of Landscape Gardening* – dating from 1816. Repton suggests fusing the room with nature by means of a glazed conservatory, extending the windows down to the ground, reducing the size of the chimney opening and softening the floor by introducing a British-made fitted carpet.

Right. Bright, confident Federal colours in use at Charles Bulfinch's Harrison Gray Otis House in Boston, Massachusetts, in the early nineteenth century.

Below. Designs for tables and dressers in the Ancien Régime style by Pierre Lefèvre-Chauveaux from an album entitled *Dessins de Meubles, Tables à Coulisses.*

shifting the balance in determining how interiors were to be shaped from the manufacturer to the consumer.

The most influential European guide of this era, which became a benchmark for all other serious works on decoration, was not in itself a bestseller. However, the 'Empire' taste that its plates promoted became the foundation for countless bourgeois interiors. The highly influential periodical *Recueil des Décorations intérieurs*, compiled by Charles Percier (1764–1838) and Pierre Fontaine (1762–1853), appeared in regular instalments between 1801 and 1812, after which it was reissued as a complete book and widely translated. Percier and Fontaine's book made 'an indelible mark on the history of design',[2] and spurred other writers and publishers into action across Europe. First off the blocks was Frenchman Pierre de la Messangières, whose *Meubles et Objets de Goût* first appeared in 1802. Five years later came Thomas Hope's

Household Furniture and Interior Decoration. Hope, who declared that he wanted to initiate a 'deviation from the prevailing style', borrowed much from Percier and Fontaine, while at the same time patriotically condemning 'the degraded French school of the middle of the last century'.[3] (France and Britain were, of course, once again at war in 1807.) His scholarly work was perhaps too austere and revolutionary for the public taste, but it did introduce the term 'interior decoration' to the language.

Over twenty years later, George Smith's comprehensive and accessible *Cabinet-Maker and Upholsterer's Guide* of 1826 popularised many of Hope's stylistic innovations, and its down-to-earth prose and copious illustrations – complete with sample paint chart, a very modern feature – made it a big success on both sides of the Atlantic. Equally influential in the English-speaking world was the London periodical *The Repository of the Arts*, issued between 1809 and 1828 by the Saxon-born entrepreneur and publisher Rudolf Ackermann (1764–1834). Ackermann's colourful plates and up-to-date styles – initially reflecting the prevailing Neoclassical taste (called Regency in Britain, Empire in France and Federal in America) but by the 1820s embracing a plethora of Early Modern revivals – proved especially helpful to the aspirational new homeowner, and can be seen as the ancestor of today's glossy home interest magazines.

The 1820s saw the appearance of the first books in Britain and America which, purveying general domestic advice on subjects ranging from interior decoration to cooking, were aimed at the

women's market. Mrs William Parkes's *Domestic Duties, or Instructions to Young Married Ladies* – first published in Britain in 1828, with the US edition appearing the following year – was the first of many. The precursor of bestsellers such as Eliza Leslie's *The House Book* (1840) and Catherine Beecher and Harriet Beecher Stowe's *The American Woman's Home* (1869), these volumes reflected women's new role as arbiter of middle-class interior decoration. The Beecher sisters in particular provided 'written descriptions and practical illustrations for creating inexpensive but fashionable interiors that fulfilled the ultimate goal – a "homelike" setting'.[4]

By 1840 there was a bewildering variety of guides and manuals on t he subject of interior decoration, making the subject into a popular occupation not merely for the grandee but for the average house owner. Most guides now advocated the concept of an instantly recognisable, comprehensive 'look' to be imposed on all the aspects of the interior, a concept which had been devised for great houses by Robert Adam and his contemporaries since the 1760s but which was now declared to be within the reach of all households. The use of 'en suite' decoration in middle-class homes was popularly promoted by Ackermann; by 1833 J.C. Loudon, in his invaluable (if less easily digested) *Encyclopaedia of Cottage, Farm and Villa Architecture*, was asserting that interior colours must be employed 'in unison, or a proper combination of parts', and that piecemeal decoration resulted simply in 'an incongruous mixture'. Carpets, he advised, should

harmonise with the furniture; wallpaper and upholstery should match the curtains; and all should match the paintwork. Loudon's *Encyclopaedia* proved particularly influential in the US, with new editions appearing there as late as 1860.

By Loudon's day, many of the fabrics that adorned fashionable middle-class interiors were being made by the revolutionary new 'Jacquard' weaving process, invented in France in 1801 by Jean-Marie Jacquard. This replaced the effort of human labour by a series of punched cards, enabling complex patterns to be produced on a large scale

and, once the initial investment in equipment had been recouped, very cheaply. An 1801 exhibition of textile machinery in the courtyard of the Louvre in Paris featured a Jacquard loom – which won a prize – in public for the first time; by 1812, a total of 11,000 Jacquards had been installed across the breadth of Napoleonic France.

In 1820, in a canny reinterpretation of the spirit of Waterloo, the Englishman Stephen Wilson employed an industrial spy to find out exactly how Jacquard's invention worked. To a collective sigh of relief from the British textile industry, the following year Wilson was able to issue a British patent for a similar Jacquard system. By 1830 Jacquard weaves were

Opposite. A sombrely coloured, soberly Neoclassical Russian bedroom of 1819 (watercolour, private collection).

Right. An 'ornamental air stove' shown in Ackermann's *Repository of the Arts* (plate 17) in 1825.

Below. A Jacquard loom, 'borrowed' from the French and in operation in Britain in the 1820s.

beginning to appear in Britain, America and Germany. As Mary Schoeser has noted, these 'muscular' new designs 'were often vigorously shaped or broken by strong outlines', and frequently copied French patterns of the period.[5]

However, while the British textile industry viewed Jacquard looms as one of many new technological advances to be exploited and perfected, French weavers were content to stay more or less as they had been in Napoleon's day. For while London and Paris were the dominant forces in terms of taste in the post-Waterloo world, it was Britain that emphatically led the West – including its cross-Channel rival – in manufacture. The British naval blockade of Napoleon's France had strangled the French economy to the extent that it only fully recovered in the 1840s. While post-Napoleonic French textile designs may have been judged by the critics to be superior to their British counterparts, it was British textiles that flooded into worldwide markets after 1815. France's textile industry even went backwards: hand-weaving increased in France, whereas in Britain power looms spread with little opposition (excepting outbursts of machine-smashing Luddism during the economic downturn of 1810–12). As early as 1816 the government banned the import of cotton cloths, and by 1860, while France boasted 200,000 handlooms, Britain had only 3,000. 'France remained, in comparison with Britain, a country of land-owning peasants, self-employed craftsmen, and small towns and villages.' Britain's manufacturing labour force had exceeded the size of its agricultural

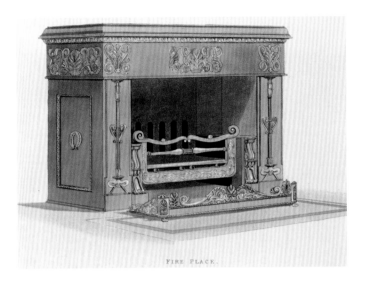

FIRE PLACE.

equivalent by 1840, but this did not happen in France until the 1950s.[6]

In Britain, cotton increasingly meant Manchester. By 1840 Manchester had established itself as the world's Capital of Cotton: the following year it was estimated that in Manchester alone 500 people were working as designers of printed cottons, with George Dodd observing that 'the drawing of [fabric] designs is an extensive branch of employment at Manchester'. In contrast, the Lyons silk industry operated much as it had in the eighteenth century, employing 'more than 300,000 people ... in a complex system of domestic outwork spread over a radius of 100 miles from the city'.

The diverging approaches of Britain and France to the technological revolution in home furnishings encouraged the French to seek different market sectors. Unable to compete with Britain in overseas markets for mass-produced products, and with a domestic market dominated by a large peasant population that consumed little, French manufacturers went upmarket, supplying luxury goods to the rich consumers of the Continent, America and above all, Britain. 'Their selling points were fashion, quality and exclusivity, rather than cheapness and technology.'[7]

The effect of this commonsense concentration on premium wares and luxury items made in Britain was often crippling. For example, the ailing British silk industry, already suffering from the shrinking of markets during wartime and the rising tide of mass-produced cottons, was virtually killed off by French competition. The 1824 Spitalfields Act terminated all artificial protection of silk-weavers' wages, thus consigning what remained of the Spitalfields silk industry to oblivion and encouraging the now jobless Huguenot community in Spitalfields to migrate east, to the burgeoning suburbs of Stepney and Hackney.

Meanwhile, it was Britain's cheap, washable cottons that paved the way to the democratic interior. Western cotton manufacture in general – and Britain's in particular – had, as we have seen, been revolutionised by the introduction of mechanisation. The patenting in Britain of the spinning mule in 1779 opened the door to the mass-manufacture of more delicate, finely woven cottons. As a result, by 1810 muslin sub-curtains – which could filter daylight so that it did not damage expensive fabrics and paintings – were a standard feature of middle-class drawing rooms.

If any furnishing fabric could be said to have epitomised the homes of the early nineteenth century, however, it was undoubtedly the vast family of cotton chintzes. Chintz – the word comes from India, where it merely means printed cloth – was particularly favoured for parlours and drawing rooms. However, in libraries and dining rooms wool fabrics were still preferred for curtains, while leather remained the accepted covering for dining-room and library chairs throughout the nineteenth century. Dining-room chairs were typically upholstered in red leather, library furniture often in green. Leather was particularly popular for dining-room upholstery in the more well-to-do households since it did not absorb food smells and could be easily wiped clean. Those households which could not afford leather used cheaper horsehair upholstery, which performed in a similar manner to leather at a fraction of the cost.

Elsewhere in the house, however, cotton chintz upholstery predominated.

A block-printed floral cotton of 1812 by Peel & Co. of Lancashire. This was just the sort of design, with architectural elements suspended in space between realistically delineated flowers, that the design reformers of the later nineteenth century abhorred.

By 1810 not only the more traditional red, green and blue cottons were used, but even striking gold, silver and black colour schemes – particularly on the sofa, where rich coverings, elaborately tufted backs and tasselled bolsters were all explicitly designed to make it the most eye-catching item in the room. The introduction of new mineral dyes in the early years of the century (see Chapter 7) was enthusiastically welcomed by the manufacturers of furnishing fabrics, and allowed designers to produce even more striking colour combinations. These could now be put into sharper contrast by the subtle use of bright white. Bleaching fabrics with chlorine to achieve a bright white had already been discovered in the 1810s in France, where by the 1820s white was used with bold black outlines to highlight the increasingly bold and luxuriant flower bunches the French designers preferred. In 1800, too, the method of printing

bright colours adjacent to each other without leaving intervening white lines (through the use of 'resist mordaunts') was discovered.

Fabric patterns became bolder, larger and more colourful. The military motifs so popular before 1815 had by 1830 given way to flowers, pillars and birds – the latter especially popular in America after the publication of J.J. Audubon's magisterial *Birds of America*, from 1827. In Britain and America, Indian flowering trees came into fashion after the appearance of Thomas and William Daniell's evocative *Antiquities and Views of India* of 1795–1808, paralleling the vogue of the 1810s and 1820s for 'drab' styles, base on the fugitive yellows and golds produced by Edward Bancroft's newly discovered 'quercitron yellow' dye, made from tree bark. Bancroft himself boasted that his new dye caused 'no discolouration to the grounds or parts intended to remain white'. Scrollwork

Opposite. A deep-buttoned sofa by Le Bouteiller, published in his short-lived consumer magazine *L'Exposition: Album de l'industrie et des Arts Utiles* of the 1830s. Such a piece would have been the quintessential element of the mid-nineteenth century bourgeois living room.

Right. French chintz design of the 1830s. Floral realism at its most confident and stylish.

and floral stripes came back into fashion in the 1820s, and eighteenth-century trellis and sprig patterns were revived in the 1830s.

It is important to remember, though, that such lush displays of colour and decoration were actually rarely seen unless important guests were present. Throughout the eighteenth and nineteenth centuries, every important item of furniture was invariably provided with a protective loose cover, to preserve the precious fabric underneath. By 1840 most middle-class interiors were shrouded in loose covers of cotton, serge or linen, whose employment became a barometer of social status: only the most prized visitors earned their removal.[8] These loose covers can be frequently seen in contemporary paintings and watercolours, and were themselves often interestingly patterned or bordered. Glazed chintz, calico, green baize, gingham and leather

covers were very common. Needlework covers, out of fashion by 1800, were prevalent again by the middle of the century, as industrialisation brought home handicrafts back into fashion. Alternatively, as the anonymous author of the *Workman's Guide* of 1838 suggested, chintz, Holland or calico covers could be used – with or without piping, possibly lined with thin calico, and tightly fastened with sewn loops and strings.

Loose covers were not only made for seat furniture. In 1803 Sheraton cited the existence of 'covers for pier tables, made of stamped leather and glazed, lined with flannel to save the varnish of such table tops', adding that 'lately they have introduced a new kind of painted canvas' to serve the same purpose. Richer families could afford damask protective covers for their tables and sideboards. Tablecloths, too, were a new feature; they should, the *Workman's Guide* confidently averred, always be of damask.

A bizarre French printed cotton of *c.*1820, featuring Daniel Defoe's story of *Robinson Crusoe*. Presumably destined for the walls of a single man's home.

Curtain design moved on apace, too. In 1803 Sheraton had noted that festoon curtains were outmoded, and that side-drawn French rod curtains – the first curtain type not to rise from the floor – were 'the most approved way of managing window curtains' in Europe.[9] With the abandonment of festoon curtains and the like, curtain poles were now often left exposed, or (in the more showy homes) dramatically draped with loose-hung swathes of inessential fabric. Curtains were, by the 1840s, even being used in the kitchen, although here they were very plain – usually of simple cotton muslin or checked dimity.

By the 1840s carpeting had come to be viewed 'as an essential part of middle-class interior decoration'. Looped-pile and cut-pile 'Brussels' and 'Wilton' carpets were now made on power looms,

such as those at Crossleys in Halifax, and by 1840 were within the purse of all middle-class homes. In America, their price plummeted only after Erastus Bigelow had in 1846 installed his new power loom in his factory at Clinton, Massachusetts; this mighty and innovative machine was exhibited at the Crystal Palace in 1851 and there earned worldwide admiration. By 1850 machine-woven carpets were widely available, particularly from new factories in New York and the Scottish lowlands.[10] The market for hand-woven, ersatz-Axminster flat carpets (often termed 'domestic Orientals') had been overtaken by that for machine-woven 'Axminsters', such as James Templeton's Glasgow-made 'chenille Axminster' of 1839 and Halcyon Skinner's Yonkers-woven 'Royal Axminster' of 1867.

Right. The height of
fashion in 1816: a
French curtain and muslin
sub-curtain fronting a pair
of French windows, which
give an excellent view
of tamed nature beyond.
The chimneypiece and
mirror in this plate from
Ackermann's *Repository
of the Arts* are suitably
minimalist – in contrast to
the overblown revivalist
fireplace designs of three
decades later.

Carpet use changed from nation to nation. In Regency and Early Victorian Britain, machine-made as well as handmade carpets were woven with borders, leaving a strip of bare floorboarding when they were laid, and did not reach into window recesses. In Federal America they generally had no borders, and did.

For those working-class households where even machine-made carpets were unaffordable, or those workaday locations where rich fabric floorcoverings were inappropriate, there was always the traditional floorcloth. In 1812 the American manual-writer Hezekiah Reynolds explained exactly how floorcloths were made: 'Canvas or common tow cloth is sewed with a flat seam, of the dimensions required; and nailed form upon a floor; then wet with water even, and thoroughly; and before dry, is primed with any common colour.' After two more coats of paint and the filling of any cracks with putty, the cloth was 'divided into squares or diamonds of which one half … are painted white; and the other half black'. In 1816 the painter Rolinda Sharples provided directions for a more durable pattern, by which the colour was stamped, hot, on to the cloth with a pearwood block and 'when it is finished, breadth ways with one colour, it is stamped with another, the pattern of the former, until completed'.

Floorcloths did not only imitate black-and-white marble flooring. In his *Encylopaedia* of 1833 Loudon mentions patterns of inlaid stone, of wainscot and of 'tessellated pavement', while other floorcloths even attempted to mimic Turkish carpet designs. To match his

oak-coloured drugget at Abbotsford in the 1820s, Sir Walter Scott bought an oak-coloured oilcloth, which, typically for the time, he placed under the sideboard to catch spillages. By 1821 the floorcloth-makers Smith and Barber were, Ian Bristow has noted, offering floorcloths in Plain Red, Yellow Mat, Green Mat, Alex Pavement, Octagon Marble, Patera, Tessellated Marble, Fancy Flower, Oak Leaf, Foliage, Carlton, Green

Cluster, Imperial, Turkey and Persian designs.[11] Floorcloths never lasted very long, however. In 1833 Loudon pointed out that 'where there is much going out and coming in of persons generally employed in the open air, and of course wearing strong shoes', floorcloths rapidly disintegrated. By the mid-nineteenth century many tradesmen specifically advertised their ability to get 'Old Cloths new Painted and Repair'd'.

The rooms that the furnishing fabrics adorned were themselves undergoing a metamorphosis in the early nineteenth century. Rooms became recognised indications of function and status. Thus, for example, by 1800 having a parlour – effectively a ground-floor drawing room – had become a mark of middle-class status in British and American homes; sometimes homes had two, one on the ground and one on the first floor, with the latter doubling as dining room. In grander houses, the

parlour was still 'a general purpose room of secondary importance', while in humbler homes it signified the best room, used primarily for entertaining visitors in the absence of a formal drawing room or (as we would say today) living room.[12]

During the 1830s the provision of libraries spread. Libraries were introduced into even modest homes not just to be useful repositories of books but, as Robert Kerr wrote in 1864, to represent 'a sort of Morning-room for gentlemen' and 'essentially a private retreat' from women, who were not of course expected to read books. 'No villa or suburban residence ... can be considered complete without a library,' declared Loudon in 1833.[13] Always gendered a very masculine space, in large homes the library was supplemented by a billiard room and, by the 1860s, a smoking room.

On the garden side of the house, too, conservatories were becoming more common, their design and construction facilitated by the invention of the curved cast-iron glazing bar in 1815 and improvements in glass technology, culminating in the introduction of plate glass in the 1820s. While libraries were seen very much as male preserves, however, conservatories – as the gateway to trammelled or untrammelled nature, and perceived as a means of blurring the distinction between nature and domesticity – were considered part of the 'female' region of the house. Robert Kerr also warned that the 'warm moist air' in plant-strewn conservatories was bad for both upholstery and health, and advocated keeping the conservatory well

Right. Federal experimentation from the Harrison Gray Otis House in Boston, Massachusetts. Gone are the pale dados and dark baseboards of the eighteenth century; in this Boston home of the 1820s, turquoises and reds complement the rich straw of the walls.

Below. This charmingly naïve watercolour of *c.*1830 demonstrates how frequently cheap, gaily coloured slip covers were used for seat furniture at the time. They would only have been removed for the most important guests: clearly the artist did not qualify for this category.

away from the living and dining rooms.

However, the most fundamental change in how average homes were used from day to day came in the actual disposition of furniture. Until the 1790s all furniture was invariably placed against the side walls, and brought out only when needed – being subsequently returned against the wall by the servants. The dado or chair rail corresponded to the top rails of chairs arranged in this customary fashion; at the same time, the backs of much eighteenth-century furniture were comparatively plain, since they were only infrequently seen. During the last decade of the century, however, leading designers began to take the revolutionary step of bringing furniture permanently out into the room, aided by such advances in lighting as the Argand lamp. The importance of the new, informal arrangement of fashionable interiors, both large and small, cannot be overstated. For the first time in the history of the interior, pieces of furniture were not stacked against the walls in stiff, serried ranks after use, but remained disposed about the whole room in a free and easy – and decidedly asymmetrical – fashion.

The consequent liberation of the interior was shockingly dramatic. It was noted by observers such as Jane Austen, who, in her novel *Persuasion* (1816), observed that 'the present daughters of the house were giving the proper air of confusion by … little tables, placed in every direction'. But it was not an innovation that aesthetic conservatives could stomach. In 1811 the American Louis Simond visited Osterley Park, to the west of London, and was horrified to

find that 'Tables, sofas and chairs were studiously deranged about the fire-places and in the middle of the rooms, as if the family had just left them. Such is the modern fashion of placing furniture carried to an extreme, as fashions are always, that make the apartments of a fashionable house look like an upholsterer's or cabinet-maker's shop.'

This new development was particularly apt for smaller households

Chair-leg designs by
Lalonde of the early
nineteenth century. The
dawn of eclecticism:
Neoclassicism tinged with
the Renaissance Revival.

that lacked sufficient numbers of
servants to continually rearrange
furniture. It also corresponded well with
the general trend towards informality
evident in the early nineteenth-century
home. As the century progressed,
more and more pieces of furniture
were introduced into the centre of the
room, resulting in the clutter that so
characterised High Victorian interiors.

It was a development that
particularly benefited from the
increasing portability and reliability of
oil lamps. Portable oil lamps were needed
until the advent of electricity at the end
of the century, since gas fittings were
static and necessarily wall- or ceiling-
based, and therefore illumination for
other areas of the room could only
come from lamps. The efficient new
Argand lamp, originally patented in
1784, was particularly helpful in this
regard. Argands could be of many
forms – they could be multi-branched;
some types were fixed to walls; some
indeed metamorphosed into rather
bulky chandeliers – and incorporated
the ingenious solution of passing the
oil through tubes in the rim of the
lampshade itself, which removed the
need for a reservoir. (The thick, viscous
colza or rapeseed oil the British used,
or the whale oil the Americans used,
still, however, remained something of
an obstacle to good design.) Thomas
Jefferson had noted the invention of the
Argand in 1784, and the design was soon
pirated on both sides of the Channel.
The fecund American inventor and
entrepreneur Count Rumford warned
that 'no woman of "decayed beauty"
ought ever to expose her face to the

direct rays of an Argand lamp'.[14]
Argand's lamp was bright, adjustable
and relatively clean. By 1800 President
George Washington owned several
examples. And by the mid-nineteenth
century, the classic Argand form of a
reservoir on a pedestal, underneath a
burner in a clear glass chimney, had
been established for table lamps – the
glass globe of the burner being etched,
coloured, cut, pressed, moulded, painted
or engraved.

The furniture that such portable
lamps helped to illuminate after dark
itself became increasingly comfortable,
as the newly wealthy middle classes
sought to create environments that,
while emphasising their owners' taste
and sophistication, also prioritised
snug security. The deeply padded,
toad-like armchair (which the French
really did call 'crapaud') which was
fashionable from the 1830s may have
looked awkward, but was very pleasing
to use. Springs were widely used in seat
furniture and beds by 1840, relegating
traditional hair stuffing to a secondary
supportive role, and the well-stuffed
upholstery was increasingly secured
by buttons rather than by tufting,
the former being easier to apply and
replace. (The quest for more comfortable
upholstery did, though, produce some
strange experiments during the early
decades of the nineteenth century.
Filling mattresses with inflated pigs'
bladders was mooted, as was the use
of oiled sacs filled with water – an idea
which clearly anticipated the modern
waterbed, and which found some use
in hospitals.) The typical seat furniture
of the 1840s was thus heavily stuffed,

with grace and elegance being happily sacrificed to the gods of ease and comfort.

Interiors of this period were not only more informally disposed and comfortably upholstered, in cheerful defiance of the order and conventions of rigid eighteenth-century classicism. They were also more convenient. Field or tent beds were suddenly popular, provided with fully enclosing curtains which could be drawn up during the day.

The confidence of the newly enriched middle classes also encouraged them to overturn accepted stylistic conventions. No longer were the austere precepts of Neoclassicism to hold complete sway: instead, the 1820s and 1830s became the decades of stylistic eclecticism. In Britain, King George IV led the way in the 1820s by creating at Windsor Castle one of the country's most eclectic sets of interiors, his predilection for diversity in interior decoration anticipating and possibly influencing the Victorian passion for mixing provenances and periods that was so prevalent in British middle-class homes by 1850. While some of the new furniture made in the 1820s for Windsor Castle, for example, was authentically medieval in inspiration, other pieces demonstrated the King's abiding enthusiasm for the French styles of the *ancien régime*. (Even George IV's architect, Jeffry Wyatville, felt moved to protest against the 'introduction of old French boiserie of the age of Louis XV, which would never have appeared in the Castle had the architect been guided solely by his own judgement'.)

By the mid-1820s, a 'Gothic' style

that was of somewhat more precision than the fanciful 'Gothick' of the mid-eighteenth century, yet was still far more light-hearted in tone than the products of the earnest Victorian Goths, was beginning to be used for everyday furniture as well as for grand baronial retreats. George Smith was the first designer to feature a complete range of Gothic furniture. However, most of the Gothic plates of his *Household Furniture* of 1808 were more reminiscent of the skin-deep 'Gothick' of the 1740s, such as Strawberry Hill and Inveraray Castle, than of truly medieval forms. Two years later Smith himself was actually warning in the pages of Ackermann's *Repository* that only the rich could afford to indulge in Gothic fantasies, since 'no person of a genuine taste' should be seen to introduce isolated examples of Gothic furniture into a house that has not been wholly Gothicised: the result, he claimed, would be 'grotesque and ridiculous'.

But the popular interest in Gothic did not abate, fuelled as it was by contemporary Gothic romances in both literary and architectural forms. In 1825 Ackermann judged that the time was right to exploit the passion for Gothic romance, mystery and historicism, and included in his *Repository of the Arts* a series of designs for Gothic furniture by the young, precocious A.W.N. Pugin, who in 1827 was still aged only fifteen. Accompanying them were claims that 'the architecture of the Middle Ages possesses more playfulness in its outline, and richness in its details than any other style' – hardly the sentiments of the committed Victorian Goth, but an

The advent of gas by no means banished candles from the average interior. This heavy cast-iron and brass chandelier is a French example of the 1830s, and was designed by Le Bouteiller to hold candles.

A design from Ackermann's *Repository of the Arts* clearly displaying the early nineteenth-century vogue for golds, yellows and drabs based on Dr Edward Bancroft's newly discovered organic pigment 'Quercitron yellow'.

invocation calculated to appeal to the more frivolous spirit of the Regency. The designs were so successful that, shortly after the end of the series, they were reprinted in a single volume under Pugin's own name, simply entitled *Gothic Furniture*.

The fashion for medieval-style furniture spread like wildfire. 'Gothic' pieces were particularly favoured in libraries and halls, undoubtedly on account of the vaguely monkish and ceremonial connotations of these rooms. As early as 1827 Ackermann was noting that 'we have now so many skilful

workers in Gothic that very elaborate pieces of furniture may be made at a moderate price'. The same period saw a Western revival of so-called 'Rococo' furniture, which used the eighteenth-century styles of Louis XV and XVI for its inspiration. Genuine Rococo pattern-books were reprinted by John Weale during the 1830s, and utilised by the leading furniture-maker Gillows. The style was particularly prominent at the Great Exhibition of 1851, where furniture inspired by Henry Whitaker's recent guides to Rococo sat unhappily cheek-by-jowl with Pugin's painstakingly authentic Gothic pieces.

The 1820s and 1830s also witnessed a fashion for the 'Elizabethan', 'Tudor' or 'Renaissance' style, an eclectic and unacademic combination of sixteenth-century forms which, in Britain, France and Holland at least, was no doubt chosen to recall the martial glories of that particular age. Since little sixteenth-century furniture had actually survived, there were few models available and thus, rather as had been the case with the 'Chinese taste', designers were able to let their imaginations run riot. The results, alas, were often rather uncomfortable, both visually and practically. Loudon warned that, while a Greek chair ought to be 'prized for its expression ... for its simplicity, and for the great effect produced in it by a very few lines', an Elizabethan chair 'wants that beauty of simplicity, or that evidence of affecting the most important ends by the simplest means'. Elizabethan furniture, Loudon admitted in the *Encyclopaedia* of 1833, was 'sometimes very rudely composed', while the architect C.R. Cockerell, himself no stranger to stylistic experiment, declared that all so-called 'Tudor' furniture was 'undoubtedly of spurious origin'.

Even more abhorrent to the aesthetic purist was the popular enthusiasm for historical and contemporary French fashions in Britain and America after 1815. In 1822 Ackermann observed that 'the Taste for French furniture is carried to such an extent, that most elegantly furnished mansions ... are fitted up in French style'. This fad – originally inspired by the passion of the Prince Regent for French

furniture – brought in its wake countless over-decorated and badly made pieces, allegedly reviving the styles of Louis XIV, Louis XV or Louis XVI, which represented the exact antithesis of Hope and Sheraton's doctrine of pure, clean lines. Hope himself had no sympathy with this style: 'that degraded French school of the middle of the last century', he termed it, which has been 'totally destitute of ... true elegance and beauty'.

Yet in spite of Hope's pleas, stylistic pluralism became the hallmark of interiors in the post-Waterloo era. By the 1830s countless historical styles were vying for attention. In the wake of orthodox Greek, Graeco-Egyptian, Louis XIV, Louis XVI, Gothic, and the newer fad for 'Elizabethan', came stranger styles still. Walter Scott's internationally successful novel of 1819, *Ivanhoe*, helped to promote a short-lived Norman Revival (originally and confusingly termed the 'Saxon Style', no doubt in deference to the nationalistic sympathies of Scott's work). Even more obscure sources were cited. Hope himself, in his Duchess Street house, included furniture not only in the 'Chinese' style of Brighton Pavilion but in 'Turkish' and 'Hindu' too. The overall effect on those who were not regular readers of the *Repository* could be quite bewildering. 'Only think of a crocodile couch and sphinx sofa!', exclaimed Miss Mitford in 1819; 'they sleep in Turkish tents and dine in a Gothic chapel, and all manner of anomalies are the consequence'.

While Britain was becoming the home of cheerful stylistic mix-and-match, Germany and Austria were turning to

less ostentatious and more dispassionate means of decorating and equipping interiors. If, by the mid-nineteenth century, the middle-class home in Europe and America had become a repository of family morality, combining the goals of comfort and display, it was in the German-speaking states that the morality of interior design was taken most seriously. Here, after the turmoil of the Napoleonic Empire, social emphasis was increasingly focused on comfort and family life, rather than on an external display of conspicuous consumption.

From the 1810s until the middle of the century, this firmly middle-class ideal was encapsulated in the so-called 'Biedermeier' style. Biedermeier – a term used for literature as well as interiors (although one not coined until the 1890s[15]) – had its origins in Vienna, spreading throughout the Austrian Empire and the German states. Biedermeier furniture was modest,

simple, restrained and easily affordable. Its designers stripped classicism down to its barest essentials, and used ornament sparingly. Proponents of the style advocated the employment of simple, multi-purpose pieces for middle-class homes. And with applied decoration being used less and less often, this provided the stylistic foundation for a range of well-built and eminently affordable items that could easily be mass-produced.

It has been alleged that Biedermeier's popularity in German-speaking Europe was due to the fact that those countries could not actually afford grander furniture, since the Napoleonic Wars had impoverished the whole area of Central Europe.[16] However, this theory does not explain the style's survival well into the 1840s. Nor, indeed, were Austria and the German states particularly raddled by warfare: even the final campaigns of 1813 were

conducted in a relatively restricted area of Central and Western Germany. Biedermeier's enduring popularity during the nineteenth century – as well as its significance as the ancestor of such twentieth-century developments as the bentwood chair, the products and ethos of the Wiener Werkstätte and the simplified classicism of Art Deco – has surely more to do with the new emphasis on modesty and propriety in Western society. It has been said that the Austrian Empire, presided over by Chancellor Metternich from 1815 until 1848, 'bred an introverted attitude that focused on family life and the cultivation of domestic accomplishments'. As a result, 'rooms now began to be equipped with countless items whose function was to divert and amuse the inhabitants'.[17] And, for the first time ever, the aristocracy now began to emulate the taste of the middle classes, rather than the other way round.

The Biedermeier style was simple, practical and linear, influenced by the rectilinear Neoclassicism of the French 'Empire' style but not by its ostentation or bluster. (For example, the Empire love of gilding was entirely absent from Biedermeier pieces after 1820.) It was economical, using veneer-cutting machines which could produce large, continuous sheets of wood. It was patriotic, exploiting the preference for inexpensive native woods which originated during the British navy's Continental blockade before 1814. It was economical of space, too, being destined for relatively small middle-class rooms. It was colourful, fuelled by the newly available organic dyes, and simply patterned, with broad stripes being used for both wallpapers and textiles.

Since the 1850s, Biedermeier has provided easy fodder for critics, who have inevitably despised its bourgeois appeal, its historicist origins, the absence of great design statements and the resultant 'uneventful calmness', and its apparent signalling of the end of the age of craftsmanship, 'and the beginning of the slide into mass-production'.[18] Yet the qualities that writer Mario Praz sneeringly termed 'the delicious awkwardness of Biedermeier' actually encapsulated the innate success of this style of sense and sensibility. Praz, like so many design historians past and present, found Biedermeier an easy target, 'with its conversation of divan and easy chairs around the tea table, the glass cabinet of porcelains, the petit-point, and the contamination of classical, Gothic and exotic motifs'. To Praz and others, the relaxed eclecticism of Biedermeier and the first half of the nineteenth century merely underlined the damage the middle classes could do to style and taste: in their hands, interior design 'becomes heavier, loses its purity and grace, thickens with curious superfluities'. Praz approvingly quoted Musset's *La Confession d'un Enfant du Siècle* of 1830, which admitted that 'Our age has no form ... Eclecticism is our taste; we take what we find, this for its beauty, that for its convenience, and that for its antiquity ... thus we live amid flotsam.'[19] It is now time to redress the balance, and speak up for this most practical and democratic of interior styles.

With luxury objects, fabrics and fittings available to all but the poorest homes, there was also a new interest in keeping them safe. Plate glass was being used for windows from the late 1820s, enabling window glass to be unsupported by glazing bars and thus improving sightlines from the interior.

The British window tax was finally lifted in 1845, by which time blank, plate-glass sashes were common across Britain and America. Plate glass, however, also made interiors even more visible and vulnerable. The poet Robert Southey noted of English homes as early as 1807 that 'each window has blinds to prevent the by-passers from looking in'. To keep prying eyes away, additional shutters and

Biedermeier anticipated: the living room of the 1795 home of German publisher Georg Joachim Göschen, in Saxony.

roller-blinds were fitted outside. Inside, snob screens – generally painted green, and made of silk, brass or wood slats – were fitted to the bottom frames of window sashes, while internal window drapery helped to keep both direct light and the over-curious pedestrian from intruding.

The perceived vulnerability of the interior proved a boon to the security industry. During the 1760s mortise locks, built into the frame of the door, had begun to supersede traditional rim locks of iron or of brass. By 1800, too, stamped brass door locks had begun to displace those of wrought iron. In 1784 Joseph Bramah patented the first door lock that required not the traditional ponderous key, but a small and easily pocketable one, the lock being operated

The corner room at the Carl Knoblauch House, Berlin (originally built in 1759 by Knoblauch for himself). Once again, the internal treatment (of *c.*1800) anticipates the simplicity of the bourgeois Biedermeier style of post-1815.

Pellatt and Green's china and glass showroom, as depicted in Ackermann's *Repository of the Arts* in 1809.

not by the traditional sliding bolt but by a rotating barrel. In 1818 the Chubb lock was invented, able to detect tiny variations in key patterns, which enabled the creation of a far greater variety of key configurations. And in 1848 the classic Yale cylindrical lock perfected Bramah's patent, effectively creating the modern door lock.

New acquisitions for the home had not only to be defended from the uninvited, but also to be properly displayed to those who were genuinely invited. In the evening, that meant improving the levels of artificial light. Gas lighting was common in middle-class homes by the 1830s – though gas-related accidents continued to flourish, particularly since many of the supply pipes were installed perilously near to

fireplaces and wall surfaces. Their gas flames were usually contained within glass bowls fixed on brackets on the wall or ceiling; the heavy metal pipes needed to supply the gas prevented the development of freestanding gaslights in the centre of the room. In lower-status rooms, the flames might be left to burn nakedly. Yet even when covered with a glass shade, the most they could hope to illuminate was equivalent to a ten-watt electric bulb.[20]

Attempts were also made in the early decades of the nineteenth century to improve the performance of portable oil lamps. The 'Moderator' lamp of 1825, for example, used a spring-activated piston to raise the oil to the wick. By mid-century, however, a far lighter substitute had been discovered for the traditional heavy, viscous fuel oils: paraffin, which was first successfully refined in 1847. The decline the of heavily hunted sperm whale during the early decades of the nineteenth century encouraged Americans to research into new substitute materials. The results were lamps which could run on cheaper fish oils, and even on lard – promoted via the promise that 'one half a pound of Lard will last Sixteen Hours, and give throughout that time a very brilliant light'.[21] The Englishman William Palmer invented a multi-wick candle which needed no tending and was equal in brilliance to an Argand.

Yet outside the homes of the relatively wealthy, the Georgian practice of using a few candles still held sway. 'Prints, watercolours and paintings of European and American domestic interiors ... strongly suggest that when not entertaining guests, a family gathered around one or two candles in the evening rather than attempting to illuminate an entire room.'[22] Where they were used, oil lamps were used to supplement candles, and not displace them.

Lamps only became widely affordable when they were able to use the two miracle oils of the late nineteenth century: kerosene and paraffin. In 1846 the Canadian geologist Abraham Gesner (1797–1864) demonstrated a new lamp run by a fuel made from distilled coal, which he called kerosene. Gesner patented this new oil in New York in 1854; by the end of the decade kerosene was being manufactured from bituminous

Colour pervaded even the most modest of middle-class interiors in the post-Napoleonic era. This view of a German Biedermeier room was painted in 1827 by Georg Friedrich Kersting.

coal and oil shale, and the kerosene lamp had taken off. Historian Roger Moss has noted a huge expansion in kerosene lamp patents from 1862, and has defined the secret of its success: 'In addition to kerosene's cost, cleanliness, relative safety and bright light, virtually any lamp of fixture could be converted to burn it'.[23] Across America, thousands of whale oil lamps were converted to kerosene use, and in many areas kerosene replaced whale and lard oil as the principal light source until electrification in the 1930s.

Meanwhile, Gesner's British contemporary, chemist James Young (1811–83), had managed to produce oil from distilled coal, the end product of which which he named 'paraffin oil'. Patented in Britain in 1850 and in the

US in 1852, it had the same effect as kerosene on the British oil lamp trade. This breakthrough was followed by an even more ominous augury of the fuel-hungry future. In 1859 Edwin L. Drake drilled the world's first oil well, in Titusville, Pennsylvania. The age of oil was just round the corner.

1. Mary Schoeser and Celia Rufey, *English and American Textiles from 1790 to the Present* (1989), 10. 2. Peter Thornton, *Form and Decoration: Innovation in the Decorative Arts 1470–1870* (1998), 166. 3. Charles McCorquodale, *The History of Interior Decoration* (1983), 155. 4. Jane C. Nylander, *Fabrics for Historic Buildings* (1990). 5. Robert and Isabelle Tombs, *That Sweet Enemy* (2006), 325–6. 6. Schoeser and Rufey, *English and American Textiles*, 67; Adrian Forty, *Objects of Desire* (1986), 47; Schoeser and Rufey, *English and American Textiles*, 77. 7. Tombs, *That Sweet Enemy*, 326. 8. Florence Montgomery, *Printed Textiles: English and American Cottons and Linens 1700–1850* (1970), 156, 79, 81. 9. Ibid., 120. 10. Helen von Rosenstiel and Gail Casey Winkler, *Floor Coverings for Historic Buildings* (1988), 120, 19. 11. Ian Bristow, *Interior House-Painting Colours and Technology 1615–1840* (1996), 41. 12. Margaret Ponsonby, 'Parlours', in Joanna Banham (ed.), *Encyclopaedia of Interior Design* (1997), vol. 2, 931. 13. Peter Thornton, *Authentic Decor* (1984), 220 14. Roger W. Moss, *Lighting for Historic Buildings* (1988), 75. 15. Two late nineteenth-century satirists, Adolf Kussmaul and Ludwig Eichrodt, invented a fictional author, Gottlob Biedermeier, 'whose self-satisfied insularity symbolized all that was regarded as being negative about his era'. 'Bieder' meant everyday; 'Meier' – 'miller' – was and is the most common name in Germany, the equivalent of the Anglo-Saxon 'Smith' (Dominic Stone, 'Biedermeier', in Banham [ed.], *Encyclopaedia of Interior Design*, vol. 1, 143). 16. Forty, *Objects of Desire*, 217. 17. Charlotte Gere, *Nineteenth-Century Decoration* (1989), 179. 18. Stone, 'Biedermeier', 145. 19. Mario Praz, *An Illustrated History of Interior Decoration* (1964), 63. By the end of the century, in Praz's view, accessories 'had finally become the protagonists' of middle-class décor. He cited Wilde's outburst against the 'strange ornaments to be seen in the houses of very charming people', including 'horrible things perpetrated in Berlin wool' and 'endless antimacassars'.(65) 20. Moss, *Lighting for Historic Buildings*, 165. 21. Ibid., 80. 22. Ibid., 35. 23. Ibid., 91.

Vulgarity without precedent.

(Charles McCorquodale, *The History of Interior Decoration*, 1983)

Opposite. The middle-class interior comes of age: London's Great Exhibition of 1851.

Right. Austrian bentwood chairs from the Thonet factories, as displayed at the Great Exhibition of 1851 and advertised in *The Illustrated London News*, 1862.

The story of the London Great Exhibition of 1851 has often been told. Opened by Queen Victoria and Prince Albert on 1 May 1851 as the world's first truly international exhibition, it was housed in Joseph Paxton's stupendous iron-and-glass cathedral, the 'Crystal Palace' (a nickname coined by the magazine *Punch*). Measuring 1,848 feet long, with a central nave span of 72 feet, and big enough to enclose trees – and their accompanying fauna – already on the Hyde Park site, the Crystal Palace was made from Lucas Chance's plate glass, patented in 1832, and iron glazing bars shaped and grooved by machine. It comprised over 100,000 exhibits, from 15,000 exhibitors, intended to reflect the world's best manufactures and fine art – or rather, to show the world what Britain could do: although there was much emphasis on the international flavour of the show, British goods were understandably pre-eminent, and products from its Empire unduly prominent. And underlying many of its exhibits were the themes of affordability and classlessness, aims taken very seriously by the show's royal patrons: the 'Model House for the Working Classes' was sponsored by Prince Albert himself.[1]

The Great Exhibition was primarily about mass-manufacture, rather than looking back to an idealised artisan past. Its emphasis was on machine-made goods rather than handmade crafts, and on art and manufacture being applied to practical, everyday objects rather than on pure fine art. In many ways the Crystal Palace's exhibits represented the high-water mark of industrial confidence in the West, and the Victorians' belief in the inevitably beneficial progress of technology. As contemporary Victorian critic Richard Redgrave (one of the exhibition judges) noted, not entirely approvingly, the exhibition's machinery 'demonstrated the ability to produce the florid and overloaded as cheaply as simple forms, and to satisfy the larger market for the multitude, who desire quantity'.

Even the exhibition's organisers disagreed about what the event was actually for. Was it to be, as Judith Flanders has noted, 'an exploration of the technology that had created, and been created by the Industrial Revolution?', or was it to be 'a supermarket, a display of all the goods, the commodities, of the age?' Was it education, or was it entertainment?[2] And how 'British' should it appear?

The Great Exhibition was a reflection of the host nation. Britain was no longer a land of contented farmers and simple craftsmen, but the manufacturing heart of the world. 'In 1780 nine-tenths of English textile workers were at home; in 1850 nine-tenths worked in factories'.[3] Prince Albert's argumentative lieutenant Henry Cole wanted the exhibition to compare handmade products from the Far East favourably with machine-made products from the West. But it was the machines that were the stars of the show, an event so successful it attracted an average of

43,000 visitors a day. The exhibition showcased steam-powered veneering machines that could cut veneers to a sliver, at a fragment of the price that veneering had cost twenty years before. It displayed the latest WCs – a feature now to be found in virtually every middle-class household – and freestanding baths (which were, predictably, more common in American homes than in their Western European counterparts by 1851). Included on a variety of national stands were an astonishing number of richly decorated pianos, features common in well-to-do middle-class interiors all over Europe and America by 1850. It was certainly papier-mâché's finest hour, with all manner of items – from piano cases (!) to seat furniture to tea-trays – on display. Design reformers' subsequent criticisms of this morally and physically lightweight material, however, ensured

An ornate brass stove and fender by Stuart & Smith of Sheffield, exhibited at the Crystal Palace in 1851 and subsequently illustrated in Wyatt's *Industrial Arts of the Nineteenth Century* (1851–3).

Machinery at the Great Exhibition. The show was as much about the methods of production as about the products that they manufactured. This colour lithograph was published by Dickinson Bros in 1851.

that by 1870 the market for papier-mâché had almost completely disappeared.

Cornelius & Baker of Philadelphia exhibited two strikingly enormous 'gas chandeliers', advertising them in the catalogue as standing 'about fifteen feet and a half high by six feet wide, having fifteen burners with plain glass globes, and are of brass lacquered'. The design, they trumpeted, 'is very rich in ornament ... the gas-keys represent bunches of fruit, thus combining beauty with utility'. Charles Eastlake was later to argue that this sort of overblown design was completely unnecessary, since the simplicity of gas fittings – consisting of a small number of interchangeable tubes, valves and joints – allowed designers to experiment more rather than stick to 'stereotyped forms' or 'the ecclesiastical shapes generally found in the art-metal-worker's catalogue'.[4]

The exhibition demonstrated what industry and ingenuity could do. There were gas-fired kitchen ranges

(portable gas ovens had to wait until the 1880s); new gelatine moulds, enabling bold, undercut plaster mouldings to be cast cheaply and quickly; and cast-iron seat furniture and even cast-iron beds (the first metal bed had appeared as recently as 1849); and enormous, one-piece plaster ceiling roses. (Fibrous plaster, cast in lengths at a factory and fixed on site, was only introduced in 1856.) John Crossley of Halifax was so impressed with Erastus Bigelow's American steam looms for making Brussels carpets that he bought the British rights from Bigelow after the exhibition and installed them in his Halifax factory. Master paper-maker Zuber of Alsace was there, with the products of his new, British-made steam press; he was also one of the exhibition judges. Also exhibiting at the Crystal Palace, alongside the highly admired display of French carpets, was Richard Whytock of Edinburgh, whose patent for a looped pile 'tapestry carpet' had been registered a few years before.

Design historians writing about the exhibition decades later, however, tended to ignore the great machines and their colourful produce – the exhibits which had won most popular acclaim – in favour of the two hugely different displays which, with the benefit of hindsight, were to make the biggest impact on subsequent design: A.W.N. Pugin's spurious Medieval Court, which helped to fuel the new enthusiasm for academically derived Gothic architecture and furniture, and, light years away from Pugin's painstakingly crafted pieces in terms of philosophy and design, the mass-produced bentwood furniture exhibited by the Viennese factory of Gustav Thonet.[5]

Bentwood was not wholly new. The first bentwood patent was taken out in Britain as early as 1720, and by 1826 (seven years after Thonet himself had opened his first workshop) the Englishman Isaac Sargent had invented a way to steam-heat balustrade railing and window glazing bars in order to bend them.[6] But it was Thonet who first successfully applied the technique to everyday furniture. Gustav Thonet (1796–1871) was born in Prussia, where by 1830 he was making 'furniture parts' from laminated veneers glued and bent in warmed wooden frames. By 1836 he was making whole chairs, and boiling his veneer strips in glue, making bending easier. Invited to Austria by an admiring Count Metternich in 1841, the following year Thonet moved to Vienna, where he set up his first factory seven years later. By 1850 he was making bentwood settees as well as

Above. Tuer & Hall's power loom for weaving carpets, made in Bury in Lancashire and exhibited at the 1862 South Kensington exhibition, as shown in The Illustrated London News.

Below. A brass bedstead of the 'Louis XVI' type popularised by the Great Exhibition, from Hampton & Sons' Catalogue of Furniture.

HAMPTON & SONS' BRASS FRENCH BEDSTEAD.

No. 2082.—ALL BRASS FRENCH BEDSTEAD IN THE LOUIS XV. STYLE.
THIS DESIGN IS ALSO KEPT IN STOCK AS AN ITALIAN.

chairs; by 1860, although his patent for bentwood furniture had expired, he was making bentwood rocking chairs – a successful design that was very popular in America – and manufacturing 50,000 pieces of furniture a year in his new factory in the heart of the Moravian forest. By the end of the century he boasted seven factories dotted across the whole Austro-Hungarian Empire; between 1859 and 1903 his firm made 45 million bentwood chairs.

The bentwood chair was a breakthrough in affordable design. Thonet's chairs 'required less labour and material than conventional carved chairs, weighed considerably less, and could be sold at lower prices'. Their cheapness and simplicity of design, with little or no ornamentation, fitted them well for Biedermeier interiors. And they were certainly well represented at the Great Exhibition. He not only exhibited two armchairs, six chairs, four tables and two what-nots, but took out a full-page advertisement in the *Official Catalogue*. The exhibition jury awarded his chairs a Prize Medal, although they rather undermined their recognition with faint praise, deeming them merely 'curious'.[7]

While Thonet's products were deliberately understated, the rest of the Great Exhibition was brash, bold and brassy. Its big themes were the possibilities of industry and how technology could liberate even the working-class household. And it was a riot of colour. *The Times* denounced Owen Jones's medieval-inspired colour scheme for the Crystal Palace as 'garish', while *The Builder* snorted that the hues 'untrue to the iron structure of the building ... the columns striped as they are, are degraded into wooden posts'. Jones's defence was explicit: 'Primaries always dominated during early periods, but as these civilisations declined, so secondary and tertiary colours began to prevail. When the secondary colours were used in the best periods in conjunction with the primaries, they were generally confined to the lower parts, following nature, who uses for her flowers the primaries. I therefore propose to use blue, red and yellow in such relative quantities as to neutralise or destroy each other: thus no one colour will be dominant.'

Owen Jones's daring scheme at the Crystal Palace was given academic sanction during 1851 when Jacob-Ignace Hittorf's *L'Architecture polychrome chez les Grecs* and Gottfried Semper's *Über Polychromie* revealed just how brightly coloured ancient Greek buildings had been – both inside and out. These volumes greatly influenced Jones, and helped him to produce his internationally successful *Grammar of Ornament* five years later, in 1856. This accessible, plate-laden volume in turn encouraged the general householder to bolder displays of colour in the home.

Not every area of interior design, however, benefited from the impetus

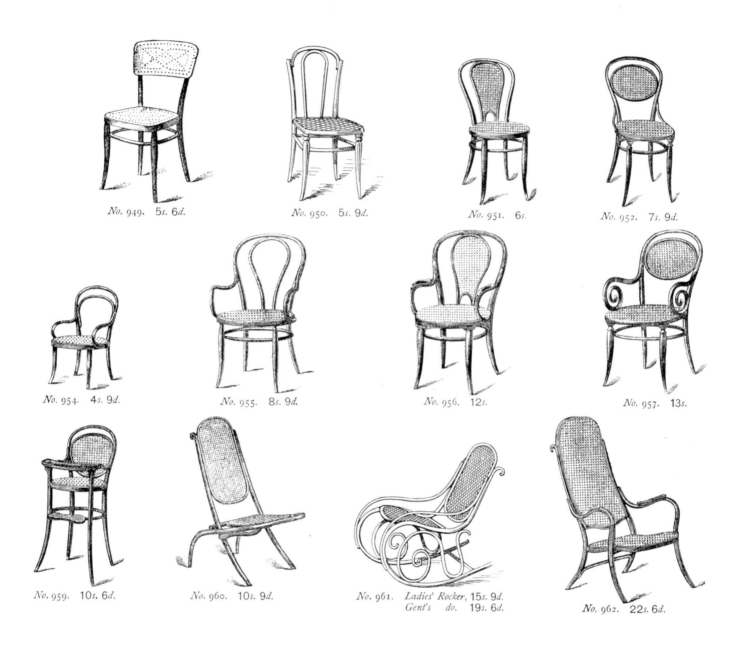

No. 949. 5s. 6d.

No. 950. 5s. 9d.

No. 951. 6s.

No. 952. 7s. 9d.

No. 954. 4s. 9d.

No. 955. 8s. 9d.

No. 956. 12s.

No. 957. 13s.

No. 959. 10s. 6d.

No. 960. 10s. 9d.

No. 961. Ladies' Rocker, 15s. 9d.
          Gent's   do.   19s. 6d.

No. 962. 22s. 6d.

Opposite. Thonet's shop: the 'Thonet-Haus' in Vienna's Stefansplatz, engraved by an unnamed artist in *Neue Illustrierte Zeitung*, 23 March 1884.

Above. Bentwood chairs from Hampton's catalogue. The rocking chair model became particularly popular in the US.

provided by the exhibition. Wallpaper designs exhibited at the show (which included the first of many papers actually featuring the motif of the Crystal Palace itself) were judged to be somewhat over-enthusiastic in their use of gaudy colours, and their manufacturers were accused of losing sight of the boundaries of good taste in the headlong rush towards full mechanisation. Having examined the exhibited wallpapers, exhibition judge Richard Redgrave bemoaned in the *Illustrated London News* that 'excellence was being reckoned in the number of colours rather than any other quality'. Significantly, the only paperstainer to receive one of the premier Great Exhibition awards was a Frenchman, M. Delicourt.[8]

And not every contemporary critic was welcoming. Ruskin, of course, disapproved of the exhibition; its celebration of the potential of industry was not in accord with his vision of the decorative arts. Walter Crane similarly lambasted the 'design-debauchery' of the 1850s which the exhibition had promoted – 'where the furniture is afflicted with curvature of the spine, and dreary lamps of bronze and ormolu repose on marble slabs at every opportunity, where monstrosities of every kind are encouraged under glass shades ... and where the antimacassar is made to cover a multitude of sins' – while in 1866 Jacob von Falke's *Geschichte des modernen Geschmacks* denounced the Crystal Palace exhibits as having displayed 'wretchedness in its full measure'. Redgrave himself subsequently inveighed against the machine-printed fabrics that had been exhibited, complaining that the undoubtedly impressive machines that made them were 'wasted on the imitation of flowers,

Nations vying for attention at the Crystal Palace. Despite the exhibition's professed internationalism, in truth it was envisaged primarily as a showcase for the goods of Britain and its growing Empire. This colour lithograph published by Dickinson Bros in 1851.

foliage and accidents of growth, quite out of ornamental character and opposed to just principles'. However, he then scored a stunning own goal by praising some of the simpler cylinder-printed furnishing fabrics – which he wrongly assumed had been handblocked – and criticising some of the fussier designs, which were in truth handmade.[9]

Contemporary criticism was timid in comparison to the brickbats that the design historians of the succeeding century hurled at the event. The pioneer interwar decorator Elsie de Wolfe, understandably rejecting the styles and approaches of an older generation, memorably denounced the furniture of the exhibition as pieces that would 'never be coveted by collectors, unless someone should build a museum for the freakish objects of house furnishing'. To Mario Praz, writing in the early 1960s, while the Great Exhibition certainly

included some 'bravura pieces of the exhibiting manufacturers', it largely comprised 'furniture of incredible complication and bad taste, where architecture and sculpture are so predominant that the pieces look more like monuments than furniture'.[10] 'Many exhibits at the Crystal Palace', declared John Gloag at the end of that same, supremely self-confident decade, demonstrated 'how ornament had got out of control'. Gloag lauded the 'refreshing frankness about the shortcomings of contemporary taste' contained within the original exhibition catalogue essay by lawyer Ralph Wornum ('The Exhibition as a Lesson in Taste'), which had complained that 'There is nothing new in the Exhibition in ornamental design' and identified that 'there is want of definite design, and [a] disregard of utility ... [and] an overloading of detail'. Such lawyerly

sentiments must, Gloag asserted, 'have badly jolted the complacency of many readers' in 1851.[11] They certainly must have enraged many of the exhibitors.

More recently, design historian John Pile has echoed the traditional chorus of the design reformers, declaring that the Crystal Palace's exhibits made 'a strange contrast' with the hi-tech building in which they were installed. He subsequently dismissed them as 'generally of the decorated or over-decorated sort that became the norm of "high Victorian" design', a period which, he cheerfully reminded his readers, design guru Lewis Mumford had characterised as 'the brown decades'. All in all, Pile concluded, the High Victorian interior design represented at the exhibition combined 'the astonishing mixture of the functional and the practical with ornamentation and sham'. Here, as usual, the term 'ornamentation' was not used admiringly but, in true Modernist fashion, as a pejorative.[12]

However, at the time even the parsimonious solicitor Ralph Wornum conceded that the most popular and successful exhibits at the Great Exhibition were not Thonet's avant-garde furniture or Pugin's mystical medieval Gothic – the displays on which most design historians of the twentieth century have preferred to concentrate – but furniture couched in the familiar 'Louis XIV' style. Indeed, as design historian Paul Greenhalgh has pointed out, until the 1925 exhibition in Paris the styles of France's long-banished *ancien régime* remained the most popular idiom for exhibits at the great international exhibitions which followed in the wake of the 1851 show. The inspiration of the styles of pre-revolutionary France actually 'outlasted most of the styles dominating design histories to date'; indeed, few subsequent exhibitions managed to exclude historical styles 'even when an exhibition brief was sent to manufacturers actively discouraging them', as at Paris in 1925 and 1937 and New York in 1939.[13] It is always extremely dangerous to attribute stylistic consistency and homogeneity in the average home based on the apparent direction afforded by hindsight. Homeowners rarely do what design critics exhort. Historicism has always been the norm for interior decoration, whatever may be reflected in the pages of *World of Interiors* or *Wallpaper*.

Disparaging critics of the Great Exhibition from Wornum to Pile have, anyway, rather missed the point of the whole thing. Most of the furniture and textiles displayed in 1851 were not intended for use or as a template for future design. Instead, they were 'specifically chosen to illustrate the capabilities of the machine, and it was probably not expected that many of these articles would be used in the ordinary home'. Great exhibitions such as the one staged so magnificently at the Crystal Palace were intended to encourage 'ingenuity and intricacy in manufacture', promoting 'a commercial decorator's style' which never intended to ape 'the relationship between functional structure and surface ornament that is the most important characteristic of architect-designed furniture'.[14]

Britain's principal industrial rivals abroad certainly saw the exhibition

Opposite. Pugin's Medieval Court is perhaps the element of the Great Exhibition that has attracted most notice from modern historians. In fact, though, it was little regarded at the time; to most visitors, its authentic evocation of the fourteenth century paled into insignificance when compared to the machinery of the nineteenth.

as a phenomenon to be imitated. The French in particular were alarmed at the exhibition's display of Britain's manufacturing prowess: 'Comparing their products with others at the Great Exhibition of 1851 convinced the French that they could outdo their rivals in design and taste. They concentrated on lavishness, in styles associated with the aristocratic past.' The French press 'urged readers to go to London and be "dazzled"'. Thereafter, determined to outdo the British – Jules Michelet had reflected the views of most Frenchmen when he affirmed in 1847 that, while 'England is ahead in strength, power, the astonishing, the enormous, the useful', France 'is incontestably ahead in all that concerns art, taste, finish, elegance, distinction'[15] – Paris staged its own version of the exhibition in 1855. Held at a time of unusual Anglo-French amity – even Napoleon III had become a favourite of Queen Victoria's – the show was deliberately modelled on the Crystal Palace event, but with more emphasis on the fine arts (*pace*

Michelet) and, of course, bigger. The 1855 show boasted more exhibitors than its London predecessor: 20,000, only half of whom were French. Although it proved a financial disaster, losing a staggering 8 million francs, Paris nevertheless staged repeat events in 1878, an exhibition which attracted 13 million visitors but lost 32 million francs; in 1889, to celebrate the centenary of the Revolution; in 1900, with an exhibition dominated by Art Nouveau; in 1925, an event which effectively created the Art Deco style; and 1937, which juxtaposed both traditional and Modernist designs.

The United States was also swift to showcase its own manufacturing strength. The New York exhibition of 1853 was held in a domed, cruciform iron-and-glass structure remarkably similar to Paxton's revolutionary Crystal Palace building. In 1876 Philadelphia used the Centennial Exhibition to mark both the centenary of the American Revolution and to show the world America's finest and newest wares. The exhibition promoted the new Arts and

Monsieur Dernière's 1867 Paris Exhibition stand of bronze clocks, chandeliers and *objets d'art*.

Stereograph card showing the 'colonial' log cabin at the 1876 Philadelphia Centennial Exhibition. This recreation was of central importance in the evolution of American Revivalism.

Crafts style: it included furniture suites designed in Charles Eastlake's rectilinear, sparsely decorated idiom, which was vaguely termed 'Gothic' (or, much to the critic's annoyance, 'Eastlake'), while visitors to the fair were also introduced to the designs of Christopher Dresser, Walter Crane and William Morris. The exhibition also successfully fused Arts and Crafts simplicity with the growing interest in America's colonial past. The simple New England log cabin was the biggest hit of the show, a 'revival of old simplicity' that Clarence Cook's *House Beautiful* later suggested was 'proof that our taste is getting a root in the healthier and more native soil'.[16]

Even larger events were held at the end of the century. The vast, Daniel Burnham-designed 'Columbian Exposition' in Chicago in 1893 marked the apotheosis of Beaux Arts classicism; its achievements were rivalled at the enormous St Louis 'World's Fair' of 1904. The Buffalo Exposition of 1901 was remembered, however, not for the diversity or quality of its architecture or its exhibits, but for the assassination of President McKinley. Leo Czolgosz, a friendless and deranged anarchist, shot McKinley twice at point-blank range while he was viewing the exhibition. One bullet was quickly found, but the second remained hidden deep in his body. As chance would have it, a recently developed 'X-ray' machine was being exhibited at the fair; yet no one dared to try it out on the wounded President. Had they done so, his life might have been spared. Similarly, while the Exposition's stands demonstrated countless examples of the newly developed

Above. 'Gothic' cabinet and chimneypiece by Cox & Sons at the 1876 Philadelphia Exhibition.

Below. Lemaire's cast iron 'revolving stove-grate', from the 1867 Paris Exposition. Unattributed engraving from *The Illustrated London News.*

Above. The Paris Exhibition of 1855 was expressly devised to outshine its British precursor of four years previously. Even its iron-and-glass hall was consciously modelled on that of the Great Exhibition.

Below. The climax of the nineteenth-century's cult of the exhibition: the 'Burnham Baroque' of the Columbian Exposition in Chicago of 1893.

electric light bulb, electricity had not been incorporated into the exhibition's temporary hospital. As a result, doctors had to use a pan to reflect sunlight on to McKinley's wounds, and never located the second bullet. McKinley died eight days later from shock, the second bullet still lodged in his body.

The age of the international industrial exhibition culminated in the great American extravaganzas of the 1930s: the 1933 'Century of Progress' exhibition in Chicago, the Golden Gate International Exhibition in San Francisco, also held in 1933, and the New York World's Fair of 1939. Exhibitions had continued in London, too. The 1862 South Kensington Exhibition, which unleashed Japanese design and Georgian revivalism on to the European stage, was a great success; the smaller sequel of 1871 less so. The British Empire Exhibition was originally slated for 1915, but was finally held in Wembley in 1924–5. This, however, was the last British portmanteau exhibition; the 1951 Festival of Britain, staged largely to convince the rest of the world of Britain's economic and aesthetic resurrection after the trials of the war, was an entirely different animal. After the Second World War the industrial triumphalism of the Great Exhibition and its progeny was understandably deemed anachronistic and inappropriate: amid the ruins of a bankrupt Europe, survival and rebuilding was deemed more important than display.

Opposite. 'Moving machinery' at the Great Exhibition, from a colour lithograph published by Dickinson Bros in 1851.

1. The royal couple were great fans, and visited the site repeatedly. Before it closed on 12 October 1851, they even asked to be present at the packing up. Albert opposed the demolition of the Crystal Palace, and helped ensure that it was bought for re-erection at Sydenham in South London in 1854. 2. Judith Flanders, *Consuming Passions* (2006), 14, 16. 3. C. Ray Smith, *Interior Design in 20th Century America* (1987), 17. 4. Kit Wedd, *The Victorian Society Book of the Victorian House* (2002), 165. 5. In the 1960s, John Gloag patronisingly reproved the original Great Exhibition catalogue editors for missing the 'significance of the table and the bentwood underframe by the Austrian designer Michael Thonet' (*The Crystal Palace Exhibition Illustrated Catalogue*, Introduction, xi). 6. Peter Lizon, 'Bentwood', in Joanna Banham (ed.), *Encyclopaedia of Interior Design* (1997), vol. 1, 131. 7. Christopher Wilk, *Thonet: 150 Years of Furniture* (1980), 8, 20. 8. E.A. Entwisle, *The Book of Wallpaper* (1970), 111. 9. Charlotte Gere, *Nineteenth-Century Decoration* (1989), 276; Peter Thornton, *Authentic Decor* (1984), 217; Adrian Forty, *Objects of Desire* (1986), 50. 10. Elsie de Wolfe, *The House in Good Taste* (1913), 263; Mario Praz, *A History of Interior Decoration* (1964), 336. 11. *The Crystal Palace Exhibition Illustrated Catalogue* (1970), Introduction viii, ix, and Wornum v, xi–xii. Wornum particularly castigated Pugin's Medieval Court as 'simply the copy of an old idea; old things in an old taste'. 12. John Pile, *A History of Interior Decoration* (2000), 244, 247, 265. 13. Paul Greenhalgh, *Ephemeral Vistas* (1988), 145. 14. Joanna Banham et al., *Victorian Interior Design* (1991), 57; Gere, *Nineteenth-Century Decoration*, 332. 15. Robert and Isabelle Tombs, *That Sweet Enemy* (2006), 326, 369. 16. Helen von Rosenstiel and Gail Casey Winkler, *Floor Coverings for Historic Buildings* (1988), 164, 169.

Everything about the Veneerings
was spick-and-span new.

(Charles Dickens, *Our Mutual Friend*, 1865)

Opposite. Holman Hunt's
celebrated denunciation
of the immorality of mass-
production: *The Awakening
Conscience* of 1853
(oil on canvas; Tate
Britain, London).

Right. Cross-section of a
'house for the bourgeoisie',
by H. Monnot, *c.*1870.
Monnot's principal
reception room has a
marbled finish of paint or
paper. From an unpublished
folio collection of original
pen and ink drawings.

While the renowned art critic and design guru John Ruskin and his followers decried the Great Exhibition's celebration of bourgeois confidence and the virtuosity of mass-manufacture, the growing availability of furniture and fittings in high street retailers helped extend the geographical and social range of their consumption. Thus 'Louis XVI' style was all the rage not only in Napoleon III's Second Empire of the 1850s and 1860s, but in High Victorian Britain and in ante-bellum America, too. In 1943, Sartre's idea of hell in his play *Huis Clos* was 'Un salon style Second Empire';[1] yet to the middle classes of the industrialising nations of a century before, this was the apogee of comfort and style.

Ruskin and the apostles of design reform fiercely resisted the tide of bourgeois consumption. In 1854 Ruskin, describing Holman Hunt's newly exhibited and eagerly awaited canvas *The Awakening Conscience* in a letter to *The Times* of 25 May, identified the 'fatal newness' and 'terrible lustre' of both the drawing room's furnishings and the moral dilemma they epitomised; all was, he declared, 'common, modern, vulgar'. Set in a small apartment in the newly built London suburb of St John's Wood – which was already beginning to acquire a reputation as a dumping ground for mistresses past and present – Hunt's picture sought to reflect the ethical hollowness of the woman's existence, as a mere plaything for her rich patron, in the moral decay of her physical setting. Everything in the small parlour – the gaudy gilt mirror, the veneered and immaculately polished piano, the brightly coloured carpet, the over-styled 'naturalistic' curtains – was designed to indicate a reliance on surface and colour rather than depth and meaning, on immediate visual gratification rather than on a more subtle and gradual appreciation. The resulting interior represented the triumph of mass-manufacture, of new over old, of the celebration of colour and texture for its own sake rather than as an expression of traditional, organic craftsmanship.[2]

Ruskin admired decrepitude, not the gleaming newness of mass-manufacture. 'Every excrescence or cleft involves some additional complexity of light and shade,' he declared; natural erosion, to him, 'lent beauty a temporal dimension'.[3] Ruskin's stringently academic and pointedly historicist viewpoint, however, was singularly out of step with public enthusiasm for the world of colour which industrialisation now brought to the everyday interior. While the adverse critical reaction from authorities such

Left. A neoclassically styled and vigorously striped French drawing room of the Second Empire. Green is predominantly paired with its complementary, lilac. From a compilation of lithographs of room sets, furniture & furnishings in *Le Garde-Meuble* (1859 to early 1900s).

as Ruskin to mass-production – and, in particular, to the allegedly 'unnatural' colour tones now being chemically produced by paint, fabric and wallpaper manufacturers – sought to draw ominous parallels between moral and aesthetic deterioration, the middle classes of Europe and America quickly seized on these bright new harbingers of an exciting new industrial future. Searing colour for fabrics, coverings and finishes was no longer the preserve of the rich or the daringly avant-garde. Both the colours and the products they adorned were now, thanks to the industrial revolution, affordable by most. In an age when the majority of interiors were lit by candles, oil lamps or gaslight, the bold new primaries and secondaries that manufacturers were able to use helped to lend some cheer to principal rooms. It has to be said that even the parlour

A modest middle-class interior captured in 1860: A. Enwood's *The First Place* (oil on canvas; private collection).

COAL TAR DYES.

SPECIMENS OF FABRICS DYED WITH
Simpson, Maule & Nicholson's
COLORS.

Concentrated Regina Purple.

Concentrated Violet with a little Roseine.

Phosphine.

Roseine.

Regina Purple.

Violet.

Phosphine.

Printers Roseine.

Regina Purple.

Nº 2 Violet.

Nº 1 Blue.

Blue.

Nº 2 Blue & Violet.

Concentrated Printers Roseine.

SPECIMENS OF FABRICS DYED WITH
Perkin & Son's Colors.

featured in *The Awakening Conscience* was made more habitable by the new furnishing fabrics – however base the motives of their purchaser. Certainly by the end of the nineteenth century, Ruskin's condescending morality was distinctly out of fashion, overtaken by the fundamental changes that had occurred in the manufacture, marketing and choosing of paint and dyes.

Despite Ruskin's antipathy, his contemporaries were eager to exploit the new potential to fabricate bright new colours and dyes. However, finding a strong, durable yellow remained difficult. Organic yellow pigments such as annatto (obtained from the seeds of the South American plant *Bixa orellana*, and used since the seventeenth century), barberry (from the roots of the British shrub *Berberis*), fustic (from the West Indian and South American tree *Chlorophora tinctoria*), quercitron (patented by Edward Bancroft in 1799 and made from the bark of the North American oak, *Quercus velutina*), weld (the dye luteolin, made from the leaves of the European plant *Reseda luteola*) and 'yellow pink' or 'Dutch pink' (chalk-based yellow pigments) were all either pale, fugitive or drab in tone. Eighteenth-century decorators looking for a bright yellow had thus been forced to use pigments that were difficult to make and toxic, both in manufacture and application. 'King's yellow' and 'orpiment' were yellows made from highly toxic sulphides of arsenic; 'Naples yellow', from lead antimonite, dated from antiquity, but was equally poisonous. Bancroft's 'quercitron yellow' was at least easier and safer to obtain than

earlier pigments, and was certainly more colourfast. The brief vogue it created in the first decades of the nineteenth century for 'drab' colours encouraged the development of new mineral yellows, olives, oranges and browns.[4]

The big breakthrough came, however, at the end of the eighteenth century, with the invention of 'Patent yellow', based on lead oxychloride. Discovered by Swedish chemist C.W. Scheele in 1771, its British patent was filed in 1781 by James Turner. By 1800 it was being widely used in Britain and France, where it was termed 'Montpellier jaune'. Only in the 1820s was it superseded by a deeper, more lustrous pigment: chrome yellow – discovered in the 1790s from experiments with Siberian chrome ore, and made by combining potassium bichromate with lead acetate. By 1831 pale, mid, deep and orange varieties were being produced; subsequent red varieties, made from a greater proportion of chromate and termed 'Chinese Red' and 'Persian Red', were widely available by the 1840s.[5]

The expanding range of colours available to the householder enabled the latter to experiment more not only with different schemes of decoration in each room, but also to effect a notional allocation of space on the basis of age or sex. The nineteenth century saw the widespread gendering of interior spaces, and their increasing use as an indicator of function and social status – indicators that were generally defined by what were perceived as 'masculine' or 'feminine' (or child-like) colours. J.C. Loudon's hugely comprehensive *Encyclopaedia of Cottage, Farm and Villa Architecture* of 1833 advocated that 'the colouring of rooms should be an echo of their uses', and of those who used them; thus his typical library was to be a 'severe' and sober masculine space, the drawing room a 'gay', feminine one (having originated from the ladies' 'withdrawing room'), and the dining room a 'grave', cross-gender arena. Other decorative guides of the 1830s recommended that bedrooms – explicitly defined as a light, clean and cheerful feminine area – should be decorated in white, tinted with pale hues of blue, rose, straw or lilac.

Technology linked arms with fashion and practicality to expand the internal paint palette yet further. Reds were not only more easily obtained through newly patented mineral and (after 1856) chemical dyes, but also imparted a finish that was both gender-free and made an excellent background for gilt picture frames. Red was held to be the best medium with which to encapsulate the effects of 'vivacity, gaiety and light cheerfulness' which D.R. Hay had specified was required for drawing and dining rooms in his popular guide, *The Laws of Harmonious Colouring adapted to House Painting* (1821). Hay had indeed concluded that 'a proper tint of crimson is the richest and most splendid colour for the walls of a room' and, he further noted, 'much used in internal decorations' of the time.[6] Red was almost universally recommended for dining rooms, as the best ground for pictures. The artist J.M.W. Turner strongly advocated red walls as the most suitable background for his own paintings, while his fellow-practitioner Sir Thomas Lawrence bemoaned the

detrimental effect that the new fashion for replacing red with yellow was having on his canvases and particularly on the gilded frames.

While red remained highly prevalent in fashionable Regency interiors, this does not mean that other colours were wholly displaced. Bold, dark greens were much used for drawing rooms and bedrooms, and were held to be particularly appropriate for libraries. Indeed, green was a constant presence inside and outside the nineteenth-century home, being the customary colour for all types of utilitarian objects: front doors, woodwork, ironwork,

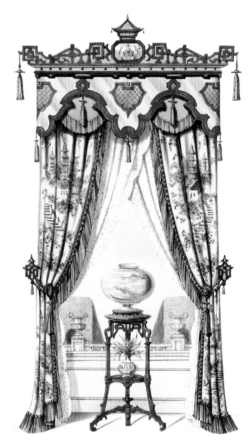

Right. A bright, ostentatious chinoiserie curtain design from the French periodical *Le Garde-Meuble* of c.1870.

Opposite. Revivalist French room designs of the late nineteenth century from *Fonde de Cabinet deTravail – Henri II,* aiming to fuse Ancient Regime with Late Valois.

window blinds, screens, fences, gates and garden rails. The architect and designer J.B. Papworth considered that 'bronze green' – the pale, olivish colour much favoured for its supposed reflection of the patinated bronze of the Ancient World – was especially suitable for verandas and related ironwork since it 'assumes a substantial, though light appearance, [whilst] every other colour bespeaks it of wooden construction, and is offensive to the eye of taste'. In his practical manual *Mechanical Exercises* (1812), Peter Nicholson included more greens than any other basic colours in his 'List of useful Colours for House Painting', citing 'grass green', verdigris, 'dark ochre green', 'blue-pea', and bright 'mineral green'. While reds were still often used for decorating the walls of the dining room, and indeed for any room in which pictures were to be hung, greens were frequently employed on the walls of drawing rooms, bedrooms and especially libraries.

Green was particularly prevalent both inside and outside the middle-class home of the mid-nineteenth century. In 1814 a bright, lasting 'emerald green' paint was invented in France by using copper arsenite. So-called 'invisible' dark greens were used for fences, gates, railings and garden furniture, while bronze greens were used for ironwork and internal woodwork. Even in the 1890s a popular paint manual was still noting that 'the commonly known commercial mixed greens are bronze greens and quaker greens, which are ochre and black or chrome and black'. Drab greens were also widely used. A guide of 1852 listed a variety of ways to

achieve the fashionable goal of a sombre, dirty, olive-brown drab: mixing French yellow and black, French yellow and Prussian blue, raw umber and Venetian red, or burnt umber and Venetian red. From the 1870s onwards rich Brunswick greens were often used to decorate not only windows and external doors but also internal woodwork.

Browns, too, were particularly common during the nineteenth

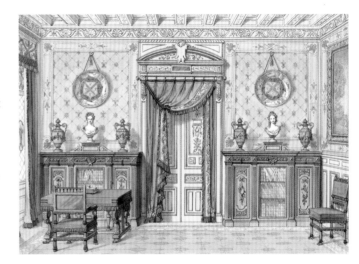

century, partly because of their resemblance to the traditional wood colours and the still-popular technique of wood-graining, and partly because of their cheapness. Olive-browns and purple-browns were very popular for joinery, and can still be detected on old window frames and doors.

The first half of the nineteenth century also saw a great increase in the popularity of yellows. The Prince of Wales inaugurated this trend by having Henry Holland fit his Carlton House with yellow paper in the 1780s. Twenty years later Soane used a striking 'Patent yellow' for the painted walls, curtains and upholstery of the drawing room at his own home in Lincoln's Inn Fields. The brighter Neoclassical colours of Ancient Rome and Pompeii came at a price, however. Eighteenth-century 'King's yellow' was fatally poisonous, being based on arsenic. The practice of covering walls in strong yellows still remained controversial. In the 1830s even the military hero and former Prime Minister the Duke of Wellington was publicly rebuked for choosing yellow for the principal rooms at Apsley House.

Faded yellows, though, were considered safer. From 1800, Bancroft's 'quercitron yellow' was widely used to create the family of greeny-yellows, yellow-browns and yellow-golds which were collectively known as 'drab' – a term which did not possess the pejorative connotations it does today. These hues were frequently used for fabrics and wallpapers of the period, as well as constituting the basis for internal paint schemes. By the 1830s these and other less vivid colours – lilacs, rose

pinks, pale terracottas – were being used in combination with stronger hues of complementary colours. As Hay observed: 'The strength of intensity of a colour is much increased by being placed near its contrasting or accidental tint.'

Certainly some of the resulting harmonies were very pleasing. In the mid-1820s Ackermann expressly recommended the combination of lilac or fawn with bright green, while in 1829 T.H. Vanherman suggested 'light yellowish buff' to complement 'light

Right. The title page of Nathaniel Whittock's influential *Decorative Painters' and Glaziers' Guide* of 1827.

Opposite. A daringly inventive stained glass design suggested by Whittock in the *Decorative Painters' and Glaziers' Guide.*

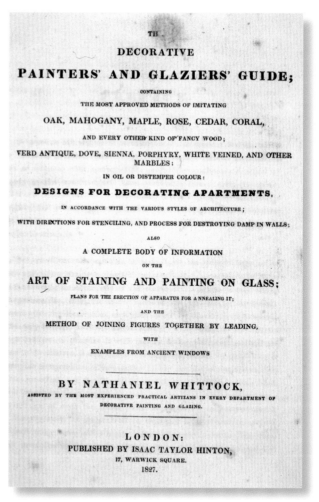

THE DECORATIVE PAINTERS' AND GLAZIERS' GUIDE;

CONTAINING

THE MOST APPROVED METHODS OF IMITATING

OAK, MAHOGANY, MAPLE, ROSE, CEDAR, CORAL,

AND EVERY OTHER KIND OF FANCY WOOD;

VERD ANTIQUE, DOVE, SIENNA, PORPHYRY, WHITE VEINED, AND OTHER MARBLES;

IN OIL OR DISTEMPER COLOUR:

DESIGNS FOR DECORATING APARTMENTS,

IN ACCORDANCE WITH THE VARIOUS STYLES OF ARCHITECTURE;

WITH DIRECTIONS FOR STENCILING, AND PROCESS FOR DESTROYING DAMP IN WALLS;

ALSO

A COMPLETE BODY OF INFORMATION

ON THE

ART OF STAINING AND PAINTING ON GLASS;

PLANS FOR THE ERECTION OF APPARATUS FOR ANNEALING IT;

AND THE

METHOD OF JOINING FIGURES TOGETHER BY LEADING,

WITH

EXAMPLES FROM ANCIENT WINDOWS

BY NATHANIEL WHITTOCK,

ASSISTED BY THE MOST EXPERIENCED PRACTICAL ARTIZANS IN EVERY DEPARTMENT OF DECORATIVE PAINTING AND GLAZING.

LONDON:
PUBLISHED BY ISAAC TAYLOR HINTON,
17, WARWICK SQUARE.
1827.

plum colour' on wall panelling – an exhortation which epitomised the recent fashionable trend towards painting stiles and rails in panelling a different colour to that of the recessed areas. Other suggestions were decidedly more avant-garde, such as Nathaniel Whittock's instructions of 1826 on to how to obtain a 'flame-colour' effect on the walls – by 'drawing a long streak of blue, then one of red, next yellow, and lastly green' on a light ground, after which 'the whole of the streaks are softened and blended together with a large dusting'.

One colour, incidentally, which rarely appeared on walls before the mid-nineteenth century was white. By 1810 chlorine was being used to create bright, bleached areas of relief in fabric patterns. With regard to paintwork, however, Hay wrote that white was 'seldom employed in house-painting', having 'entirely given way to shades of various colours and imitations of the finer kinds of wood'. Whites were still used for ceilings, but even then they were often tinted with pinks, blues or yellows. In the opinion of the influential furniture designer George Smith, by 1828 white was 'but bad taste'. Black-painted woodwork, however, was made fashionable by the uncompromising 'Egyptian' designs of Thomas Hope, published in 1807, and by the 1830s was frequently being used in combination with Pompeian red or a similar terracotta variant to produce a so-called 'Etruscan effect' – also creating a rich background against which both paintings and prints prospered.

By the 1830s the use of restrained, secondary tints such as beige, lilac and pink was commonplace. These were

often used in combination with stronger versions of their complementaries, resulting in colour schemes featuring combinations of buff and blue, lilac and green and so on. Nathaniel Whittock's *The Decorative Painters' and Glaziers' Guide* of 1827 suggested as complementaries 'light plum colour' with white or straw, 'dark red' with 'warm green', 'light delicate green' with pink, and mauve-grey with straw, while T.H. Vanherman's *The Painter's Cabinet, and Colourman's Repository* of 1828 recommended a light

plum colour, complemented by a 'light yellowish buff', for the drawing room – observing that principal rooms should always display the brightest (i.e. the most expensive) colours.

The concept of complementary colours was a relatively new one. In 1810 Goethe published his influential *Zur Farbenlehre...*, a study of the natural ordering of colours (not published in Britain until 1840) which suggested the theory that every colour naturally had a complementary one. Perfect harmony in the drawing room as well as the orchard was thus to be achieved when one primary was combined with two subordinate complementary colours. Goethe's ideas were adapted for the English-speaking world by David Hay in his *The Laws of Harmonious Colouring* of 1828. Hay stated that a direct union of two full-blooded opposites would

be too harsh; instead, a subdued complementary was needed, together with a third, 'neutralising' colour.

Mid-Victorian interiors were by no means always the dark and gloomy rooms of popular caricature. Gaslight provided a depth of illumination that oil lamps and candles could never match (see below, Chapter 9). Accordingly, householders began to pick out individual wall and ceiling mouldings in bright colours or gilt, or to use different (generally darker) shades for recessed wooden panels, in direct defiance of Georgian custom. White-painted doors often had mouldings picked out in tints matching the wall paint or wallpaper. And while the average ceiling remained white, by 1840 it was occasionally tinted pink, lavender, light grey or light purple, with ceiling roses and associated plaster ornamentation being picked out in stronger hues. H.W. and A. Arrowsmith's *The House Decorator and Painter's Guide* of 1840 indeed suggested that 'Louis XIV' or 'Louis XV' interiors (whatever those actually meant in practice) decorated in white should have all their architectural detailing picked out with pale tints – a look which, as we will see, greatly appealed to the new professional interior decorators of the early twentieth century.

But joinery did not always have to be white: Charles Dickens, for example, painted all the joinery in his wallpapered drawing room at Doughty Street in a bold lilac. And by 1830 the paint techniques of marbling and graining were back in favour for the first time since the late seventeenth century. In 1826 Whittock had written that 'the very great improvement that has been made within the last ten years in the art of imitating the grain and colour of various fancy woods and marbles, and the facility and consequent cheapness of this formerly expensive work, has brought it into general use'. By 1840 the gardener-cum-decorator J.C. Loudon was reporting that 'the rage for painting the mouldings in a different kind of wood from the general graining' was 'now discontinued', but that the technique of graining itself was still very popular – as testified to by the wealth of manuals available on the subject. The idea spread beyond paint finishes too: in his vastly influential *Encyclopaedia* of 1833, Loudon noted the fashion for oak-grained floorcloths and carpets the 'colour of

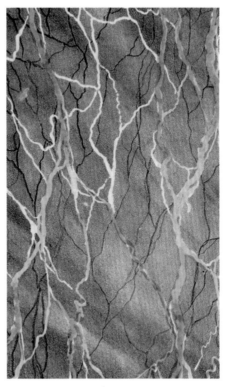

Marbling suggestions from a consumer's guide of the 1880s. Using this type of manual, householders could achieve paint effects such as this by themselves, without recourse to tradesmen.

bolder contemporaries experimented with silvering; the latter never really caught on, however, as even the most assiduous servants found brightening the constantly tarnishing silvered surfaces a tiresome chore.[7]

By the mid-nineteenth century, the fashion for inserting a decorative wallpaper frieze at dado level, and then lightening the paint shades as the wall rose, had become prevalent in middle-class homes. Increasingly, the average wall was used as a vehicle for patterned wallpaper, with paint being relegated to the framing woodwork. Here the colours could be green, brown, white or even blue. However, very few strong blues are evident in the colour cards that survive from the period, suggesting that mid-blue was not extensively used in the Victorian home.

Mid-nineteenth century householders, in marked contrast to accepted Georgian practice, often picked out individual elements of the cornice in different, and often surprisingly strong, colours – which, from the 1860s, including 'gilded' paints, mimicking gold leaf. At the same time, dado rails were often eradicated as picture rails were installed above, a practice which destroyed the classical analogy of the domestic wall but allowed homeowners to hang heavier pictures more easily (and reversibly), as well as to hang newly affordable wallpapers from the cornice or picture rail right down to the skirting. In some cases, though, dado rails were retained – the design reform guru Charles Eastlake extolled the practical and visual use of the dado – and the area below the rail was decorated

wainscot' in libraries. Grained woodwork and marbled walls (often covered with a marbled paper if painted marbling was considered too expensive or time-consuming) represented a decorative combination which continued in widespread use in Western households right up until the Second World War.

To brighten the mid-nineteenth century interior further, grained and marbled surfaces were generally varnished. Even gilding was fashionable in middle-class homes by the 1830s. Dickens placed a gilded fillet below his drawing-room cornice in his Bloomsbury home in 1837, while some of his

with wallpaper (often one of the many embossed varieties available) or painted in a darker version of the colour used above the dado.

The huge possibilities afforded by new chemical dyes turned mid-nineteenth century interiors into riots of bright, confident colour. This in turn reflected the era's confidence in (and indeed the consequent territorial ambitions of) the burgeoning industrial economies of Europe and North America. In 1856 the first of the wholly inorganic, chemical 'aniline' paint dyes appeared, William Perkin's 'mauve'. Made from coal tar (helpfully, the waste product of the gas industry), its hue was far more potent and vibrant than the washed-out 'mauves' popularised in the twentieth century. The following year came 'alizarin red', which replaced the traditional, natural madder dye, and in 1859 'magenta', a French product named after the recent, crushing victory of Napoleon III's army over the Austrians. In 1877 came the first 'azo' dye, red, which obviated the need to use cochineal.

While aniline dyes were initially ignored by the more conservative paint manufacturers – from the evidence of contemporary colour cards and paint manuals, it seems that the new chemical dyes were not taken up with any great alacrity by the paint manufacturers and decorators – European and American wallpaper and fabric producers were eager to embrace the new possibilities afforded by this chemical technology. And by 1900 their horizons were even further broadened by the appearance of new paint and print colours based on colourfast coal-tar dyes. The first of

these, 'Congo red', was launched in 1884. Now, too, dyeing could be carried out cheaply and simply at home, leading to a minor revolution in the easy provision of and swift alteration in the colours of domestic textiles.

By the end of the century paint preparation, too, was taken out of the realm of the professional, as pre-tinted paints became available to individual consumers. The earliest ready-mixed paint available in the US was a mid-green, 'French Imperial Green', marketed by Lucas & Company from 1866. In 1869 F.W. Devoe followed with a 'Park Lawn Green'; by the mid-1870s paint

Above. From royal seat to domestic throne: a washable sanitary wallpaper, marketed as 'Jubilee', made in celebration of the fiftieth (Golden) anniversary of Queen Victoria's accession, in 1887.

Opposite. Delicate and humorous wallpaper designs from René Binet's *Esquisses Décoratives* of 1895.

manufacturers in America and Britain were selling resealable cans directly to consumers rather than, as before, solely to tradesmen. The result was a significant empowerment of householders, enabling families – and, increasingly, women – to take decorating choices into their own hands. To help the consumer further, paint companies were soon distributing catalogues featuring approximated paint samples. The problem was that these printed samples actually bore little relation to the tone of the actual paint. Thus Devoe in the US initiated the laborious and expensive process, still followed by the best specialist paint suppliers today, of gluing actual paint samples into the catalogues.[8]

By 1900 non-toxic oil paints were available in addition to the more traditional, lead-based products. Many of these were zinc-based, or used combinations of zinc and lead. However, although zinc-based oils were more flexible than lead paints, they were also more brittle, and thus harder to apply. Nevertheless, both zinc and, after 1900, titanium produced a far brighter white paint than had been possible with the use of white lead. Robert Tressell's celebrated socialist polemic *The Ragged Trousered Philanthropists* of 1914 reflected contemporary suspicion of the composition of these new products, the tradesman Philpot reflecting that 'they might appear to be all right for a time, but they would probably not last, because they was mostly made of kimicles'.[9]

The appearance of the first of the new chemical aniline dyes heralded a new age of paint production, during which increasing numbers of synthetic pigments vastly expanded the range of paint colours available to the average householder. Inevitably, though, there was a reaction against the most garish of the new aniline colours. Thus during the last decades of the nineteenth century, paint colours used for interior decoration appear if anything to have been more restrained than in previous years, despite the increasingly wide range of colour possibilities which technology now offered.

The Anglo-Saxon enthusiasm for the so-called 'Queen Anne' style of the 1880s and 1890s, characterised by white-painted joinery for windows, both inside and out, skirtings, stair balusters and internal doors, established a trend for white and tints of white which has lasted to this day. The effect of this sudden lurch away from bright colour in the direction of what Mark Girouard has aptly termed 'sweetness and light' is demonstrated in comments written by a visitor to Oscar Wilde's home in 1885: 'The walls, all white, the ceiling like yours a little (gold) but with two lovely dragons painted in the opposite corners of it. All the white paint (as indeed all the paint used about the house) was of a high polish like Japanese lacquerwork, which has great charm for one who hates paper on walls as much as I do.'[10] The bright, clean effect of these whites was further enhanced by the introduction of electricity, installed in average homes from the 1890s onwards (see Chapter 9, below). Gloss paint, too, began to be widely used for the first time since the early eighteenth century.

The nineteenth-century

English (Lancashire) roller print wallpaper design of c.1830, after John James Audobon's magisterial *Birds of America*.

revolution in domestic colour was seen to its best effect in furnishing fabrics and wallpaper. The floorcoverings, wall-coverings and curtains of the mid-nineteenth century epitomised how far taste, influenced by the possibilities of manufacture, had changed. Not only were new secondary and tertiary colours being introduced; the sizes of the pattern, too, became ever larger. In 1970, American fabric historian Florence Montgomery acknowledged that 'whether or not Victorian principles of design and color conform to the taste of today's consumers, one cannot help admiring the flair and verve with which designers invented new patterns and color combinations and the high standards of engraving and meticulous attention to detail'.[11]

The possibilities of technology, in particular the newly invented mineral dyes, had by 1850 loosed a flood of brightly coloured carpets and drapes on to Western markets – many of them, sadly, 'all too often lacking in harmony of colour, design and motif'. To some observers the new mineral colours 'brought about a new palette of harsh shades, thereby destroying the former harmony of colours created by vegetable dyes' – although 'one cannot

help admiring their flair and verve'. Brightly coloured, stylised foliage of the sort that never graced a branch or bush was lovingly detailed in increasingly bold ways – the manual writer Mrs Orrinsmith subsequently condemning carpets on which 'vegetables are driven to a frenzy to be ornamental'.[12]

Colour made a huge impact on the floor too. The growing market for utilitarian floorcoverings, from flatweave 'Kidderminster carpets' to stamped footcloths, was given a further boost in 1861 with the patenting of 'linoleum', a strong basic covering, made from linen fibres, which lasted longer than the traditional floorcloth. Like its predecessor, it could be overprinted with all manner of garish and ambitious patterns. Its brightly coloured, imitative patterns indeed remained hugely popular until in the 1960s, when plastic vinyl substitutes became available.

Equally colourful, though more durable, than linoleum were ceramic floor tiles, which by the 1840s were undergoing a spectacular revival. From 1793 Herbert Minton of Stoke-on-Trent had been experimenting with medieval-style stamped tiles, with patterns filled with slip. In 1830 Minton bought a share in the patent of Samuel Wright for the industrial production of these indented tiles, and by 1840 his Minton Pottery was producing large numbers of them. The Gothic Revival provided Minton with a vast market: by the time of his death in 1858 over 150 churches had been paved with Minton's encaustic tiles – many of which were copied directly from examples in the Westminster Abbey Chapter House and other repositories

of medieval tiling. However, encaustic tiles soon found a ready secular market, too, in the middle-class front path and hallway. In 1840 Richard Prosser invented clay dust pressing, which enabled large numbers of tiles to be produced with just a decorative relief or transfer-printed surface. Mass-produced encaustic tiles, first made by Minton in 1842, were essentially made in the same basic manner as their handmade medieval ancestors. The basic terracotta form was stamped with a pattern and fired. A second colour was then poured into the stamped hollow, and the result was fired again. The process was simply repeated if another colour was required; indeed by the 1860s encaustic tiles were being produced in up to six colours.

The liberation of the middle-class interior by technology in the middle of the nineteenth century, though, was perhaps best illustrated by the development of wallpaper. The first primitive machine for making wallpaper – formerly printed with wood blocks – was patented in 1799 by the Frenchman Louis Robert. In 1820 Michael Spoerlin devised a tinting technique which enabled the same motif to be printed in a variety of colours. Yet the first large-scale machine – excepting William Palmer's 1823 pattern for a device that was effectively just a mechanical block-printer, and Jean Zuber of Rixheim's horse-powered cylindrical press of 1826 – was not perfected until 1839. In that year the calico-printing Potter Brothers of Darwen in Lancashire unveiled the first commercially scaled, four-colour, roller-driven wallpaper-manufacturing machine. Coming three years after

Vivid tile designs by Maw & Co. of Brosley, Shropshire, of c.1870.

any fabric; 'wood' and 'marble' papers; 'landscape figure' papers, invariably made in France and very popular in the American market, featuring scenes printed between vertical stripes; and paper that even imitated deep-buttoned upholstery. By the late 1840s 'satinising' machines could produce satin-effect backgrounds by running dampened paper under high-speed revolving brushes. The prestigious Alastian firm of Zuber was using Manchester-made six-colour rollers to produce designs of astonishing hues and complexity; in 1858 the same company introduced 'gravure' printing and matt and coated effects. The French author of *Grammaire des arts décoratifs*, Charles Blanc, subsequently boasted that wallpaper could now assume 'the sheen of silk or stain ... the thick substance of drapery or the glaze of ceramic finishes, but also the grain of fabric, the texture of old tapestry, crochet or Genoese velvet, the regularity of brocade and even the swell and curve of upholstery'.[13]

By the 1840s, only the grandest homes still retained fabric wall hangings; elsewhere, wallpapers were invariably preferred. As the colour range available to the producers of what was now a mass-market item expanded through the addition of organic and inorganic dyes, so the public were offered an increasingly bewildering array of designs and hues. So much so, indeed, that aristocratic homes turned away from what they now perceived as a mass-market product towards traditional wall finishes such as paint stencilling – a handmade finish which could always, of course, be suitably aged or distressed.

The furniture of the middle-class home was also changing.

Orientally influenced curtain treatment suggested by the French periodical *Le Garde-Meuble* in c.1870. If executed, such a bold feature would undoubtedly have overpowered a modest room.

the last of the wallpaper excise had been slashed by Lord Melbourne's government (though it was not until 1861 that the tax was finally abolished), this put colourful wallpaper designs within reach of almost every household. In America, the first mechanically printed wallpaper was produced in 1844 by Howell & Brothers in Philadelphia – though using a British machine.

Spurred on by these technological leaps forward, wallpaper manufacturers could, by 1840, achieve almost anything. Flower motifs got bigger and blowsier, especially in France – one of whose best export markets remained the United States. 'Décor' paper was available to imitate pilastered walls, as were papers that imitated stamped leather or oriental lacquer; papers that imitated drapery of

Machine-cut veneers for tables and legs and supports for seat furniture made contemporary and increasingly fashionable reproduction furniture more affordable. Manufactured veneers were indeed chosen for special attention from Charles Dickens, whose *Our Mutual Friend* of 1865 gently satirised the brightly coloured, mass-produced furnishings and fittings of the 'Veneering' family: 'Everything about the Veneerings,' he observed with glee, 'was spick and span new'. As in Ruskin's reception of *The Awakening Conscience* – though rather more affectionately – Dickens implicitly contrasted the eagerness with which the lower middle classes embraced new industrial fashion with the persistent distaste of Old Money for mass-produced items.

Much to Ruskin's distaste, furniture became more colourful. Gaily coloured papier-mâché furniture – light, easily painted, and often inlaid with mother-of-pearl – won favour as seating for children. Significantly, it also became more comfortable. By 1850, springing

– introduced on a wide scale from the 1820s – had become commonplace, as did the new, pan-European fashion for deep buttoning, which (particularly after the spread of the use of coiled springs in the 1860s and 1870s) helped to ensure a more pleasingly padded landing for the well-fed bourgeoisie of the industrial West. No wonder that design historian John Cornforth astutely characterised this age's primary goal as the 'quest for comfort'.

As seats themselves became more comfortable, so did their immediate context. Rooms were draped with fabric to soften the environment and create a sense of cosiness and comfort, muffling sounds and filtering light. Cushions were added to sofas in increasing profusion; tables were now covered with tablecloths. Room corners – 'considered the epitome of discomfort' – were concealed, and the outside world was gently shut off.[14] Comfort and colour predominated. Regrettably, though, the next century and a half was to be devoted to eroding these laudable design aspirations.

1. Charlotte Gere, *Nineteenth-Century Decoration* (1989), 222. 2. Ibid., 295. 3. John Ruskin, *Modern Painters* (1886), quoted in David Lowenthal, *The Past is a Foreign Country* (1985), 165. 4. Ian Bristow, *Architectural Colour in British Interiors 1615–1840* (1996), 33; Florence Montgomery, *Printed Textiles: English and American Cottons and Linens 1700–1850* (1970), 135. 5. Bristow, *Architectural Colour in British Interiors*, 37. 6. D.R. Hay, *The Laws of Harmonious Colouring adapted to House Painting* (1821), 36. 7. Bristow, *Architectural Colour in British Interiors*, 255. 8. Roger Moss, *Paint in America: The Colors of Historic Buildings* (1994), 35. 9. Robert Tressell, *The Ragged Trousered Philanthropists* (1914), 378. 10. Mark Girouard, *Sweetness and Light: The Queen Anne Movement, 1860–1900* (1990), 125. 11. Montgomery, *Printed Textiles*, 289. 12. Ibid., 35, 287; Penny Sparke, *As Long As It's Pink – The Sexual Politics of Taste* (1995), 38. 13. Richard C. Nylander, *Wallpapers for Historic Buildings* (1992), 100. 14. Sparke, *As Long As It's Pink*, 40.

Why cannot people understand that good taste and simplicity go hand in hand with common sense?

(R.W. Edis, *The Decoration and Furnishing of Town Houses*, 1881)[1]

Opposite. Staircase detail from Philip Webb's influential Red House in Bexleyheath, of 1859–60. The prototypical Arts and Crafts interior, dominated by whitewashed walls, plain woods and occasional rugs.

Right. A trade advertisement for the famous firm of Jeffrey & Co., of the 1890s, trumpeting the virtues of their arsenic-free 'artistic' wallpapers.

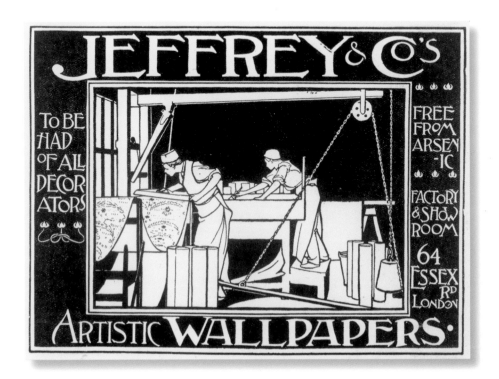

Design reform, and the peculiarly Anglo-Saxon Arts and Crafts movement that it spawned, undoubtedly revolutionised Western interior design. But they were not, as is often supposed, merely the creation and achievement of the designer-cum-poet-cum-utopian socialist William Morris in the aftermath of the Great Exhibition. As early as 1836 papier-mâché manufacturer Samuel Wiley testified to a British government Select Committee that 'public taste is bad' and that 'I can sell them the worst things [and] the most unmeaning'.[2] The committee subsequently recommended that a benchmark collection of decorative art be established for the instruction of professionals and householders alike. This laudable goal finally came to fruition with the opening of the South Kensington collections, conceived by Prince Albert and Henry Cole as 'a repository of the design works of past and present to provide inspiration for designers and manufacturers and to influence the taste of the general public', which took the best of the 1851 exhibits and proved a great inspiration to Morris and his followers.

In the ensuing decade, as we have seen, both Ruskin and Pugin inveighed against 'newness' and naturalism, against pattern and colour. Design reform declared itself the enemy of untrammelled nature; through the sustained and ultimately successful attack on naturalistic floral imagery and 'direct imitation', its protagonists 'committed ideologically to honest use of materials and appropriate ornament'.[3]

The new ideology addressed both industrial manufacturers (Cole himself was one) and individual craftsmen; its child was the Arts and Crafts movement – which, in the words of one recent historian, was 'expressive of a whole way of life'.[4] (The movement's name actually derives from the Arts and Crafts Exhibition Society, launched in 1888 by Walter Crane, painters George Clausen, Holman Hunt and others.) In the view of Morris and his followers, to whom the Great Exhibition had been an aberration, the Arts and Crafts initiatives of the 1860s represented a return to 'a respect for the achievements of craftsmen'.[5] The movement represented a fusion of simplicity and functionalism. Unfortunately for its practitioners, this synthesis, when expressed in the guise of handmade objects, proved far too expensive for the everyday home.

Design reform was also emphatically a masculine reaction. By the 1870s women were taking

Left. Consciously simple Arts and Crafts brick chimney surround at the Red House.

Opposite. An Arts and Crafts Morning Room shown in a Morris & Company advertisement of the turn of the century. The floor is, in the best Morrisian tradition, left bare except for the provision of a small flatweave rug.

a leading part in determining the decoration and disposition of the home. Yet Morris, Eastlake and his fellow design reformers 'circumvented the question of taste completely and placed all discussion about the material world in the masculine sphere of manufacture'. From Eastlake onwards luxury was invariably gendered as 'she', and the stereotype evolved of women 'preoccupied with surface rather than with substance': 'thus did culture attempt to control nature and the masculine take dominance over the feminine'.[6] This identification of women with the petty concerns of taste helped to marginalise taste as an issue and created a stereotype of smug Victorian bourgeois life which the Modern movement was later happy to exploit.

The first effective salvo fired by the design reformers came not with William Morris's Arts and Crafts principles of the 1860s but during the previous decade, with the publication of Owen Jones's influential pattern-book *The Grammar of Ornament* in 1856. Jones (1809–74), who had studied architecture under Lewis Vulliamy and had visited Europe and the Middle East, was one of the first design reformers to publicly acknowledge the poor quality, as he saw it, of much contemporary interior design. One of the principal designers of the Crystal Palace, Jones was one of the primary instigators of the permanent exhibition of decorative art, designed for the guidance of homeowners and professionals alike (and the forerunner of the Victoria and Albert Museum), which opened as the Museum of Manufactures in Marlborough House, London, in 1852.

Four years later, Jones unveiled his compendium of 'approved' styles. His *Grammar* championed the use of 'honest' two-dimensional ornament. He also, more controversially, argued that 'elements of different styles could be brought together according to these "grammatical" rules, so as to create new ornamental languages'. Jones denounced 'copying ... without attempting to ascertain the peculiar circumstances which rendered an ornament beautiful'.[7] But he was no enemy of mass-production, designing everything from mass-manufactured carpets to biscuit-tin lids.

MORRIS & COMPANY, 449 OXFORD STREET, W.

DESIGN FOR MORNING-ROOM OR LIBRARY, IN LIGHT OAK OR WALNUT, BY MORRIS AND COMPANY.

ESTIMATES FOR DECORATIVE WORK.

MORRIS & COMPANY employ a staff of good workmen—joiners, plasterers, paper-hangers, painters, etc.—many of whom have been a great number of years in the firm's service, and were trained under its traditions of workmanship. The firm will be pleased to submit schemes and estimates for all kinds of decorative work, classical as well as in their own special style, including :—

INTERIOR CONSTRUCTION	PARQUETRY
PANELLING	FRIEZE PAINTING AND WALL-DECORATION
FITMENTS OF EVERY KIND	PLASTER MODELLING AND CEILINGS
PAINTING AND PAPERHANGING	SANITARY WORK, ETC.

Six of Jones's 'General Principles' from his *Grammar* were originally explored in a series of articles he wrote in 1851, *Gleanings from the Great Exhibition*, which were initially reworked as lectures for the Society of Arts in 1852. His well-illustrated *Grammar* was effectively a manifesto along the lines of Pugin's acerbic *Contrasts* of 1836; but it was far better illustrated and far more comprehensive than Pugin's polemic (the *Athenaeum*'s review declared it 'beautiful enough to be the horn-book of angels'), and as a result proved far more palatable to the average householder. It consequently became the definitive sourcebook for ornamental motifs, going through ten editions before 1910. The American edition, which first appeared in 1880, was equally influential, both Louis Sullivan and Frank Lloyd Wright later acknowledging their debt to its plates and prose. Wright made painstaking tracings of Jones's designs on to onionskin paper when training as a young architect, and took them into Sullivan's office to help get his first real job.[8]

Jones's message was not a proto-Modernist one. He admired ornament – 'whenever any style of ornament commends universal admiration, it will always be found in accordance with the laws which regulate the distribution of form in nature' – and sought to harness, not reject, history. To work 'independently of the past', he declared, 'would be an act of supreme folly'. He merely sought to elevate honesty as the primary goal of interior decoration. His thirty-seven published 'General Principles' included such straightforward

sentiments as 'Construction should be decorated. Decoration should never be purposely constructed' (Principle 5); the precept that 'In surface decoration all lines should flow out of a parent stem' (Principle 11); and the advice that 'Flowers or other natural objects should not be used as ornaments, but conventional representations founded upon them' (Principle 13). His views on colour were, as we have seen, particularly controversial. 'Primary colours should be used on the upper portions of objects, the secondary and tertiary on the lower,' he affirmed in Principle 17, yet 'No composition can ever be perfect in which any one of the three primary colours is wanting' (Principle 23). The colour of every medieval surface, he believed, must have been 'an effect which must have been glorious beyond conception'.

Jones also pleaded that 'we may return to nature for fresh inspiration'. The last section of his *Grammar* was entirely about 'Leaves & Flowers'. (In compiling this, Jones was assisted by a young Christopher Dresser [1834–1904], who was already lecturing on botany.) Jones's promotion of the systematic use of flower motifs was very influential not only on William Morris but on a whole generation of designers.

Owen Jones was not the only mid-Victorian to decry the ostentation of mid-century interiors. Elizabeth Gaskell's powerful novel *North and South* of 1855 gave a number of examples of the 'overloading of ... a house with colour'. ('Speaking of vulgarity and commonness, you must prepare yourself for our drawing-room paper. Pink and blue roses, with yellow leaves! And such

a heavy cornice round the room!') In the Thorntons' house, as devised by Gaskell, 'Every cover was taken off, and the apartment blazed forth in yellow silk damask and a brilliantly-flowered carpet. Every corner seemed filled up with ornament, until it became a weariness to the eye, and presented a strange contrast to the bald ugliness of the look-out into the great mill-yard.'[9]

At the time that Gaskell's novel was published, designer, poet, conservationist and socialist William Morris (1834–96) was also reacting against the heavyweight colours, superfluous ornament and illusionistic flower and vegetable designs of mid-Victorian manufacturers. Rejecting many of the new, commercially produced dyes, he was particularly virulent on the subject of the typically Early Victorian drab colours: 'Do not fall into the trap', he warned in the 1880s, 'of a dingy, bilious-looking yellow-green, a colour to which I have a special and personal hatred, because (if you will excuse my mentioning personal matters) I have

been supposed to have somewhat brought it into vogue. I assure you I am not really responsible for it.' Morris's colours were obtained from traditional, organic sources such as madder (from the roots of the European and Middle Eastern plant *Rubia tinctorum*), weld (from the plant wild mignonette), saffron or quercitron bark for yellow, walnut roots or husks for brown, cochineal (from crushed insects) for red and indigo (also known as woad) for blue. From 1875 he experimented with ancient vegetable dyes; significantly, though, his late fabric of 1891, 'Daffodil', used a bright yellow aniline dye.[10] His wallpapers were all woodblocked in the eighteenth-century manner, and the number of colours he used in their design was deliberately restricted. His fabrics, however, did not always eschew modern technology. While the company's chintzes were still handblocked by Wardle and Company, the Morris-designed woven textiles were made elsewhere on power looms.

Nevertheless, Morris believed that manufacture, as well as design, needed reform, and rejected mass-production. He did not blame the machines, as many of the critics of the Great Exhibition had done, nor the craftsmen, but the workings of capitalism itself: capitalism's pursuit of profits, he believed, invariably lowered standards of design. Honesty was his keyword: there was to be no false naturalism, and no shading designed to present the illusion of three dimensions in a two-dimensional product. He aimed to evoke nature, not to copy it. Thus his seat furniture expressed its construction, and did not try to hide it behind the sinuous lines of comfortable upholstery.

Left. Making chintz the old-fashioned way: hand-blocking at Merton Abbey, *c.*1900.

Opposite. Morris wallpaper designs. Clockwise from top right: 'Pimpernell' (1876), acanthus and rose design (undated), 'Daisy' (1864) and 'Pomegranate' (1866).

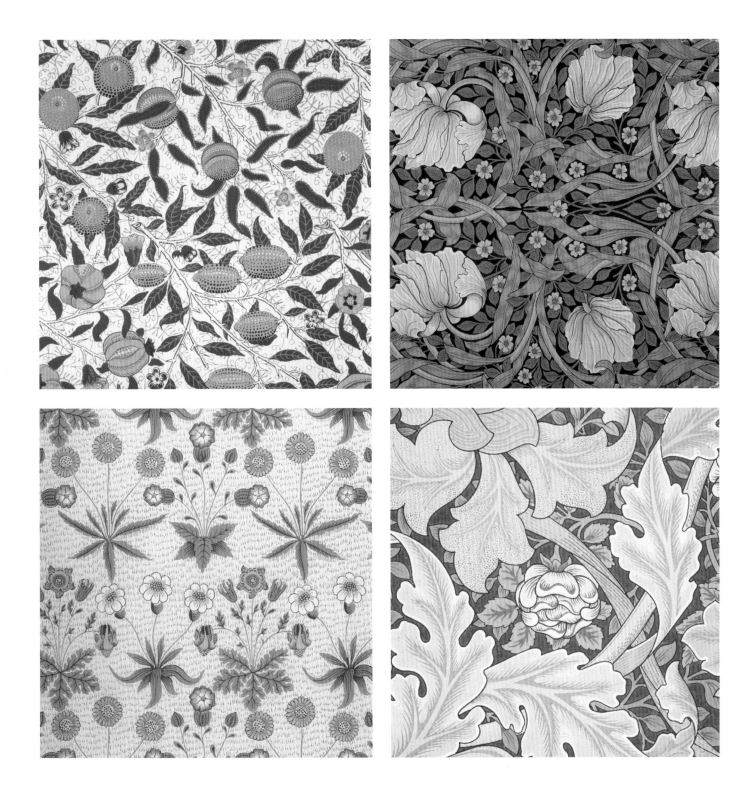

As Morris's *Times* obituary noted in 1896, he had sought 'to express the beauty of colour, line and material' based on the direct observation of nature rather than exploiting the technological possibilities of mass-production.

Morris's own design vehicle, Morris, Marshall, Faulkner & Company, was founded in April 1861, and by 1862 was producing wallpapers. By 1870 it was finally profitable – though only by appealing to wealthy customers. Morris used old-fashioned woodblock manufacturing techniques, and took care to use only the best and purest naturally obtained colours (red and blue were generally predominant) and simple, strong designs much in the Chinese vein, usually featuring birds and flowers. Where shadows were needed, Morris did not introduce an excessive number of supplementary colours, as many of his commercial rivals were wont to do, but simply used the device of hatching.

His deliberately flat and stylised designs were made to appear three-dimensional by using different, lighter shades and a smaller scale for the backgrounds. Morris & Company's products enabled British wallpaper design to reclaim the high ground it had abandoned earlier in the century. Many of Morris's papers were made not in his own workshops but by the firm of Jeffrey and Company, whose director, Metford Warner, subsequently founded the firm which still bears his name. (When Morris & Company foundered in 1940, however, it was not Warners but the firm of Arthur Sanderson and Sons which bought up Morris's archive of designs, blocks and papers. It still survives at Sanderson's archive in Uxbridge, West London.)

However, despite Morris's vigorous championing of Arts and Crafts principles, he failed to reconcile the virtues of craftsmanship with the social accessibility that industry afforded.

Morris's handmade 'Hammersmith' carpets were vastly more expensive even than the oriental or Donegal carpets they purported to rival.[11] During the last decades of his life, Morris expressed his great disappointment at having found only rich patrons for his work.[12] The Home Arts and Industries Association of 1884, together with the quaintly named Peasant Arts Society of 1885, attempted to apply Morris's teachings in order to bring handmade goods within the financial reach of the average family; but, once again, the economics of manufacture were always against them. This pattern was to be repeated throughout the twentieth century.

Lambasted by Morris's criticisms and stung by the publicity afforded to his 'organic' wallpaper designs, wallpaper manufacturers, while understandably refusing to return to the age of the woodblock, began to replace the often grating colour combinations of the 1850s and 1860s with lighter, more harmonious tones, and the naturalistic flower and vegetable patterns of the mid-nineteenth century with more abstract, geometric designs. For the popular market, designers adapted and simplified Morris & Company patterns and presented them to sympathetic manufacturers, who were able to produce Morris-style 'Arts and Crafts' wallpapers and fabrics at a fraction of the cost of the handmade originals. As Turner and Hoskins have noted, 'With their vigorous acanthus scroll work patterns in gloomy secondary and tertiary colours, these [quasi-Morris papers] were felt to be ideal for narrow suburban halls.'[13]

One of the most prominent of these new wallpaper designers was the Englishman Arthur Silver. He founded the Silver Studio in 1880 and provided the firm of Liberty & Co. with some of its most characteristic and successful designs for papers and fabrics – most notably the famous 'peacock feather'

Opposite, above. The carpet looms at Morris's factory at Merton Abbey in the early 1900s.

Opposite, below. Dutch 'Persian flower' tiles and Morris & Company 'Cray' curtain fabric in the Oak Room at Wightwick Manor, Staffordshire.

Right. Highly fashionable Japanese-influenced aesthetic furniture, offered by Liberty in a newspaper advertisement of the 1880s.

pattern, successfully revived by Liberty in 1975. Their exquisite, high-quality Arts and Crafts and Art Nouveau wallpaper designs 'raised the status of wallpaper to something near art and was a useful marketing ploy at a time when "artistic" was the main term of decorating approbation'.[14] On Arthur's death in 1896, the Silver Studio was taken over by his son Rex, who continued to promote radical new design throughout the early decades of the twentieth century.

Liberty – founded in London in 1875, and an immediate champion of new Arts and Crafts (and, subsequently, Art Nouveau) designs – was only one of the companies which, following the lead of Morris & Company, were actively encouraging good, 'reformed' design on both sides of the Atlantic during the 1880s and 1890s. Liberty's great achievement was to commercialise Arts and Crafts furniture – to make the designs of Morris and his followers accessible to a mass audience.

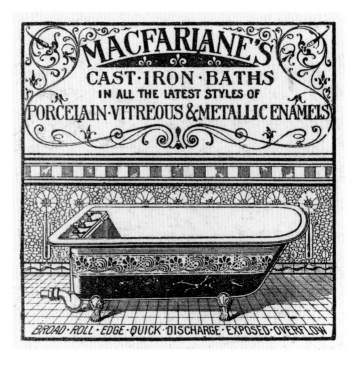

The egotistical Arthur Lasenby Liberty (1843–1917) was not a design connoisseur himself, but promoted what he thought would sell. (Despite calling Art Nouveau the 'exotic imaginings of morbid brains', he was happy to adapt and promote it after 1900.) He opened his Regent Street shop, specialising in oriental silks, in 1875; by 1880 he was selling all types of oriental furniture, and by the 1890s pieces from the Silver Studio. Liberty was knighted in 1913, by which time he had factories reinterpreting the latest designers' work in London, Birmingham and Paris, and Liberty furniture could be bought in Paris, Brussels, Berlin, Vienna and all over Europe and America.

Liberty was not the only London retailer to purvey ready-made furniture and fabrics to an eager middle-class audience. By the end of the 1870s

Simple, straightforward Arts and Crafts bedroom furniture and Morris's 'Pomegranate' wallpaper at Cragside, Northumberland. The wallpaper was reprinted in 1978 from original blocks of 1864.

a number of stores had opened in London's West End, among them James Shoolbred's impressive emporium in Tottenham Court Road. In 1877 Morris & Company themselves moved from their Bloomsbury premises to a location on burgeoning Oxford Street. The new wave of shoppers coming to the area encouraged the construction of electric underground railways after 1890; they in turn attracted more customers into the centre of London, with the result that the character of famous thoroughfares such as Oxford Street and Piccadilly changed completely, from residential to retail. Meanwhile, on the other side of the Atlantic, America's retail barons were trying something very new. In 1872 Aaron Montgomery Ward opened the first mail order firm in America.

While Owen Jones and William

Morris inspired the early design reformers, undoubtedly the biggest reforming influence on middle-class interiors in the wake of the Arts and Crafts movement was Charles Locke Eastlake's book *Hints on Household Taste*, first published in Britain in 1868. Born in Plymouth in 1836, Eastlake (1836–1906) had a good artistic and architectural pedigree: the nephew of the celebrated artist Sir Charles Eastlake PRA, he was also the pupil of the classical architect Philip Hardwick. The book originated in articles penned for the magazine *The Queen* from June 1865. It proved not only a big success in Britain, its fourth edition appearing as early as 1878, but was an even bigger success in the US, where it launched the design reform movement, went through six editions between 1878 and

not a craftsman like Morris. (He did, though, make detailed drawings for the upmarket decorating firms of Crace & Son and Jackson & Graham, including some for pieces intended for the Great Exhibition.) As a result, he did not rail against the evils of mass-production as Morris did. He was, though, very critical of the morals of the furniture trade, and of the more nakedly venal traffic in faked antiques. But he took care not to seem highbrow. His great talent was to take the ideas of Pugin, Ruskin, Jones, Morris and the other design reformers and make them accessible and attractive to a general audience.

Eastlake declared at the outset of the book that he wanted to 'disturb the visual complacency of the public'. Current taste in interiors, he opined, was based 'upon eclecticism rather than in tradition', was 'capricious' and was 'subject to constant variation', and patronised design 'of such a vulgar and extravagant kind'. Like Morris, he put his emphasis on honesty of manufacture: 'Every article of manufacture which is capable of decoration treatment should indicate, by its general design, the purpose to which it will be applied, and should never be allowed to convey a false notion of that purpose.' What he found in the typical middle-class home of the 1860s did not adhere to these high-flown aims. He saw ugly, British-made Brussels carpets disfiguring the drawing room; 'gaudy chintz' in bedrooms; 'vulgar' and 'flimsy' Birmingham metalwork in the chimneypiece and on the doors ('the present cast-iron knocker is a frightful invention') and 'silly representations of vegetable life' on wallpapers.[16]

1881, and lent its name to what was soon called the 'Eastlake' style. (Eastlake himself was rather embarrassed by this nomenclature: 'I find American tradesmen,' he later wrote, 'continuing advertising what they are pleased to call "Eastlake" furniture, with the production of which I have had nothing whatever to do, and for the taste of which I should be very sorry to be considered responsible'.[15])

Eastlake had trained as an architect under Hardwick, and was

Opposite. An elaborately tiled fireplace by Minton & Co., designed for the 1876 Centennial Exhibition in Philadelphia.

Left. Detail of a fireplace, with Dutch-style tiles made at the local Liverpool factory, and Morris's 'Pomegranate' wallpaper *in situ* at Speke Hall, Liverpool.

But Eastlake was not wholly pessimistic. He did laud 'the remarkable change which has taken place within the last few years in the character of domestic furniture'. But he despaired of the British public being able to recognise the wheat from the chaff. There was, he declared, an 'unfortunately large class of the British public who are indifferent to art of any kind, and who care only to secure "novelties" (which may be remarkable for ugliness as beauty) in furnishing their homes': 'The British public are, as a body, utterly incapable of distinguishing good from bad design', he advised, and 'As long as gaudy and extravagant trash is displayed in the windows of our West-end thoroughfares, so long will it attract ninety-nine people our of every hundred to buy.' He did, however, suggest that 'we may one day aspire to the formation of a national taste'.[17]

Setting a precedent that was to be enthusiastically endorsed by the Modern Movement, Eastlake blamed women for all this. Women were responsible for the 'assemblage of modern rubbish' that disfigured so many middle-class homes, and for the technologically fuelled obsession with novelty and fashion. Sadly, women, with their innate lack of aesthetic appreciation and education, knew no better: 'the ladies like it best when it comes like a new toy from the shop fresh with recent varnish and untarnished gilding'. Unsurprisingly, he also denounced the gendering of internal spaces through the use of particular colours and forms as 'an absurd conventionality', and raged against the 'insipid prettiness' that women insisted upon, and their introduction of unnecessary additions such as 'flimsy and extravagant' antimacassars.[18]

What Eastlake advocated, in line

with the precepts of Morris's Arts and Crafts principles, was honest simplicity. He asked that 'the internal fittings of a house may be made picturesque and interesting without being rude and clumsy in form, and that it is not necessary to sacrifice the refinements and comfort to which we are accustomed in the nineteenth century in order to secure simplicity of style'. He particularly targeted graining – 'an objectionable and pretentious deceit, which cannot be excused even on the ground of economy': why, he asked, should we paint joinery in imitation of oak, when 'Everybody can see that it is not oak'?[19] All ornament, he declared, should relate to 'the character and properties of the raw material'. Thus iron should not be painted to imitate wood or plaster ('Almost all cast-iron ornament ... is hopelessly ugly'). No furniture or fabrics should feature naturalistic carved or printed plants ('why should we lapse into the vulgarity of garlands and bouquets for the decoration of our drawing-room floors?'); here he cited the good example of Indian chintzes: 'Did you ever see any *picture* of bird, beast or flower on these specimens?' Floorcloths should not imitate anything ('I have even seen a pattern which was intended to represent the spots on a lion's skin,' he spluttered); wall tiles were always to be preferred to marbled papers in halls; and floorcoverings 'should be decorated after a manner which will belie neither its flatness nor solidity'.[20]

For Eastlake, objects should do what they were supposed to do, and not pretend to be anything else. He therefore condemned all glued-on decoration ('this trash is only lightly glued to the frame'); impractical modern drapery that was 'seldom drawn'; gas fittings that assumed 'the ecclesiastical shapes generally found in the art metal-worker's catalogue'; naturalistic iron ornament that 'more closely resembles a friendly group of garden slugs'. However, he was on occasion cheerfully inconsistent and even iconoclastic, suggesting at one point that 'stamped leather' French wallpapers were suitable for friezes – and thus dismissing the 'principles illumined by what Mr Ruskin has called the Lamp of Truth'.[21]

Unlike Morris, Eastlake was equivocal in his judgement of the value of technological advance. The fact that 'the arts of design had sunk into their lowest degradation' was, he supposed, 'an almost inevitable result of machinery'. However, he took care not to blame the workmen: 'It would be absurd, however, to suppose that English capacity has deteriorated in the same proportion as English taste. Our artisans have as much intelligence as ever; it only wants proper direction and employment.' While no Morrisian socialist, Eastlake did instead take a faltering sideswipe or two at capitalism. He suggested, for example, that 'the decline of our national taste must be attributed to ... competition', since 'if our ordinary furniture has cheapened in price, it has also deteriorated in quality'. And he did praise much of what machines could do, lauding the 'skilful combinations of colour in secondary and tertiary tints, which it would have been impossible to procure a few years ago', and the 'very great improvement of late' in wallpaper manufacture (though

'of course', he added, 'many wretched specimens continue to be displayed').[22]

Like Jones and Morris, Eastlake had his own views on colour. Carpets, he recommended, should contrast with, and not match, the wall colour. 'White dimity curtains' were best for bedrooms, especially if surrounded by strong colours (and bare bedroom floors, which he advocated as 'a healthier and more cleanly, as well as a more picturesque, fashion than that now in vogue'). For wallpaper backgrounds, 'the paper can hardly be too subdued in tone', such as a light stone or light green: 'In colour, wallpapers should relieve without violently opposing that of the furniture and hangings by which they are

Maples was one of the most successful of the furniture stores which sprang up along London's Tottenham Court Road in the 1880s. This advertisement shows a classic Late Victorian iron-and-brass bed, a design still hugely popular today. From *The Illustrated London News*, 1892.

surrounded'. In general, 'There should be one dominant hue in the room, to which all others introduced are subordinate'.[23]

His conclusion was aimed at homeowners rather than designers and manufacturers. The public, he exhorted, 'must do their part. If they will insist on the perpetuation of pretentious shams ... no reform can possibly be expected. But if they encourage that sound and healthy taste which alone is found allied with conscientious labour, whether in the workshops or the factory, then we may hope to see revived the ancient glory of those industrial arts.'[24]

Eastlake's *Hints* was a huge success across the English-speaking world. It was reprinted five times in the US between 1872 and 1881; there his appeal for 'honest' and 'moral' interiors,

and denunciation of practices such as veneering and fitted carpets, fitted the moral and increasingly hygiene-aware mood of the times. By 1880 the *Cornhill Magazine* was labelling him 'the oracle of domestic taste', though Christopher Dresser did dare to reprove him for his apparent determination 'to despise finish and refinement'.[25]

The success of *Hints* prompted a great flood of home advice books and periodicals. Most of these were by and for women, demonstrating the new role women had as arbiters of the disposition and decoration of the home. In Britain, the periodicals *The House Furnisher and Decorator* and *The Furniture Gazette* were launched in 1871 and 1872 respectively; in 1881 came *The Journal of Decorative Art* and in 1885 *The Lady*, followed by the

Opposite. Fabric or wallpaper design by Christopher Dresser from his *Studies in Design* of 1874.

Far left. In R.W. Edis's design a small chimneypiece is dwarfed by rows of overmantel shelves groaning with blue-and-white china, in the seventeenth-century fashion. As well as being an enthusiastic proponent for the Arts and Crafts style, Edis was also an extremely successful Regimental Colonel of the Artists' Rifles.

Left. 'Morning Room' design by Lewis C. Tiffany, published in 1881 in the popular American guide *Woman's Handiwork in Modern Homes* by Constance Cary Harrison of New York.

equally upmarket *Country Life* in 1895 and the more down-to-earth *Woman's World* in 1903.

Books were also thick on the ground. Possibly the most successful was Mrs Haweis's *The Art of Decoration* of 1881. Haweis was a polymath socialite – 'tiny, vivacious [and] an expert on Chaucer and a friend of painters' – and her book, intended as a sequel to her *Art of Beauty* of 1876, called for architects to involve themselves in all interior decoration issues.[26] In the same year came R.W. Edis's *Decoration and Furnishing of Town Houses*, which offered a more accommodating and less didactic version of Eastlake's gospel. Edis, an architect for the Grosvenor Estate in London who was keen to highlight the links between good aesthetics and physical health, followed it up with the highly topical volumes *Our Homes and How to Make Them Healthy* in 1883 (in which he raged in Eastlakeian fashion against 'shams and deceits' in the home) and *Healthy Furniture and Decoration* in 1884. The latter advised against 'jarring colours and patterns' on the grounds that this would cause

'nervous instability'.

In France, Eastlake's *Hints* was imitated by Emile Cardon's all-embracing *L'art au foyer domestique* of 1884 – Viollet-le-Duc's *Habitations Modernes* of 1877 having already declared Britain and Scandinavia to represent the best in domestic design. In America, Rhoda and Agnes Garrett's *Suggestions for Home Decoration* (1877) and the American edition of Edis's *The Decoration and Furniture of Town Houses* (1881) promoted the Arts and Crafts message. The Arts-and-Crafts-influenced mass-market periodical *House Beautiful* was launched in 1897, and Gustav Stickley's incisive magazine *The Craftsman* in 1901. The latter was so influential that Arts and Crafts interiors became popularly known in the US as the 'Craftsman Style', even after the periodical itself foundered in 1916. Stickley (1858–1942) adapted Morris's ethos to advocate a colonially derived style based on a darkened natural oak finish, a decorative approach which he termed 'Golden Oak' or (more lastingly) the 'Mission Style', an idiom which proved particularly popular on the north-eastern and western seaboards. In his hands the precepts of the Arts and Crafts movement were cannily harnessed to the growing self-confidence of the American nation and interwoven with the emerging popularity of the Colonial Revival.

The architect Frank Lloyd Wright (1867–1959) went further than Stickley, using only the colours of the materials he used – terracotta from bricks and tiles, beige from undyed fabric – for his simple and muted interiors. In 1901 he issued a call to arms to American designers and

Opposite. American 'Mission Style' staircase at the David B. Gamble House, Pasadena, California, by C.S. Greene of 1908–9. Detail of the central staircase, constructed in Burmese teak, where the rails and corbels are held by clearly visible pegs. The teak and mahogany used in construction and decoration of the house are symbolised by the Tree of Life, depicted in the leaded glass hallway doors.

Left. 'Mission style' hall by Gustav Stickley's 'United Crafts' of Eastwood, New York, founded in 1898. The term 'Mission' was historically evocative but stylistically misleading: the furniture shown here has little to do with the old Spanish 'Mission' architecture of the West and South.

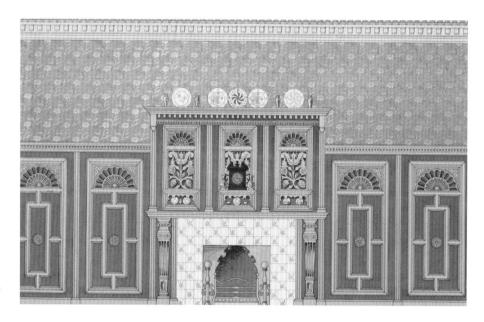

householders in his public lecture 'The Art and Craft of the Machine', given at the Hull House in Chicago, exhorting them to eschew the products of mid-Victorian mass-production and instead observe the lessons of Eastlake and the Arts and Crafts movement. However, as with most cases where designers or craftsmen espoused design reform ideals, the economic consequences of rejecting mass-manufacture could not be reconciled with the goal of bringing the best of design to a popular market. Wright's style may have been deliberately pared down, and his message egalitarian; however, his domestic clients were invariably very wealthy.

The American popularity of Arts and Crafts ideas was paralleled in Germany, Austria and Scandinavia. Here, too, Arts and Crafts ideology became intertwined with the simplicity of colonial revival and the notion of national identity. While the fruits of

this synthesis were not properly seen until the twentieth century (see Chapter 9, below), they did help foster a new internationalism in interior decoration, partially forged by the widespread interest in the Orient.

What is now called the 'Aesthetic' movement originally developed in Britain and America from the seeds sown by the Arts and Crafts pioneers and the rediscovery of Japanese manufactures. Japanese art and design was first seen comprehensively in the West at the 1862 South Kensington exhibition, Japan having been forcibly opened to Western trade by Commodore Perry's warships eight years earlier. (After the exhibition closed, most of the exhibits were offered for sale.)

Aesthetes argued that beauty uplifted the spirit and the mind. Boston design guru Charles Wyllys Elliott saw a time, not far off, when 'in every house, the Beautiful married to the Useful shall make life truer, finer, happier'.[27] In practical decorating terms, though, Aestheticism developed into a craze for greens and yellows, and with peacock blues, for ebonised furniture and sunflowers. It was light-hearted, accessible and cheerfully non-academic – 'essentially a decorative fashion with little ideological content other than an overt demonstration of sophisticated taste'.[28] At the high end of the market, the style was developed by E.W. Godwin (1833–86) and Christopher Dresser (1834–1904), who in 1876 became the first European designer to visit Japan. In middle-class households, the movement encouraged women to get more involved with decorative arts in general, and home design in particular.

By the 1880s Aestheticism, now 'developed into a cult of beauty [with] a tremendous influence on virtually all levels of society', had its very own Japanese manual in the form of J.W. Cutler's *A Grammar of Japanese Ornament and Design*, published in 1880. Using other helpful manuals such as Eastlake's *Hints*, the Household Art movement disseminated the principles of Aestheticism, to help consumers to create 'artful' interiors of their own. What Eastlake called 'art furniture' – which by his definition involved an artist or architect, and a degree of craftsmanship, at some stage in the process – was soon appropriated by the larger commercial manufacturers. Art furnishings have often been described as

The playwright Henrik Ibsen photographed in his remarkably uncluttered Oslo study, a view unearthed by an Italian magazine in 1928. Period photographs should not always be used as a template for historic decoration: rooms were often partially cleared for the photographer, so that the subject and the architecture could be seen more plainly.

'the first interior design style to reflect middle class, as opposed to aristocratic, taste', though this conveniently forgets the age of Biedermeier.

The popularity of Aestheticism and 'art furniture' at the end of the nineteenth century encouraged the rise of the professional interior decorator and the development of women's role as domestic arbiters of taste.[29] 'Art furnishing' retailers opened all over Britain and the US, where in 1882–3 Oscar Wilde toured, lecturing on his own vision of the 'House Beautiful'. Art furniture on both sides of the Atlantic was ebonised and gilded, lightly upholstered and revealing of its construction. Matching furniture was still popular, but there was an increasing tendency to furnish 'with individual pieces in a variety of styles and towards mixing antique and modern furniture within the same scheme'.[30] Elsewhere in the room, architectural woodwork was often painted in the same colours as the furniture itself; even druggets and linoleum were available in 'art colours' such as peacock blue, mustard, olive or

sage. In good, no-nonsense Arts and Crafts fashion, fitted carpets were frowned upon – they could not be beaten and thus properly cleaned, and were recommended to be replaced by more hygienic movable rugs. And the apostles of art furniture entreated readers to eliminate cluttered surfaces and to install more fitted furniture, which opened out interior space and cut down on dust.

By 1890 the Japanese aspects of Aestheticism had withered, and Arts and Crafts interiors began to adopt more of an eighteenth-century look both in Britain and the US, where they were happily fused with the newfound popularity of Colonial Revival. Stylistic niceties aside, though, art furniture had undoubtedly pointed the way forward. The first truly 'modern' form of interior design, its middle-class appeal, appropriation of named designers, exploitation by the larger retailers and promulgation through a network of books and journals, all foreshadowed how the average interior was to be shaped in the next century.

1. Quoted in Mary Schoeser and Celia Rufey, *English and American Textiles from 1790 to the Present* (1989), 153. 2. Penny Sparke, *As Long As It's Pink – The Sexual Politics of Taste* (1995), 52. 3. Ibid., 63, 65; Schoeser and Rufey, *English and American Textiles from 1790 to the Present*, 83. 4. Julian Holder, 'Arts and Crafts', in Joanna Banham (ed.), *Encyclopaedia of Interior Design* (1997), vol. 1, 61. 5. Charlotte Gere, *Nineteenth-Century Decoration* (1989), 276. 6. Sparke, *As Long As It's Pink*, 49, 55, 66. 7. Madeline Estill, 'The Aesthetic Movement', in Banham (ed.), *Encyclopaedia of Interior Design*, vol. 1, 13. 8. Owen Jones, *The Grammar of Ornament* (1865; new edition 2001), 326. 9. Elizabeth Gaskell, *North and South* (1855), 62, 66, 159. 10. Oliver Fairclough and Emmeline Leary, *Textiles by William Morris and Morris & Co., 1861–1940* (1981), 16. 11. See Kit Wedd, *The Victorian Society Book of the Victorian House* (2002), 253. 12. Gere, *Nineteenth-Century Decoration*, 11. 13. Mark Turner and Lesley Hoskins, *The Silver Studio of Design* (1988), 122. 14. Ibid. 15. Charles Locke Eastlake, *Hints on Household Taste* (1868), Preface, xxiv. 16. Ibid., x–xi, xxiii, 91, 2–3, 44. 17. Ibid., 118. 18. Sparke, *As Long As It's Pink*, 67; Eastlake, *Hints on Household Taste*, 71–3, 54, 97. 19. Eastlake, *Hints on Household Taste*, 42–3. 20. Ibid., 47, 51, 72, 141, 68, 52, 115. 21. Ibid., 59, 96, 148, 124. 22. Ibid., 104, 61, 295, 103, 118. 23. Ibid., 211, 119–20. 24. Ibid., 296. 25. Jeremy Cooper, *Victorian and Edwardian Furniture and Interiors* (1987), 94–5. 26. Isabelle Anscombe, *A Woman's Touch* (1984), 17. 27. Madeline Estill, 'The Aesthetic Movement', in Banham (ed.), *Encyclopaedia of Interior Design*, vol. 1, 11. 28. Estill, 'The Aesthetic Movement', 13. 29. Ibid., 11; Gere, *Nineteenth-Century Decoration*. 30. Nicholas Shaddick, 'Art Furnishings', in Banham (ed.), *Encyclopaedia of Interior Design*, vol. 1, 46.

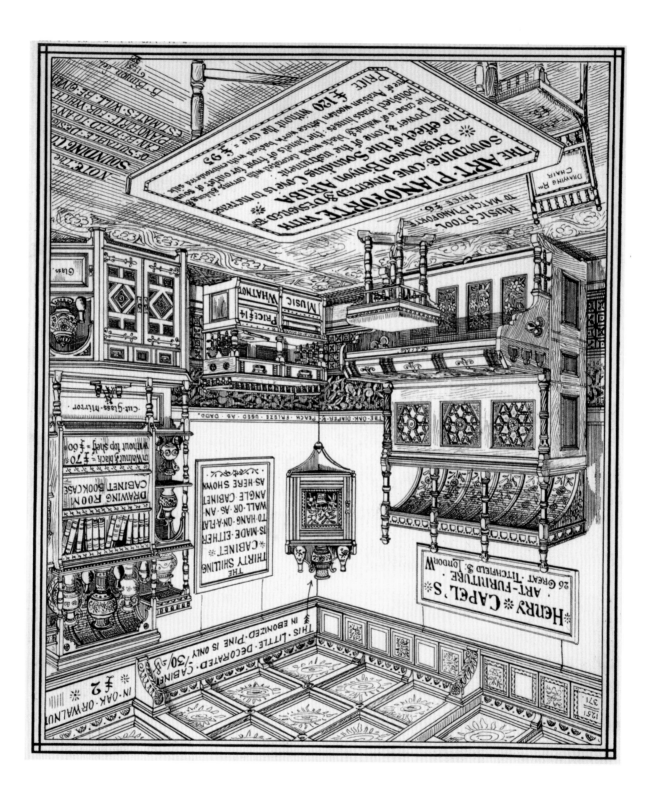

CLEAN AND BRIGHT
The Age of Electricity

6

Dear Lady, spend all your fortune on a gas apparatus.

(Sydney Smith)

"ELECTRIC" "ARGAND" BURNER

Opposite. A temple to Art Nouveau: Victor Horta's own house in Brussels, begun in 1898.

Right. The form and reputation of the venerable Argand oil lamp borrowed by an American electricity advertisement of c. 1890 to infer historic pedigree.

Arts and Crafts principles reinterpreted for a new century: Leonard Wyburn's spacious and immaculate design for a drawing room of c. 1900.

B y 1900 the attraction of no-nonsense Arts and Crafts interior design was very powerful in almost every Western nation. British influence extended everywhere, in terms of both design and manufacture; in particular, Britain unarguably led the world in the quality and quantity of furnishing textile production. In Britain itself, William Morris's designs were now held by some to be a little too quaint,[1] However, the early years of the twentieth century saw a vast expansion in the promotion and sale of Morris & Company fabrics in the US and Southern Europe.

The style which has come to be most associated with the Western world at the turn of the century, however, had little to do with the emerging Arts and Crafts tradition. Art Nouveau (originally termed 'New Art' in Britain and North America, and 'Nieuwe Kunst' in the Netherlands) was characterised by elegant and sinuous, curvilinear lines; by simplicity of subtly varying patterns; by the improbable fusion of Japanese and Celtic idioms in an ahistorical idiom; and by the rejection of three-dimensional realities. It was feminine, where the rectilinear certainties of homely, Arts-and-Crafts-influenced styles were distinctly masculine. It was founded on a unity of style based on a biological correlation between small and large features,[2] and its protagonists aimed to blur the social and aesthetic distinctions between fine and applied arts. To historian Mario Praz, Art Nouveau finally offered householders the first distinct decorative language since Neoclassicism: in his eyes, it rose from that swampy mess of all styles in which taste had become stuck.[3]

Yet Art Nouveau was rarely used for whole domestic treatments. It was best expressed in fixtures, fittings and finishes such as wallpaper, and in the rapidly developing field of home services. In particular, it was excellently suited to the curved forms of the newly developed fittings used for the electric lighting. To that end, Art Nouveau was an entirely appropriate harbinger of the Age of Electricity.

A charming turn-of-the-century inglenook design by Tom Merry.

Art Nouveau developed everywhere in Northern and Central Europe during the 1890s except Britain: Vienna, Glasgow, Prague, Brussels and particularly in Paris. Art periodicals promoted the style all over Continental Europe, from *L'art moderne* in Brussels (founded in 1881) to *Dekorative Kunst* in Munich (1897) and *Mir Iskussta* in St Petersburg (1899). In turn-of-the-century Paris, it was the decorative idiom used for the new retail stores and for the rapidly developing, electrically powered Paris Métro. On 19 July 1900 the first line of the Métro opened, from Porte de Vincennes to Porte Maillot, with impressive Art Nouveau entrances by Hector Guimard (1867–1942). Simultaneously, the Paris Exposition of 1900, while featuring much traditional and Arts and Crafts furniture, went out of its way to celebrate Art Nouveau and its exciting new possibilities, with Guimard's designs again very much to the fore. In Brussels, the pioneering interiors of Victor Horta (1861–1947)

showed what could be done with swirling tendrils of metalwork and the lightness of cast iron.[4] In America, Art Nouveau provided 'a democratic and American antidote to European aristocratic values' for young iconoclastic architects Louis Sullivan and Frank Lloyd Wright.

Ironically, though, the virtuosity of many Art Nouveau pieces put them far beyond the range of the average European or American purse. At the Palais Stoclet in Brussels (1905–11), for example, Josef Hoffmann happily used exotic woods, marbles, copper, enamel and gold leaf to create a stunning, sumptuous set of interiors that clearly could not be reproduced on a mass scale.[5]

As a result, the fad for Art Nouveau was relatively short-lived. By 1905 even Horta had abandoned the Art Nouveau style, preferring to join the Renaissance revivalists at the Paris Académie des Beaux Arts. The style's demise in the early years of the century, incidentally, also prompted a disappointed Mario Praz to bring an abrupt halt to his epic journey through the history of Europe's grandest interiors.

Art Nouveau survived in Paris largely in commercial premises and in the Métro. In Germany it evolved into the 'Jugendstil' movement, named after the magazine *Die Jugend* (founded in Munich in 1896), which championed its cause. It even made an impression in Russia, where it was combined with the revival of national folk arts to create the 'Stil Moderne'. It also continued to flourish, ironically, in one corner of the city which had emphatically

turned its back on its suggestive curves. London's Liberty store, best known for its championing of the Arts and Crafts movement, took to Art Nouveau enthusiastically, and indeed continued to market Art Nouveau fabrics throughout the interwar years. Where the style survived in Italy, it was actually called the 'Style Liberty', so influential was Arthur Lasenby Liberty's retailing genius. Further north, it was eagerly espoused by the architect and designer Charles Rennie Mackintosh (1868–1928), who took the sinuous lines of Art Nouveau and made them into an extended grid. Mackintosh's peculiarly British, rectilinear Art Nouveau manner was ridiculed in his native country – *Ideal Home* did illustrate some of his interiors as late as 1920, but without mentioning his name – but Mackintosh was hailed as a genius in Continental Europe, and was especially admired by Teutonic critics such as Hermann Muthesius (1867–1921).[6]

Opposite. Sinuous turn-of-the-century Art Nouveau ironwork betrays the hand of Victor Horta, seen here in his own Brussels home of 1905, offsetting the painted wall and Art Nouveau stencilled paint effects of the walls behind. Art Nouveau was especially suited to the curvilinear, almost organic forms of staircase balustrades and electric light fittings.

Below. Art Nouveau ceramics and glassware in the French section in the Palais des Arts et Manufactures at the 1900 Paris Exposition.

KAPUZINERKRESSE.
NATURSTUDIE
UND
ANWENDUNG.

In general, the Germans, like the British, eschewed the lithe and dangerously sexualised forms of Art Nouveau, which they preferred to associate with the excesses of the decadent, fin de siècle French. The bright light of the twentieth century encouraged them instead to harness the Anglo-Saxon Arts and Crafts legacy. The result was the founding in 1907 the 'Deutscher Werkbund' as a reaction against the perceived elitism of traditional design in general, and Art Nouveau in particular. Its emphasis was not on naturalistic curves and organic growth but on simplicity and rusticity. Its rigid, rectilinear forms certainly owed much to Mackintosh, but were without his virtuosity and feeling for line. The Werkbund originated in Munich; its founders included architect Peter Behrens (1868–1940) and theorist Hermann Muthesius. The Werkbund achieved something its ancestors in the Arts and Crafts movement had never attained: a coalition of designers and industrialists, jointly dedicated to the improvement and promotion of design. It was not an especially democratic movement, however: while professing an interest in the holy grail of post-industrial design – the development of good, commercially successful craft-based design for a mass market – by 1909 membership of the Werkbund was by invitation only.[7] The Werkbund's swansong was the Cologne exhibition of 1914; submerged by the First World War, it found after 1918 that, like Morris himself, it was unable to reconcile crafts-manship with affordability, and found itself designing merely for wealthy patrons.

Above. A stylised floral pattern from the German 'Jugendstil' pattern book entitled *Kapuzinerkresse, Naturstudie und Anwendung.*

Below. A Mackintosh watercolour design for the dining room in a 'house of an art lover', first published in Germany in 1902.

Window grids, Arts and Crafts furniture and bare floors at C.R. Mackintosh's Hill House in Glasgow of 1902–3.

Things developed rather differently in Britain. One of the key figures in the Deutscher Werkbund, Hermann Muthesius, had a few years previously been sent to London to study British domestic design. As a result of his studies he published a monumental, three-volume analysis of *Das Englische Haus* in 1904–5, showcasing the work of architects such as Richard Norman Shaw and C.F.A. Voysey.

Although some Austrian designers, largely based in Vienna, were enticed by the lubricious appeal of Art Nouveau, many of their colleagues preferred the staid sobriety of the Arts and Crafts tradition and of straight lines. In 1903 Josef Hoffmann (1870–1956), one of the 'Vienna Secessionist' designers who had resigned from the

Vienna Academy in 1897 in protest at the Academy's refusal to exhibit radical modern works, helped to found the Wiener Werkstätte, a guild of craft shops which reinterpreted the ethos of the Arts and Crafts movement for a more austere, modern age. It based itself on the Guild of Handicraft set up by Arts and Crafts pioneer C.R. Ashbee. However, Hoffmann helped to steer the Werkstätte in a more radical direction than Morris's and Ashbee's, declaring that he aimed to develop a 'style of today' through individual craftsmanship, not by machine production – an ethos unveiled in the Werkstätte's ambitious 'Work Programme' of 1905.

The furniture produced by the Wiener Werkstätte was typically rectilinear and severe. Its clean, unornamented surfaces in turn helped

to inspire Adolf Loos (1870–1933). In 1908 Loos, the shady godfather (or, better still, the wicked fairy) of Modernism, published his notorious article 'Ornament and Crime', in which he famously declared that all ornament was 'a needless expression of degeneracy'. Ten years earlier, in a refrain that was to become very familiar during the Modernist years, Loos had also denounced 'women's natural inferiority'. During the 1920s he continued to condemn popular interior design for its corrupting, innately bourgeois 'feminine aesthetic' – a misogynist approach which, as we will see, was to become all too common over the next fifty

years. Fashion's 'murder' of design, he ranted, 'is feminine whim and ambition – and ornamentation at the service of woman will surely live forever'. While the nineteenth century has witnessed the emergence of women as important consumers for ideas and products for the everyday interior, the twentieth century was already showing itself to be the era of misogynist reaction.

Not all the new designers sought to eliminate feminine influence in the home. Josef Hoffmann's rationally planned kitchen in the Villa Hochstatter of 1907 included carefully planned storage areas, open shelving and glazed cupboards. Nevertheless, Hoffmann's increasing use of large, undecorated rectilinear spaces and severely geometric forms for furniture was ultimately 'more influential in the decoration of public buildings such as cinemas than in a domestic context'.[8]

The ascetic (if brightly coloured) works of the Wiener Werkstätte suffered from the same problem as all their Arts and Crafts forbears. The Werkstätte soon collapsed under the weighty contradiction of attempting to make costly handmade pieces for a mass audience. Unable to confront the ogre of mass-production head-on, it remained mired in the nineteenth rather than the twentieth century. As a result, like Morris's own business, it found itself dependent on rich backers who could afford its time-consuming craftsmanship. It folded in 1931, nine years before its original inspiration, Morris & Company, also went bankrupt.

From Hoffmann's grid-like furniture, it was a short walk to the

Mondrian-inspired chair of 1917 designed by Gerrit Rietveld (1888–1964). In 1917 a group of designers, architects and artists, led by Rietveld, launched a movement called simply 'De Stijl'. The group looked to reject what they perceived as outmoded historical designs from an aristocratic past, and to substitute severe rectilinear forms that were affordable by all. Sweden's Society of Craft and Industrial Design (Sjlodføreningen) did much the same, its ideas proving highly influential to

Western European designers during the 1920s. Significantly, it was in those European nations that remained neutral during the First World War that the machine ethic began to triumph over the Arts and Crafts tradition.

Britain and America, however, remained solidly behind the mainstream Arts and Crafts tradition of historically derived interiors. One of the idiom's biggest Edwardian champions was Ambrose Heal (1872–1959). He was that rare animal: a retailer (he had founded

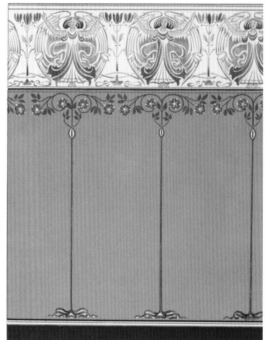

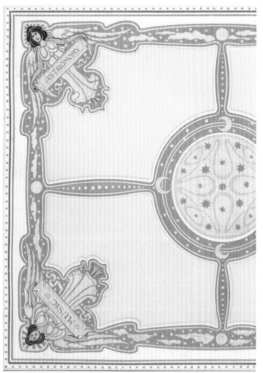

his Tottenham Court Road store in 1896) passionately concerned about interior design. He remained devoted to the Arts and Crafts, 'and an influential figure in the early days of scholarly research into the history of furniture making and other crafts'.[9] Exhibiting at the 1900 Paris Exposition, he cited Morris's dictum 'have nothing in your houses that you do not know to be useful or believe to be beautiful' as his inspiration. In 1915 he founded the Design and Industries Association in emulation (which, in the second year of the war, was of course not publicly admitted) of the Deutscher Werkbund. However, he was too canny a retailer to side with the uncommercial asceticism of the emerging German Modernists. His most famous pre-war furniture range was of pale, untreated oak – anticipating the furniture of Terence Conran, fifty years later – and after 1918 he abandoned the heavy, dark furniture associated with the Victorian era to concentrate on pieces of lighter woods and with minimal decoration, 'laying the foundation of 1950s British interior design'.[10] However, Heal also manufactured more nakedly populist items, such as painted furniture in the 'Old French' style promoted by novelist Edith Wharton and professional decorator Elsie de Wolfe – emphatically non-Modernist products which he continued to offer until his retirement in 1953.

In America, more fashionable households turned not to Art Nouveau or the more utilitarian interpretations of the Arts and Crafts vision, but to Old Europe. And for published advice they turned either to Eastlake or to the more recent decorating gurus: Edith Wharton, John Ogden Codman, or Elsie de Wolfe.

Wharton and Codman's *The Decoration of Houses* of 1897 unashamedly looked back into history for its prime inspiration, using European pieces as exemplars, while also taking care to combine this veneer of historicism with sound Arts and Crafts principles on functionalism, clutter and hygiene. Novelist Edith Wharton had toured Europe with her husband; the subsequent book, intriguingly, was allegedly written 'to alleviate the boredom and frustration of an unsuccessful marriage'.[11] Codman was an established architect, with offices in Boston and Newport. In Wharton and Codman's world, all was disposed according to rules of proportion, order and propriety. Isaac Ware's venerable *Complete Body of Architecture* of 1756 was lauded for its typically Anglo-Saxon 'restraint and conduct of judgement'. And historical revivals were to be shunned. 'Every house should be decorated according to a carefully graduated scale of ornamentation culminating in the most important room in the house', the authors maintained, while advocating that there should never be a 'violent break in the continuity of the treatment'. Echoing the previous generation of design reformers, they deplored the 'thirst for novelty, not always regulated by a ... sense of fitness': 'the quest of artistic novelties would be encouraging were it based on the desire for something better, rather than for something merely different'. Each room should be based on one colour only, 'which [should] at once and

Opposite. Art Nouveau wall and ceiling schemes proposed by the Edwardian periodical *Modern Ornament.* Note the excessively deep friezes, whose exuberant decoration now dominates the design.

unmistakably assert its predominance [and] which should be expressed in furnishing fabrics as well as in carpets and wall finishes', which should ideally be in 'neutral tones'. Classical solecisms such as over-high dado rails, which destroyed the essentially Palladian proportions of a room, were derided. Wallpaper was scorned as insanitary, liable to efface the architectural lines of a room and submerge everything under 'a flood of pattern'. In the best Arts and Crafts tradition, the authors mocked three-dimensional carpet designs as 'vulgar' and, following late nineteenth-century custom, suggested that rooms should ascend in colour scale from dark in the carpet to light in the ceiling. Rejecting much of the past century, they declared that plain colours were always to be preferred to patterns: 'Masses of plain are one of the chief means of producing effect in any scheme of decoration.'[12] They observed that the fashion for smoking rooms was waning – the feature was 'no longer considered a necessity in the modern house' – and denounced the popular taste for inglenooks and corner chimneypieces ('a misplaced attempt at quaintness'), the 'modern litter of knick-knacks' (all so dust-collecting), the current 'plague of golding', and 'excessive pattern in modern decoration'. Plain was best: unbleached cottons, 'plain panelled walls', the virtues of simplicity, moderation, fitness and relevance.[13]

The Decoration of Houses was a huge success in America, where it almost rivalled Eastlake's sales. And Wharton and Codman's championing of the 'Old French' look exerted a considerable influence over the wealthier households. However, their book had only a limited sale outside the US. Wharton and Codman themselves admitted their advice was really relevant only to American homes; for example, they acknowledged that far more prominence was given to halls and stairs in the US than in Europe, since American houses generally enjoyed more floor space than their necessarily more cramped European contemporaries.

Wharton and Codman's example was enthusiastically taken up by the new breed of professional interior decorators, led by the formidable Elsie de Wolfe (1865–1950). De Wolfe can justly be termed the world's first true professional decorator, and 'among the first aesthetic practitioners in the modern era to understand the close relationship between taste and social status'.[14] Yet she turned to interior decoration only in her forties. A well-known fitness fanatic and

King cotton at work: an American cotton mill in Lawrence, Massachusetts, pictured in 1905.

design eccentric (who famously dyed her hair lime green on one occasion), in 1910 she organised a series of lectures on interiors at the highly fashionable Colony Club in New York, which she adapted into book form and which was published three years later as *The House in Good Taste*. De Wolfe's decorating manual 'emphasized simplicity, harmonious colors and good proportion', and recommended light-coloured walls, Louis XVI furniture and a lavish use of chintz.[15] Refusing to align herself with the emerging Modernist style, she rejected the harsh, masculine face of Bauhaus design for more amenable, feminine values. Aiming at more of a mass market than Wharton and Codman, while using *The House in Good Taste* as a means of building a wealthy clientele for her own practice, she happily mixed antique and reproduction pieces in order to create rooms that were comfortable and practical. She wanted 'comfortable and sensible furniture' and sedate but cheerful colour schemes, whose inspiration was usually to be taken from the floorcoverings. (Imagining a room decorated in red, white and pale blue, she chirruped that 'You can imagine how impossible it would be to be ill-tempered in such a cheerful place'.) She particularly favoured gaily printed chintzes: 'Now there are literally thousands of these excellent fabrics of old and new designs in the shops', she declared, 'I am using more chintz than anything else'. It was said that de Wolfe's prodigious use of handblocked chintzes in her commissions kept this industry alive. She certainly helped kick-start the international revival of the silk trade.

Departing from historical precedent, de Wolfe declared that apartments 'should have the same finish throughout'.[16] But, she borrowed most frequently from the 'Adam' style or, more precisely, from the pages of Sheraton and Hepplewhite.

A year later de Wolfe's great rival, Ruby Ross Goodnow, also published her opinions on interior decoration, in a volume rather cattishly called *The Honest House*. Goodnow's recommendations were less prescriptive than de Wolfe's, but followed the same parameters: furniture that was 'comfortable and beautiful and of sound construction', pale walls (though never bright white: 'all physicians and oculists deplore the distressing effect of the white glare on the nerves'), and the reintroduction of dados and cornices to give a proper sense of proportion.[17]

De Wolfe and her imitators did more than just help a generation of American homeowners to decorate and

A strikingly bold hall design of *c*.1900 by the German architect Gertrude Kleinhempel, one of the leading designers associated with the Dresdener Werkstätten für Handwerkskunst (Dresden Workshops for Arts & Crafts) which grew from ideals of the Arts and Crafts movement. The Teutonic classical tradition is here reduced to its simplest elements.

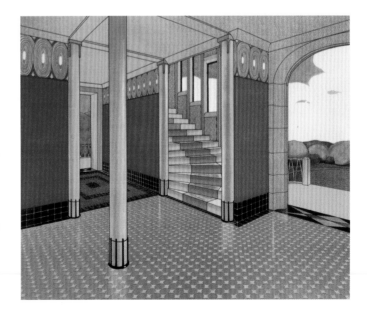

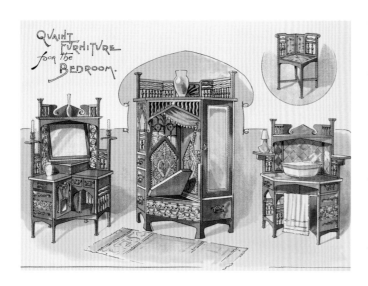

furnish their houses. They also helped to establish interior design as a serious discipline, both in professional and educational terms. De Wolfe was one of the prime instigators of the Decorators Club of New York, founded in 1914 and, even more significantly, of the New York School of Interior Design, founded by Sherrill Whiton in 1916.

Yet whether looking for their inspiration to *ancien régime* France, medieval England, Parisian Art Nouveau or Teutonic utilitarianism, the middle-class interiors of the newly born twentieth century were transformed not by the adoption of one particularly historical, or anti-historicist, style, but by the provision of electric light.

Gaslight had been around for nearly a century when electricity made its debut. The first gas lighting had been installed in an English factory as early as 1798. But householders had always been rightly ambivalent about this volatile fuel. Gasoliers or (as they were called from the 1850s) 'gas chandeliers'

were unavoidably heavy, and were themselves linked to the gas supply by necessarily cumbersome metal pipes. Thus domestic gaslight was not portable, a difficulty which in turn made gaslit interiors frustratingly static. The relative brightness of gas also encouraged the provision of more shutters and curtains to shield the effects of direct light on valuable fixtures and fittings; thus the average home 'was turning its back on natural illumination for the first time'.[18] Gaslight was rarely used in the bedroom, where its fumes and smuts could easily discolour light-coloured fabrics; in these rooms the candle and oil lamp still predominated.

Humphry Davy had first discovered the 'electric arc' light in 1808. The next seventy years saw numerous attempts to bring a thin metal filament to incandescence without destroying the metal or its glass container, a process which, it was eventually grasped, would be best achieved within a vacuum. Thomas Alva Edison in the US and Joseph Swan in Britain simultaneously produced the first successful light bulbs in 1878; by 1882 light bulbs were commercially available (with Edison and Swan combining forces to sell them in Britain from 1879); and by 1890 stable multi-looped and curled filaments had been introduced. In 1880 the arms tycoon Lord Armstrong converted the gas lamps at his vast Northumberland retreat of Cragside to electricity, although many of the fittings remained naked bulbs until shades were fitted in the early 1890s. Armstrong's innovation was soon followed by other go-ahead country houses such as Wightwick Manor, near Wolverhampton, where electric light was installed in 1887. And electricity was first generated for general sale in Britain in the unlikely technological crucible of Godalming in Surrey, in 1881. The age of electricity was thus well and truly launched.

Early electric light bulbs were rarely provided with shades, but were left exposed. In grander houses they were grouped together in chandelier form, called 'electroliers'. Many early fittings indeed took their design cue from existing gas products. However, it was soon realised that direct light from the bulbs was too glaring for the naked eye; thus the whole paraphernalia of shades and reflectors was introduced, with cut or coloured glass being (as with earlier gas fittings) regarded as most popular materials for reflective shades.

At the same time, it was soon appreciated that new electric fittings were far lighter and more flexible than those used for gas. Thus, while gas fittings remained static, electrically lit lamps could be moved with ease around the room. Electric lights were also more economical, as they could be instantly turned off and on, and they were safer, involving no danger of suffocation or poisoning from gas fumes.

Electric light was rightly hailed in the press as the illumination of the future. *The London Globe* welcomed the Electrical Exhibition held at the Crystal Palace (by now located in Sydenham in South London) in 1882: 'its universal adoption', it declared of electricity, 'must be held to be an absolute certainty'. The paper had to warn consumers, though,

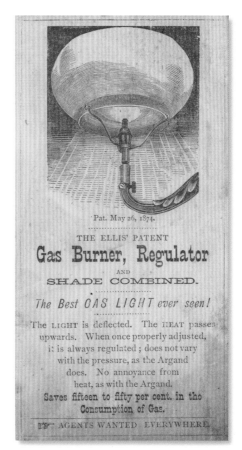

Left. The gas trade fights back: an advertisement of the 1880s featuring a patent gas burner, regulator and lampshade. Such relatively cheap and remarkably efficient advances in gas technology helped to stem the tide of electric light fittings for a decade or two. Patented in 1874, Ellis's design claimed superiority over the traditional Argand format.

Below. A page from a Hampton's catalogue of 1902, delineating a range of fabric window blinds.

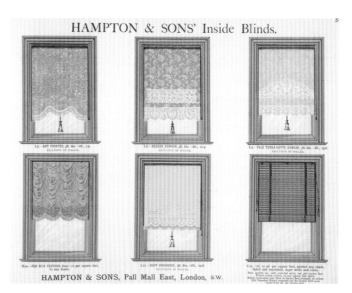

not to light the fittings with a match – much as Belling advised its customers, as late as 1912, not to use a poker for their new electric fire.

Yet many old-fashioned consumers distrusted the new form of lighting, and there were numerous predictions (as with gas in the 1830s) that its introduction would blind a generation. Less alarmist critics still believed electric light was harsh and over-bright. In 1891, for example, Lady Monkswell visited a house in Portland Place, London, and commented that 'I was not much … pleased on arriving at the Bryces' to be ushered into a drawing room as cold as charity & lighted by some eight or ten electric lights so that it was considerably lighter than daylight and most unbecoming'. In 1897 Wharton and Codman were in no doubt that 'Electric light … with its harsh white glare, which no expedients have as yet overcome, has taken from our drawing rooms all air of privacy and distinction'. They ultimately judged that electricity was best left to 'passageways and offices'.[19]

Despite these forebodings, by 1914 the electric light bulb had gained widespread acceptance, and interiors had begun to be wholly reappraised using this dramatic new form of illumination. Colours could now be subtler; mouldings of lower relief; ceilings could now be lower: gaslight had required high ceilings so as to enable the fumes and smells to escape. And interiors could be lit without fear of the permanent soiling of expensive textiles and furniture.

The gas suppliers initially tried to fight back. In 1885 the brighter, more gas-efficient and fabric-based Welsbach burner, invented by Austrian chemist Karl Auer von Welsbach, was introduced. Its mantles were 'little drawstring bags of cotton net that were tied around the gas vent [which] were impregnated with thorium and cerium so that, on first being lit, they puffed up and the cotton burnt away, leaving a brittle bulb of metal oxides that glowed in the heat of the flame. Thereafter they had to be lit with great care, as the slightest touch of the match would cause the mantle to crumble.'[20] These were followed by improvements such as inverted mantles, intended to produce 'downward light

Left. Edison's 'electric lamp', as illustrated in *Scientific American* in January 1880. This demonstrates the 'on/off' switch which now controlled the flow of electricity to the lamp.

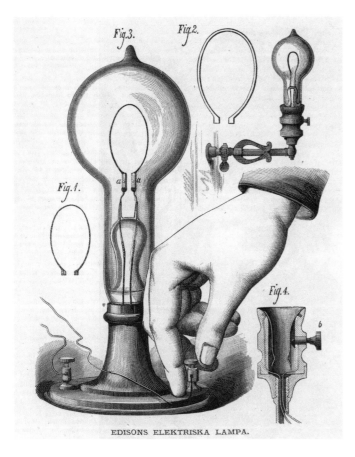

Fig.3. Fig.2.

Fig.1.

Fig.4.

EDISONS ELEKTRISKA LAMPA.

free from shadows', and pendant fittings, made adjustable by a counterweight. Penny-slot gas meters were also common by 1914.

By the outbreak of the First World War, however, it was obvious that electricity had won the battle of the drawing room. Growing familiarity with electric fittings prompted some manufacturers to a 'stylish use of electric light bulbs and their flex to dictate the ... light fitting'. Electricity was especially appropriate for the sinuous curves of Art Nouveau; however, fittings designed in this idiom could easily become over-elaborate. *House Beautiful* in America warned in 1897 that modern manufacturers had combined 'all the decorative motives [*sic*] which the original designers would have spread over half a dozen different objects, and the result is most appalling in its ugliness'.[21]

Electric light encouraged a trend to paler colours. One commentator even tried to fuse the introduction of electric light with the fashion for hygienic interiors, claiming in 1902 that 'Light papers are conducive to health as opposed to dark ones'.[22] In a similar vein, bright, wipeable enamelled paints and, for plasterwork, distemper paints – which could also be easily washed – became highly popular.

Artificial dyes multiplied, particularly in Germany, which by 1900 had become the centre of the clear, colourfast vat dyeing industry. And it is surely no accident that the modern, scientific classification of paint colours occurred at the beginning of the age of electricity. Prior to the twentieth

Above. Plates from an electric light catalogue of 1890 from Lea & Company of Shrewsbury. These examples were all fitted by armaments tycoon Lord Armstrong at his technologically sophisticated house of Cragside, Northumberland, one of the first houses in Britain to have electric lights.

Right. Early electric hanging lamp at a Parisian shopworker's home of 1910.

century, colour terminology and mixing formulas were vague, personalised and unspecific. In 1878 Hering had developed the first four-colour paint wheel, the basis of today's National Colour System and 'a fundamental influence over fabric, product and furniture design of the last five years'. But in 1909 Arthur Jennings's book *Paint and Colour Mixing* included the first precise formulas and names for colours plus, unusually, eight pages of paint swatches.[23] Before Jennings, guides to paint had been small enough to fit into your pocket. The introduction of printed paint swatches made them far larger and far more useful, though

unwieldy. Standardised, ready-mixed paints became common after 1918, though some tradesmen were still wary of them, justifiably warning that you could not guarantee that every can would contain a product of exactly the same tint as the last. In Jennings's wake, William Oswald invented an orderly system of colours based on an eight-colour wheel, featuring four primaries and four secondaries: violet, orange, dark green and light blue.[24] It was the American Albert Munsell (1858–1918), though, who developed the classic colour codification system still used today. Munsell's classification, unveiled in 1915, used letters to describe hues based on the three basic, natural primaries – red, yellow and blue – and added numerical values according to quantity.

Electricity's influence on the average home extended far beyond the light bulb, the chandelier and the colour of the walls. The opening of electrically powered subterranean railways in many major cities at the end of the nineteenth century transformed downtown shopping streets, which were now easily and cheaply accessible to those in the suburbs and beyond. In London, the advent of the 'Twopenny Tube' (today part of the Central Line) in 1900, and the Brompton and Piccadilly Circus Railway (now part of the Piccadilly Line) in 1902, completely altered the faces of Oxford Street, Regent Street and Piccadilly, along which general department and home interest stores now sprang up. Exactly the same happened in key thoroughfares in Central Paris after the opening of the Métro in 1900, and in Midtown Manhattan after the first subway lines appeared there in the early years of the century.

Back in the home, the growing interest in personal and domestic hygiene encouraged the development and enlargement of the bathroom.

Above left. Turn-of-the century Arts and Crafts Interior at Craigauchty in Aberfoyle, Scotland. Note the fashionably deep wallpapered frieze.

Above right. An immensely stylish early electric fitting by Philip Webb at Standen, Sussex, with opalescent fluted shade, glass twists and a copper sconce-plate.

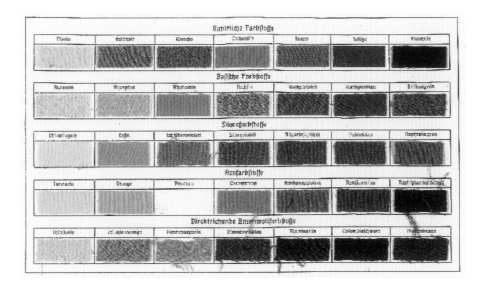

Natürliche Farbstoffe						
Flavin	Gelzbolz	Katechu	Cochenille	Krapp	Indigo	Blaubolz

Basische Farbstoffe						
Auramin	Phosphin	Rhodamin	Fuchsin	Viktoriablau	Methylenblau	Brillantgrün

Säurefarbstoffe						
Chinolingelb	Eosin	Echtsäureviolett	Säureviolett	Alizarinsaphirol	Patentblau	Naphtalingrün

Azofarbstoffe						
Tartrazin	Orange	Ponceau	Chromotrop	Echtmanganbraun	Azosäureblau	Naphtylaminschwarz

Direktziehende Baumwollfarbstoffe						
Chlorophenin	Chloinorange	Benzopurpurin	Diaminreinblau	Diaminerin	Columbiaschwarz	Diaminbraun

A brave new chemical world: a German dyestuff sample card of 1890, with cotton colour samples stuck into the original version. From M. Geitel's *Der Siegeslauf der Technik*, volume 2 (1890).

The modern WC had been patented in 1778 by Joseph Bramah – who, as we have seen, went on to sell thousands of examples and secure his fortune. It was not until 1853, however, that Joseph Adamson patented the modern siphonic flush, and 1885 that Thomas Twyford brought out the first one-piece ceramic pedestal toilet.[25] (The WC was already complemented by perforated toilet paper, introduced into America in the 1870s. It was not until the 1930s, however, that Western bottoms were relieved by the invention of soft toilet tissue.) And in 1904 Hermann Muthesius noted that, in Britain at least, toilets were still kept in a separate closet, and not admitted into the bathroom. Forty years earlier, indeed, Robert Kerr had advised that keeping the two separate avoided 'unpleasant associations of ideas' as well as the 'awkward and inconvenient consequences' of not being able to use the WC when the bathroom was occupied.[26]

The bathroom had by 1900 become something of a status symbol. If you didn't have one, it was time to convert a surplus bedroom. And central to the furnishing of an up-to-date bathroom was a plumbed-in bath. Baths of painted zinc, copper or tin were a common feature by the 1850s; by the 1880s, though, the familiar enamelled, freestanding cast-iron bath, often with ball-and-claw feet, was becoming prevalent. By 1900 British suppliers dominated the market for cast-iron bathroom fixtures, and names such as Twyford, Shanks and Doulton had become household names the world over. And, to keep everything spotless, bathroom walls were invariably tiled, or gloss painted if tiles could not be found.

In his painstaking study of *The English House* of 1904, German architect Hermann Muthesius declared that a well-equipped, middle-class English bathroom had 'a bath, shower-bath, wash-basin, hip-bath, heated towel rail, mirror, clothes hooks, a shelf for towels and a receptacle for used towels'. Note the heated towel rail – as early as 1904. And American bathrooms were even better equipped, Americans having always been more attentive to personal hygiene than their transatlantic cousins. The washstand was still an important feature in the room by 1900, but was ultimately replaced by plumbed-in, freestanding or bracket-held washbasins. Bathroom fittings – which, Muthesius held, should be 'simple in construction and easy to clean' – were increasingly made of metal rather than wood since, as Muthesius advised, 'modern sanitarians condemn woodwork enclosures' as unhygienic traps for dirt and germs.[27]

The same obsession with hygiene revolutionised the bedroom, too. The influence of Arts and Crafts precepts had led to a sharp decline in the provision of bed curtains, and to the proliferation of iron bedsteads and their machine-made wooden cousins. Bedroom floors of 1900 were frequently uncarpeted, the exposed woodwork being scrubbed and left bare but for the provision of a rug or two. Bedrooms were increasingly painted white, allowing dust to be seen as well as maximising the amount of light entering what was often a poorly fenestrated space at the top of the house.

Elsewhere, too, the 1900 house was very much the Healthy House. It was lighter, brighter and cleaner than its predecessors. There was a new emphasis on clear spaces and more austere, less ornamental furniture. Mid-Victorian clutter was definitely on the retreat. Fitted carpets were removed and floorboards – stained, varnished, painted or polished – were partially exposed, with smaller carpets or rugs strewn across them. Deep buttoning

The very latest in sanitaryware: British firms such as Morrison, Ingram and Twyfords took the bathroom world by storm at the turn of the twentieth century. Colour lithographs from the catalogues of Morrison, Ingram & Co., c.1890 (bottom left), and Twyfords (*Twyfords' XXth Century Catalogue*), c.1902–4 (bottom right).

was abandoned for sofas and chairs, and simple curtains and pelmets replaced their heavy, swag-laden predecessors. Internal woodwork was increasingly painted off-white to show the dust.

Despite Wharton and Codman's encomium, fitted furniture became common. The International Health Exhibition in London in 1884 had energetically promoted fitted furniture as minimising areas where dust and dirt could collect. Built-in inglenooks, portable 'cosy corners' and conversational groupings of chairs were very popular in Northern Europe and North America by the end of the nineteenth century. Originally designed as a warm, enclosed space for those sitting by the fire, by 1900 inglenooks – complete with brick arches, herringbone-pattern brick panels and even beaten copper hoods – had migrated to the further corners of the living room.

'Cosy corners' were for those whose rooms were not big enough to accommodate inglenooks; these features could moreover be employed as de facto room dividers.

Not every turn-of-the century domestic development was dictated by the desire for cleanliness. Dado rails were simply reintroduced as a useful way of defining the space in which to hang pictures and prints. Wooden overmantels grew in height and complexity towards the end of the century, and were increasingly designed as multi-tiered, historicist confections (what *Furniture and Decoration* magazine termed in 1891 'spindled absurdities') in order to display a bewildering variety of *objets d'art*. A passion for revivalism was also the factor that often determined the purchase of off-the-peg seat furniture by 1900. As Turner and Hoskins have noted: 'armchairs that bore no resemblance to 18th-century French furniture were

Decorated washbasins from Twyfords' *XXth Century Catalogue*, c.1902–4.

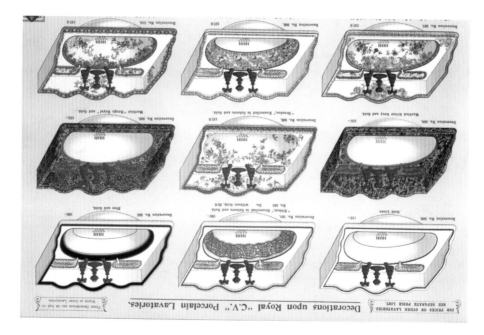

grew so quickly at this time.'²⁸

In America, it was the burgeoning interest in Colonial Revival and Stickley's 'Mission Style', allied to the new obsession for health, which saw the rejection of wood panelling in favour of plastered walls. The chimneypiece became the focus of the Northern European and North American room – signalling, in good Arts and Crafts fashion, a return to the medieval or colonial practice of regarding the hearth as the heart of the house. Enamelled slate or 'Marezzo marble', a composite product a tenth of the cost of real marble, and patented in 1868, were used for chimney surrounds alongside bare or painted wood or, cheapest of all, cast iron. If exposed wood was used, Arts and Crafts followers on both sides of the Atlantic preferred plain oak rather than fancy foreign woods, though more pretentious middle-class households boasted South African mahogany examples by 1900. Simple pine surrounds were always painted – usually, again, (off) white – and increasingly, at least in Britain and America, adopted a square, Adam-style neoclassical form. Timber and plaster fire surrounds were still painted, however: the stripping of old woodwork in vague emulation of Arts and Crafts practice fused with Scandinavian Modernism only came after 1945. Iron surrounds were often cast to mimic wood carving, something Eastlake and his followers found atrocious (Eastlake had labelled such surrounds 'curvilinear and elaborate monstrosities'), and could be used with a variety of tiled or copper insets. Copper was favoured around the late nineteenth-century fireplace as, unlike brass, it didn't need polishing.

glibly labelled Louis XVI and massive and be-mirrored sideboards with storks carved on the panels of the doors were sold as Anglo-Japanese. The ordinary public usually had no idea what a Louis XVI chair looked like and were obliged to follow the advice of the salesman or the recommendations of writers in magazines. It is small wonder that the demand for practical furnishing guides

Above. Bedroom design of c.1910 by Curjel & Moser of Karlsruhe, with a revivalist four-poster bed and properly bare wooden floor.

Below. A more traditional ensemble, allegedly belonging to 'a country bachelor'.

This made it particularly popular after 1918, when servants were no longer readily available.

The simplification of ceilings was instrumental in the quest for a healthy interior. Ceiling roses were coming under increasing criticism from hygiene-obsessed households as places where dust, dirt and germs loved to collect. Before the spread of electricity, they tended to harbour the smuts thrown out by centrally hung gasoliers. But by 1900 the Western trend was to have plain, flat ceilings of plaster, possibly covered with embossed wallpaper, or sheets of fibrous plaster. Stamped metal ceilings, painted white, were rare in Britain and France, but common in Germany and the US. In 1904 Hermann Muthesius's *The English House* noted that 'simple rooms in England have smooth, plastered ceilings with no "rosette" and no stucco moulding' and that 'the ceiling is either plain white or papered'. ('Papering is very popular,' he continued; 'in simple houses especially, the drawing-room ceiling is usually papered since this is considered superior to a plain white finish.'29)

Unsurprisingly, the hygiene revolution also affected the floor. By 1900, too, ceramic tiles were extremely popular for floors and walls. They were cheap, brightly coloured and versatile, and also responded well to concerns regarding both household and workplace hygiene, being easily cleaned and resistant to grime. After 1861 Morris & Company began to produce exquisite tile designs, hand-painted on to Delftware blanks. These Arts and Crafts tiles, designed by Burne-Jones and by Morris himself, were inevitably expensive, but still much in demand. By the 1870s even Morris & Company's products were being eclipsed by the exotic and colourful hand-painted products of their former designer William de Morgan, whose lustre-glazed designs mark the zenith of Victorian tile manufacture. The 1880s saw an interest in 'oriental' tiles, prompted by creations such as George Aitchison's Arab Hall' at Leighton House, London, of 1877-9. By 1890,

Left. In dramatic contrast, the Viennese 'hall in a modernist style' of 1910, by Otto Prutscher, Richard Geyling and Heinrich Vollmer, anticipates the angular rhythms and stark colour contrasts of a new age.

Above. The eighteenth century lives on in George Rémon's room setting for *Intérieur de Style* of 1900, phrased in what the magazine called the 'All-the-Louis' styles.

mass-produced Art Nouveau tiles, with graceful but simple patterns, raised clay paste borders and rich glazes, were flooding the market, and had become commonplace on hall dados, inside porches and on chimneypiece surrounds of the early twentieth century. Attempts by the Omega Workshop shortly before the First World War to popularise hand-painted craft tiles in the Morrisian manner, however, failed commercially.

In the quest for washable, utilitarian floorcoverings, linoleum had, by 1900, virtually seen off the traditional floorcloth. Linoleum was not only more hygienic than the floorcloth, but it was also more durable. During the 1860s it had begun to be introduced into British homes, a development which effectively sounded the death knell for all traditional types of utilitarian floorcovering, whether cloth, paper, cork or fabric based. (Revealingly, by 1900 the term 'drugget' had come to denote a glazed linen sheet used to cover expensive carpets, rather than the simple fabric floorcovering of previous centuries.) Invented by Englishman Frederick Walton in 1863 and manufactured in Britain from 1864, and in New York from 1875, linoleum was a natural floorcovering made from the tough shaft fibres of the linen plant mixed with linseed oil, cork dust, gum and pigments, which was roller-pressed like floorcloths or wallpaper and backed with canvas. By the 1890s linoleum could be printed in

Cheerfully coloured domesticity; a dining room from Carl Larsson's *Lasst Licht Hinin* ('Let in More Light') of 1908.

The grid-like layout of this dining room by Friedrich Glaser of Berlin is typical of German Werkbund-influenced designs of the early twentieth century.

just as many imitative patterns as the old floorcloths, 'marble' floors proving very popular. A household manual of 1889 recommended 'tiny squares of black and white marble, which looks very well down' – although quickly adding the Eastlakeian proviso that 'Of course it is a sham, and as such is to be deprecated.' Felt-backed versions of linoleum, marketed as 'Congoleum', were available from the 1910s. Production of linoleum was already mechanised by this time, and by 1914 Germany, France, Canada and the US rivalled Britain in the variety and scale of linoleum manufacture.[30]

By the time of the outbreak of the First World War, the provision of furnishing fabrics had also undergone a hygiene-driven transformation. Loose covers and antimacassars were often dispensed with, as was much of the elaborate fringing and tasselling which so characterised nineteenth-century beds and seat furniture. As with so many aspects of the fashionable Arts and Crafts interior, the emphasis was now on simplicity. Brightly coloured fabrics (often reproducing or mimicking Morris & Company or other Arts and Crafts-inspired designs) were still being used to cover seats, but were being applied in a plain, unfussy manner. Glazed chintzes and other fabrics redolent of Victorian upholstery were quickly replaced by more modest fabrics: simpler cottons or, by the 1920s, new, industrially produced hybrids such as the easily washable cotton and rayon mix.

The wallpaper market also responded to concerns about cleanliness. The great wallpaper success stories of the years before and after 1900 were the utilitarian embossed papers which, when painted (and, for added protection, sometimes varnished), provided extremely durable, washable and thus hygienic coverings for walls and ceilings. The rigorously repetitive patterns of these papers were often based on stylised flower motifs or scroll- and strapwork. Their simple repetition and tough character made embossed papers particularly suitable for large areas of wall space in public buildings. In more domestic contexts, they were often pressed into use as dado papers – the dado being the area of the wall that suffered the most regular punishment. 'Lincrusta Walton', a high-quality moulded covering launched in 1877 by

Frederick Walton (who had previously failed to register the name 'linoleum' as a trademark, but was not caught napping twice), is the only heavy-relief wall covering to have survived the era. Other similar, branded products such as 'Tynecastle Tapestry', an expensive product which imitated gilded and embossed leather, 'Lingomur', made from wood fibres, 'Salamander', made from asbestos, and promoted for its fire-resistance, and 'Cameoid' have long since ceased production.

Not all embossed wallcoverings were as rigid and heavy as Lincrusta or Tynecastle. Thomas Palmer, formerly an employee of Walton's, took out his own patent for a paper he called 'Anaglypta' in 1886. By 1888 Anaglypta, a lighter and more flexible wood-pulp covering, had failed to impress Walton, but by 1897 the *Journal of Decorative Art* was noting that 'so quickly did the new material "catch on" that within two years of that time it had slipped into its place as one of the necessaries of a modern decorator's establishment, [having] seized the taste – and the pocket – of the public and literally jumped into vogue'.[31] It was made in a variety of styles, from 'Adams' (*sic*) to 'Arabian' and 'Old English'.

There were also numerous 'sanitary' papers on the market by 1900, generally used for kitchens, passageways and staircases. In 1807 the first varnished paper was patented by Crease & Company of Bath, but it was not until 1853 that the first washable paper became commercially available, and not until the end of the nineteenth century that its use became widespread. From the 1880s wallpaper – much of it washable – was additionally made specifically for use in children's rooms, with designers such as Walter Crane (first President of the Art Workers' Guild in 1884) and Kate Greenaway being asked to compose designs.

Within two decades, however, the 1900 house – at least in Europe – was to be transformed by factors even more fundamental than the introduction of electric light and the quest for sanitation. By 1920 many of the accepted practices of the pre-war, average home had disappeared. For so had the servants.

The years before the First World War were, in retrospect, the heyday of the house servant. After 1914, the carnage of the war and the influenza epidemic of 1918–19 – which killed far more than all of the war dead combined – ravaged the populations of Europe so effectively that, after 1919, servants

were far more difficult to come by and, inevitably, cost far more than they had done before the war. The resulting servant shortage, combined with the tendency to build smaller homes after 1918 and the restricted budgets with which many postwar families had to contend, significantly changed the way Europeans lived. In 1891 servants represented over 15 per cent of the English workforce, numbering 1,550,000; by 1918 the figure was down to under 5 per cent.[32]

The lack of servants not only encouraged the trend towards eradicating dust-collecting fabrics and furniture, and towards the replacement of sooty gaslight. It also brought the reign of the labour-intensive coal fire to an end in many homes. Gas fires had been in evidence since the 1860s, but gas and electric fires began to

Frederick Walton's London showroom, showing his Lincrusta, Anaglypta and similar wallpaper products, as photographed for *Decorative Art* in 1900.

LE STYLE DANS L'AMEUBLEMENT.

Modern Style.   Véritable Extrait de Viande LIEBIG

Right. This charming French scene on a Liebig card of 1900, purportedly of a 'modern interior', underlines how popular revivalist furniture remained into the twentieth century.

Opposite. Contrasting reds and greens and a Mackintoshian grid are used to great effect here in a reinterpretation of the traditional inglenook, part of Leopold Bauer's Darmstadt design for a 'children's room with totally washable surfaces' of 1902.

replace traditional coal or wood ones after 1918.[33] In northern Europe, as we have seen, the fireplace had for centuries been the notional heart of the house. Now, for the first time, it was left untended by servants in all but the grandest homes. The era of the democratic interior had arrived.

1. David Brett, 'Art Nouveau', in Joanna Banham (ed.), *Encyclopaedia of Interior Design* (1997), vol. 1, 52. **2.** Ibid. **3.** Mario Praz, *An Illustrated History of Interior Decoration* (1964), 66, 383. **4.** Hilary Grainger, 'Victor Horta', in Banham (ed.), *Encyclopaedia of Interior Design*, vol. 1, 583. **5.** Brett, in Banham, 52–3. **6.** Anne Massey, *Interior Design of the 20th Century* (1990), 58. **7.** Hilary Grainger, 'The Deutsche Werkbund', in Banham (ed.), *Encyclopaedia of Interior Design* (1997), vol. 1, 372. **8.** Stephen Calloway, *Twentieth-Century Decoration* (1988), 75. **9.** Ibid., 150. **10.** Anne Massey, *Interior Design of the 20th Century* (1990), 88. **11.** Isabelle Anscombe, *A Woman's Touch* (1984), 69. **12.** Edith Wharton and Ogden Codman, *The Decoration of Houses* (1897, reprinted 1978), 24, 27–9, 37, 44, 101–2, 118, 115. **13.** Ibid., 151, 154, 150, 168, 193, 171, 198. **14.** Penny Sparke, *An Introduction to Design and Culture* (2004), 64. **15.** Jane C. Nylander, *Fabrics for Historic Buildings* (1990), 88. **16.** Elsie de Wolfe, *The House in Good Taste* (1913), 16, 83, 94, 96, 241. **17.** Ruby Ross Goodnow, *The Honest House* (1914), 142, 156, 171. **18.** Roger W. Moss, *Lighting for Historic Buildings* (1988), 103. **19.** Charlotte Gere, *Nineteenth-Century Decoration* (1989), 56; Wharton and Codman, *The Decoration of Houses*, 126. **20.** Kit Wedd, *The Victorian Society Book of the Victorian House* (2002), 165. **21.** Moss, *Lighting for Historic Buildings*, 130. **22.** Helen Long, *The Edwardian House* (1993), 155. **23.** Kevin McCloud, *Choosing Colour* (2003), 62; Caroline Alderson, 'Recreating a 19th Century Paint Palette', in *Association of Preservation Technology*, vol. xvi, no.1, 1984, 47. **24.** Roger W. Moss (ed.), *Paint in America* (1994), 56, 62. **25.** Wedd, *The Victorian Society Book of the Victorian House*, 188. **26.** Quoted in ibid., 192. **27.** Quoted in Long, *The Edwardian House*, 96, 98. **28.** Mark Turner and Lesley Hoskins, *The Silver Studio of Design* (1988), 70. **29.** Quoted in Long, *The Edwardian House*, 133. **30.** Pamela Simpson, 'Floorcloths', in Banham (ed.), *Encyclopaedia of Interior Design*, vol. 1, 432. **31.** Wedd, *The Victorian Society Book of the Victorian House*, 233. **32.** Long, *The Edwardian House*, 130. **33.** Wedd, *The Victorian Society Book of the Victorian House*, 152.

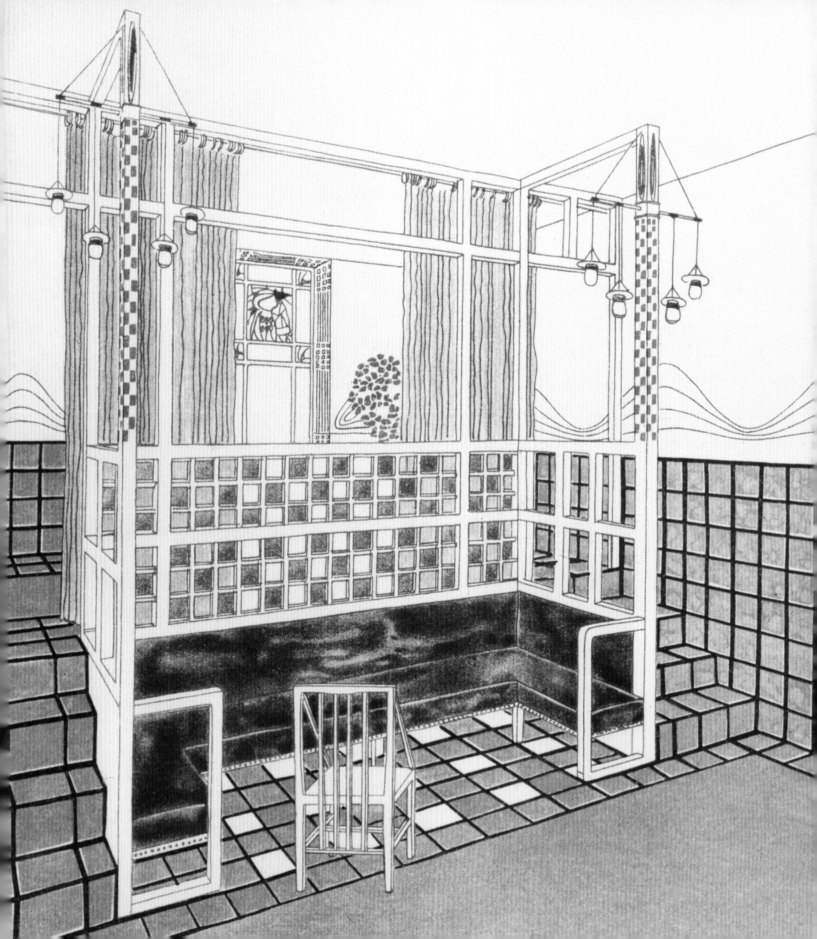

FORM AND FUNCTION

Modernism and Art Deco

10

But do you realize what a passing fancy that so-called modern movement is...?

(Ayn Rand, *The Fountainhead*, 1943)

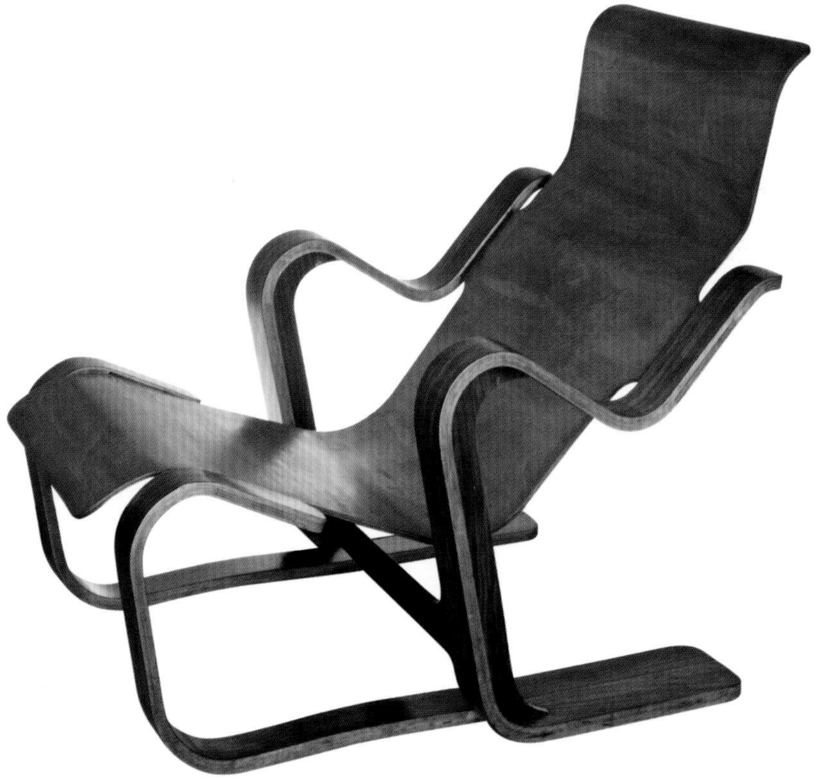

Men And Their Chairs: tubular steel chairs of 1929 by Mies van der Rohe at the Tugendhat House in Brno in the Czech Republic, left, and right, a classic laminated plywood Breuer design, for Isokon of London, of 1936.

The Modern Movement that grew out of the ambitions of young designers and architects in pre-war Germany and Holland was very much about erasing the past. The horrific experience of the First World War seemed merely to confirm their belief that the nineteenth century needed consigning to the dustbin. In the view of the early Modernists, innovation – not comfort, convenience or even cheapness – was the primary goal. The much-repeated maxim that 'form follows function' did not allow for comfort. Charles Eames's Modernist chairs were unusual in the demanding context of the architect-designed seat furniture of the mid-twentieth century, in that they were actually pleasant to relax in.

The term 'Modernism' was originally used by architects and critics of the 1920s to describe the architectural shell, and not interior design. But it has become so entangled with our perception of twentieth-century interiors that the two concepts are now indissoluble. Modernism was a doctrine of certainty. Interiors, and the objects placed within them, were considered either 'good' or 'bad'.[1] And both the past, and historically sourced national or regional decorative styles and forms (together with regional geography), were to be entirely disregarded.

The wish to discard the past was by no means a new one. As early as 1856, the American Nathaniel Hawthorne, on visiting the treasures of London, judged that 'The present is much too burdened with the past ... We heap up all these old shells, out of which human life has long emerged, casting them off forever. I do not see how future ages are to stagger under all this dead weight.'[2] In 1893 Arts and Crafts architect C.F.A. Voysey had suggested 'discarding the mass of useless ornaments and banishing the millinery that degrades our furniture and fittings' and 'reducing the variety of patterns and colours in a room'.[3] In his 1923 Modernist manifesto *Vers une Architecture*, Le Corbusier (1887–1965) took this Arts and Crafts hypothesis further, raging against 'your bergères, your Louis XVI settees, bulging through their tapestry covers' – 'are these machines for sitting in?' – and finding favour only with Morris's multi-purpose cane furniture and Thonet's bentwood products.[4] Alas for Corb, the vast majority of Western householders disagreed with him, and continued to buy historic reproductions in large numbers before and after the Second World War.

An early refrigerator, of 1912 (the icebox is in the middle), designed by McCray of Kendalville, Indiana, USA, from an advertisement in *The Printing Art*. Its cheerful functionalism and graining hark back to the Biedermeier style.

The Modernists of the twentieth century followed Nietzsche in reckoning that over-attention to the past turned men into impotent spectators, 'the latest withered shoots of a gladder and mightier stock'. Deifying the present 'without loving the past' was anathema to Nietzsche. 'Let the dead bury the living', he had declared; the 'mad collector raking over all the dust heaps of the past', with his 'insatiable curiosity for everything old', was, he held, only able to preserve, thus hindering 'the mighty impulse to a new deed' and 'paralyzing the doer'.[5]

The brave new Modernists of the 1920s based their designs on the two concepts that had dominated the thoughts of the Arts and Crafts designers of the turn of the century: technology and health. The entire movement was permeated by a deep concern for health, while 'the new emphasis of the technology-based rationalism of Modernism seemed to require that designers, at least, deny an interest in aesthetics and, at most, claim that the form of their work was reliant solely upon function or programme'.[6] Fuelled by Modernist support, the turn-of-the-century passion for hygiene had metamorphosed by the 1930s into a widespread belief in the therapeutic benefits of sunlight and the open air, and internationally popular vogues for sunbathing and naturism.

The Bauhaus, the German school of art and design that first opened under the directorship of Water Gropius in 1919, has come to epitomise the uncompromising ethos of Modernism. Indeed, many of its

designs for furniture and wallpaper were deemed saleable to consumers only from the 1960s. The Bauhaus allowed its students 'the freedom to experiment with production processes and formal solutions, uninhibited by traditional practice',[7] and its avowed aim was 'to reunify all the disciplines of practical art'. More generally, it was intended as a celebration of the machine. Students were asked to 'purge themselves of the inessential', a goal Bauhaus architects

The cramped kitchen so beloved by male Modernists. This example, phrased in the Bauhaus style, dates from 1930. Even the kettle has to be neatly stacked away.

were subsequently to demand of their clients. The Arts and Crafts emphasis on individual craftsmanship was rejected in order to embrace mass-production. When Hannes Meyer succeeded Gropius as Director in 1928, he urged the Bauhaus's weaving workshop 'to develop prototypes for manufacture' rather than rely on the handcrafted, Arts and Crafts tradition. Under the leadership of the Bauhaus lecturer László Moholy-Nagy (1895–1946), 'a concentrated effort was made in the metal workshop at the Bauhaus to design industrial products that could be put into manufacture'. The admirable notion was that a limited range of standardised product types would lead to better design and cheaper products, a concept labelled in German 'Typisierung'. Standardisation also implied that far fewer items needed to be produced. In Le Corbusier's extreme and disastrously impractical vision, apart from chairs and tables (and, presumably, the odd bed), the only item of furniture that a home should need was the storage box.[8]

Given that most of the driving forces behind the international Modernism of the 1920s and 1930s had been trained as architects, it is unsurprising that their view of the interior was one very much dictated by its external envelope. The architecture of the house should, the early Modernists believed, dictate the planning of the interior and the nature of the interior furnishings. The repercussions of this approach were significant. Possibly Modernism's most influential (and, in terms of existing buildings, subsequently most damaging) message was the

Opposite. An interior from the 1930 Stockholm Exhibition by designer Erik Chamberg and architect Kurt von Schmalensee.

Left. Sven Markelius and Gunnar Asplund's minimalist living area, as exhibited at the Stockholm Exhibition of 1930.

exhortation to open up internal spaces and to dispense with traditional room partitions. A principal Modernist concern – which tended, as we will see, to ignore piffling concerns such as noise, smells and privacy – was that interior space should be open and 'free-flowing'. To this end seat furniture was made visually transparent – Breuer declared that furniture should 'neither impede movement nor the view through the room' – and interior space was maximised for unspecified functions by building seat and storage furniture into the perimeter of the room.

In the context of interior design, the history of Modernism during the 1920s and 1930s can be seen primarily as a stirring tale of Men And Their Chairs. As design historian Christopher Wilk has noted, 'no era had produced so many designs for chairs by architects ... Virtually every architect and designer

of note ... felt compelled to turn their
attention to the design of at least one
chair'. Wilk goes on to suggest that the
explosion in architect-designed furniture
after 1918 had a very pragmatic origin:
the postwar depression and resulting
scarcity of architectural commissions.[9]

Designs by male architects such
as the tubular steel 'Wassily' chair
designed by Marcel Breuer (1902–81) in
1927, Le Corbusier's chaise longue of
1928 and Mies van der Rohe's X-framed
steel-and-leather Barcelona chair of 1929
had all become Modernist icons by the
hero-worshipping 1960s. Pure of form
and material, they sacrificed comfort to
line, and gave little heed to affordability.
Dutch architect Gerrit Rietveld (1888–
1964) boasted that 'Form has resulted
from material', but few of the products
of interwar Modernism (with notable
exceptions such as Rietveld's own,
ingenious 'crate furniture' of 1934, the
ancestor of today's ubiquitous flatpack
furniture) reached the average home.

Marcel Breuer has been hailed
by his English-language biographer
as 'the most influential designer of
furniture in the twentieth century'. His
pioneering wooden chair of 1924 actually
'allow[ed] for a degree of comfort, while
highlighting the distinction between

the supporting framework and the main seating elements'.[10] The following year he made his first tubular steel chair, having allegedly got the idea from bending bicycle handlebars, as you do. Tubular steel was strong, light and reflective. It was not, though, especially cheap. As a result of its expense, together with its avant-garde design, Breuer's first steel chair was first mass-produced only in the 1960s, when it was inexplicably marketed as the 'Kandinsky' chair. (Breuer had designed furniture for the Kandinskys, but not this particular chair.)

Tubular steel was bright and reflective. Redolent of a shiny new age of technological triumph, it had few technological links with traditional materials. It was seen, as Penny Sparke has observed, as 'the marker of a progressive democratic and benevolent technology [which] came to be valued above nature'. Steel was, of course, naturally cold and uncomfortable; but the sitter did not necessarily have to come into contact with the steel frame: 'the idea of separating, in constructional and visual terms, frame and support became embedded in Modernist furniture designs'.[11]

Steel furniture was, importantly, also demonstrably hygienic. 'The hygienic qualities of tubular steel were frequently commented upon by designers and contemporaries, and this description was used in both polemic and in advertising of the period to advocate use of this type of furniture'.[12] Metal furniture carried with it strong associations of medical hygiene, of a visit to the doctor or dentist – hardly, of course, the most relaxing or reassuring of concepts.

Hygiene was, as we have seen, even more important to the Modernists than it had been to their Arts and Crafts forbears. Loos had eulogised the spotlessness of American bathrooms; Le Corbusier stressed the hygienic and therapeutic value of all-over whitewash. Interestingly, the Modernists' emphasis on cleanliness and health both influenced, and borrowed heavily from, the health movement of the 1930s. Indeed, it dovetailed nicely with Nazi Germany's emphasis on health and fitness after 1933. Although the Bauhaus (which had moved from Weimar to Dessau in 1925) was forced to close by Von Papen's government (and not Hitler's) in 1932, the dogmatic certainties of the Modern Movement still influenced theories of planning in Nazi Germany and Fascist Italy up to the late 1930s.[13]

It has been argued that the interwar metal cantilevered chair achieved 'a symbolic importance beyond

Right. Modernist chairs and vertically stacked storage units – the acme of Corbusian Modernism. A design by Louis Dignot from the *Répertoire du Goût Moderne* of 1928–9.

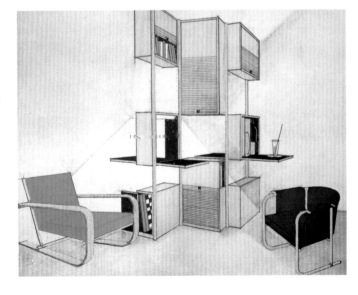

its commercial success'.[14] However, this judgement is made very much from hindsight, and from the viewpoint of design historians rather than consumers. At the time, the lack of comfort, the high price and the difficulty of manufacture dissuaded both householders from buying metal chairs and industry from mass-producing them.

Nor did the design critics of the time universally welcome this radical new departure. The British writer John Gloag, though himself no design conservative, described tubular steel furniture in *The Studio* in 1929 as 'coming from the robot modernist school [which] expresses with lucidity and relentless logic its utter inhumanity' and 'about as interesting as modern sanitary fittings'. Declaring that the metal construction 'gives no comfort to the eye', he hit the nail on the head when he suggested that, in the Modernist room, 'human beings appear intrusive', and that 'there is no sympathy between them and the setting'. Two years later, the French critic

Maurice Dufrène attacked the stateless impersonality of Modernist furniture: 'The same chair, mechanical and tubular, is to be found in almost every country ... It is the anonymous, neutral, universal chair ... and this is the root of Dullness.' Even designer Mart Stam inveighed in 1935 against the overcomplicated 'steel macaroni monsters' which he saw as both 'effete and decadent' – damning criticism indeed of Corbusian egalitarianism. Famously, the English novelist Aldous Huxley also weighed in, opining that the 'aseptic, hospital style of furnishing' promoted by Le Corbusier, Breuer and Mies was 'not my idea of domestic bliss', and suggested that 'the time, I am sure, is not far off when we shall go for our furniture to the nearest Ford or Morris agent'.[15]

The British, as usual, attempted to reach a comfortable compromise.

THE NEW ISOKON CHAIR

Left. An advertisement of 1937 for Breuer's new plywood chair (the 'Long Chair') for Isokon. Wooden chairs such as this fared better in pre-war Britain and Europe than did the more institutional-looking tubular steel models.

Below. A bathroom from Pilkington's *Glass Age Exhibition* of 1937: Art Deco fused with Classical Revival and Modernism to beget 'Moderne'.

Jack Pritchard of design pioneers Isokon lamented in 1931 that 'Much recent modern furniture has failed to give the traditional English comfort though its form and shape has been pleasing'. Architect Hugh Casson was one of those who rose to Pritchard's challenge, designing for 'comfortable Modernism' in 1936. Breuer himself, with his lounge chairs for Isokon of the same year, also tried to provide comfort as well as aesthetic simplicity, abandoning rigid tubular steel for a more flexible plywood frame. The 1933 exhibition of 'British Industrial Art in Relation to the Home' had attempted to reconcile Modernism to everyday life: Wells Coates's radical 'Minimum Flat' couched its model kitchen and bathroom in a 'strictly functional Modern style'.[16] However, few homeowners were prepared to make the leap from the comfortable and

convenient to the daringly impersonal.

Given the Modernists' obsession with eradicating ornament and with chairs, it is unsurprising that they eagerly seized on the potential of bentwood furniture, thus promulgating

a bentwood revival in the 1920s. As Christopher Wilk has noted, leading Modernist designers 'chose the "humble" Thonet Chair and endowed it with a moral significance granted to few pieces of furniture in history', choosing to applaud 'a finished product designed strictly according to function, manufactured from low-cost parts by modern methods of mass production, and available at a low cost to make it accessible to the working class'.[17]

Bentwood furniture, much of it bought from Thonet's factories (which became part of the world's largest furniture conglomerate, Thonet-Kohn-Mundus, in 1922), was used by Le Corbusier in his house designs after 1923. It featured prominently in the same architect's revolutionary 'Pavillon de l'Esprit Nouveau' at the 1925 Paris exhibition, and was

employed by Mies van der Rohe at the Deutsche Werkbund's Stuttgart show 'Die Wohnung' of 1927. Encouraged by this patronage, Thonet's factories moved into the manufacture of tubular steel furniture, much of which was designed for them by Marcel Breuer, Mart Stam and Le Corbusier. Here, however, Thonet-Kohn-Mundus and their stellar architects tripped over the eternal contradiction of interior design in the industrial age: the resulting products far exceeded the cost of their bentwood cousins, and consequently never sold well.

Modernism turned the clock backwards as well as forwards. Most damagingly, its pursuit of open-plan interiors eradicated gendered spaces in the interior. As Penny Sparke has noted, in the idealised Modernist world the interior was

Far left. Betty Joel's carpentry workshop in the mid-1930s.

Left and opposite, left. Refreshingly colourful French designs for a bathroom and kitchen from the French pattern-book *Répertoire du Goût Moderne* of 1928–9.

now merely to be 'an extension of the exterior'. Le Corbusier's advocacy of using storage facilities as much as possible eliminated 'any kind of display' – which, of course, invariably smacked of feminine bourgeois values and 'iconolatory'. Female amateur decoration was dead; long live male professionalism. A hundred years of women's advance as arbiters of interior taste and disposition was to be swept away in an instant. Rejecting Victorian values also meant 'marginalising feminine culture as it had developed in the nineteenth century'.[18]

Nor did women have much of a place or voice in training the designers of the future, a goal which of course had been central to the purpose of the Bauhaus. 'Although the Bauhaus in theory espoused the notion of gender equality (a quarter of the students who enrolled in 1919 were women), the school found it difficult to incorporate them fully into the workshop structure. Initially they were relegated to a women's class ... [which] was merged with Weaving in March 1922'. In 1920 Walter Gropius himself took formal steps to confine women students (of whom, he believed, there were already too many) to weaving. By 1926 the weaving workshop was accorded inferior status, 'despite the considerable revenue that the dyers and weavers brought to the strained Bauhaus coffers'.[19]

Modernism also drove a wedge between the work of interior decorators, a trade generally dominated by women and recently professonalised by the likes of Elsie de Wolfe, and that of so-called 'serious' designers and architects, who were invariably male and trained in

Far right. Humour infiltrates the Modernist interior in the mid-1930s. Predictably, it is a lounge designed by a woman – Betty Joel.

architecture practices or schools. The inevitable result of this development was seen after 1945, when – again, at a time of dearth for more conventional architectural commissions – male architects successfully promoted the superiority of the organised 'interior design' profession, and saw off (for the time being, at least) the challenge from the women-dominated field of interior decoration. Unsurprisingly, though, the individual 'classic' chairs and other furniture that the leading Modernist architect-designers produced during the 1920s and 1930s did little to influence the design development of whole rooms. As historian Stephen Calloway has observed, by the time of the outbreak of the Second World War, the Modernist aesthetic had in practice 'impinged on the everyday interior … on a more comfortable and less uncompromising

level' than that promoted in earlier years by the prophets of the Bauhaus.[20]

Not all Modernists were as misogynistic or didactic as the Germans at Dessau. Scandinavian Modernists attempted to humanise Modernism by sensibly combining its message with that of the Arts and Crafts tradition from which it had in many ways sprung. They used traditional, warm woods, rather than hard, cold metal, for seat furniture. Pioneering Finnish designer Alvar Aalto (1898–1976) acknowledged that metal 'transmitted heat and cold too readily [and] reflected too much light', as well as impairing internal acoustics. Aalto's chairs were accordingly less hard-edged than their German contemporaries, possessing a natural subtlety not found in the works of Breuer or Mies. Unsurprisingly this 'natural Modernism' found a

Opposite. The Bauhaus's Wood Carvers' Workshop in Weimar, photographed in 1923. Women dared not set foot in this hallowed male temple.

Left. Modernism domesticated: a forward-looking room set by Heal & Son of the 1920s. Heal's courageously championed lightwood furniture between the wars, when the public taste was generally for dark historical reproductions.

ready market in Britain: in 1933 critic P. Morton Shand organised an exhibition of Aalto's seat furniture at the upmarket London department store Fortnum & Mason, entitled 'Wood Only'.[21]

Warm, colourful furnishing fabrics had little place in the Modernists' world. Few Modernist designers sought to incorporate fabrics into their interiors; the gifted female designer Marion Dorn (1896–1964) was a rare exception. Thus, despite the invention of the vacuum cleaner (in 1909), and its rapid proliferation in the West during the 1920s and 1930s, carpets were in decline. By 1930 Brussels carpets – seen by the Modern Movement as unhygienic, overly expensive and redolent of a bygone age – were, significantly, no longer made in America. When Paul Nash advised his readers to purchase simple modern rugs for their homes, he acknowledged that there 'were few suitable examples from which to choose'. Textiles were considered as 'equipment' rather than embellishment for the Modernist interior. Furniture was now ideally grouped around the central rug, which replaced the fireplace (now relegated to the periphery or even abandoned altogether) as the focus point of principal rooms. For rugs or carpets, rectangular shapes were preferred, to fit with the rectilinear nature of the ideal architectural shell; they were also designed so as not to compete with the lower furniture that was emerging from the Modernist studios.[22]

Even colour itself was seen as an iniquity to be shunned. In their 1932 exhibition at the Museum of Modern Art in New York, academic Henry-Russell Hitchcock and architect

Right. Art Deco dining room by Michel Guillemard, from *Ensembles Choisis* of 1930. Fun and historical quotation have returned to the domestic interior.

Below. Duncan Grant fabric design of 1932, 'Grapes', from the Omega Workshop.

Philip Johnson (launching what they termed the 'International Style' with a book of the same name, their version of Le Corbusier's *Vers une Architecture*, and a travelling exhibition) warned householders about the evils of using colours other than white on their walls. 'There is', they advised, 'no better decoration for a room than a wall of book-filled shelves'.[23]

As a recent scholar has observed, to many householders both then and now, the Bauhaus's products seemed 'coldly theoretical, over-analytical and lacking in human comfort'. Two centuries of rapid advance in terms of standards of comfort were happily thrown away. As *The Studio* commented in 1930, the prime consideration in designing seat furniture should be comfort; yet instead, we are exhorted to sit 'in dignified but disconsolate fashion on chairs designed apparently for the mortification of the flesh'.[24]

Here lay the fatal contradiction of Modernism. Its rigid rules of aesthetics were neither sufficiently inclusive to express the character of the inhabitants, nor flexible enough to allow the degree of comfort that twentieth-century consumers increasingly believed

was their right. As design historian Adrian Forty has noted, 'The pursuit of individualism cannot be compatible with the observance of preordained principles of design'.[25] At the same time, the materials that the early exponents of Modernism used so enthusiastically during the 1920s and 1930s were simply not compatible with contemporary technology. It was only in the 1960s that industry caught up, enabling the mass-production of some of the more lasting, iconic products of early Modernism.

Despite what most design histories imply, Modernism was never a mass movement before or even after the Second World War. Steel furniture was prohibitively expensive: before 1939 it 'only penetrated the most avant-garde of interiors, especially in Europe'.[26] And Modernist pieces were never popular in the homes of Britain, Sweden, Southern Europe or, significantly, North America. In truth, the middle classes of the interwar West were far more eclectic and historicist

in their taste than contemporary Modernists and subsequent historians would have wished.

In America it was French Art Deco, rather than European Modernism, that caught the public imagination. Although the US refused to participate in the 1925 Paris Exposition (Commerce Secretary Herbert Hoover astonishingly claimed that America was not yet in a position to offer 'new and really original' design[27]), the fashion rapidly took hold. In 1926 the Metropolitan Museum in New York organised an American touring exhibition of Art Deco objects, which proved a huge success, and the following year Saks, Macy's and other leading New York department stores opened displays of contemporary French furniture. In 1930 Joseph Urban (who in 1922 had set up a mirror Wiener Werkstätte in the US) created the brash 'Century of Progress' exhibition in Chicago 1930, and it was the Art Deco style, and not Corbusian Modernism, which dominated. Art Deco subsequently became the dominant style

for commercial interiors in America; in the shape of the Chrysler and Empire State buildings, it even dominated the New York skyline.

Art Deco had everything that Modernism lacked: historicism, flair and humour. As with early Modernism, though, its products could be prohibitively expensive. Its origins, as we have seen, lay in the 1925 Paris Exposition. However, the organisers had not originally intended this to be so: they had envisaged an exhibition which would showcase the sort of proto-Modernist pieces that De Stijl were producing in Holland. The exhibition brief for the event explicitly stated that the show was 'open to all manufacturers whose produce is artistic in character and shows clearly modern tendencies', and that 'all copies or counterfeits of historical styles will be banned'. There were undoubtedly two radical statements of 'modern tendencies' at the exhibition: Le Corbusier's 'Pavillon de l'Esprit

Left. Living room from the Art Deco Exhibition in Paris of 1925.

Below. Heal & Son offering 'inexpensive' chromium-plated steel furniture in c.1930.

Opposite, above. An unashamedly revivalist bedroom design by André Groult of 1925, as shown in *L'Illustration* in September of that year.

Opposite, below. Art Deco influences are clearly discernible in this smart and functional bathroom of *c.*1935. Even the weighing scales match the idiom.

Nouveau' and the unapologetically Modernist USSR Pavilion. Yet Le Corbusier's building was largely ignored at the time by critics and public alike. And, much to the organisers' horror, the Art Deco style which emerged and predominated at the exhibition was both eclectic and historicist.[28] Most of the French exhibits at the show celebrated the native cabinetmaking tradition rather than the international potential of Modernism. (Interestingly, the home of the Bauhaus was not represented at the show, either: the invitation to Germany was sent 'too late' by the French, whose troops then still occupied the Rhineland.) And the idiom could also be very costly: Art Deco designers such as Jacques-Emile Ruhlmann (1879–1933) delighted in using prohibitively expensive materials such as ivory, shagreen, lizard-skin and mother-of-pearl.

Art Deco was a bizarre synthesis of the old and the new: a combination of the avant-garde furniture of the day with Neoclassical French furniture styles; eighteenth-century orientalism; Mackintosh's vertical, geometric forms (themselves based on Japanese interiors fused with the Scottish baronial style and with Arts and Crafts principles); the products of the Wiener Werkstätte, particularly their enthusiasm for angular forms and expensive materials; and even African forms. The style's use of colour was, in contrast to the monochrome designs of the emerging Modernists, highly adventurous. Yet in the event, the expense of the labour and materials involved in creating Art Deco objects resulted in few domestic interiors being couched in this idiom

A Ruhlmann bedroom design exhibited at the 1925 Paris Exposition and subsequently published in *Ensembles Mobiliers II*, photographed by Chevojon.

outside the homes of the seriously wealthy. By 1939 the rare and exotic finishes characteristic of French Art Deco 'were replaced by mass-produced, modern materials', with velveteen, moquette and veneering being used in place of silk, shagreen and ebony.[29]

A handful of designers did try to reconcile the style and flair of Art Deco with the functionality of Modernism. The most successful of these was the Irish-born Eileen Gray (1879–1976), who after 1929 sought to inject comfort and humour into the rigidly masculine Modernist canon. Gray walked a precarious tightrope between Art Deco and Modernism, experimenting with tubular steel and glass while selling Art Deco products. Her comfortable 'fauteuil transatlantique' of 1929, of sycamore frame with leather upholstery and metal fixtures, took its inspiration from the deckchairs of ocean liners – an environment soon dominated by Art Deco design.[30]

Ultimately, though, Art Deco remained anti-Modernist, rebuffing the

Left. An Art Deco interior as displayed at the 1925 Paris Art Deco Exposition.

Opposite. A masculine American wallpaper design of the early 1930s, featuring cigars, pipes, golf and yachts. Even the base colour is described as 'tobacco'.

Modernists' rejection of individuality and craftsmanship and turning instead to traditional classical inspiration and ostentatious showmanship. It was 'deliberately outrageous in both cost and effect'.[31] And it consciously turned its back on mass industry: its only mass-manufactured products were furnishing fabrics and wallpaper. While it is a style which is still regarded internationally with great affection, the exigencies of the Second World War ensured that it was the machine, and the comfortingly familiar, that triumphed.

1. See Penny Sparke, *As Long As It's Pink – The Sexual Politics of Taste* (1995), 81. **2.** Nathaniel Hawthorne, *English Notebooks* (1856), quoted in David Lowenthal, *The Past is a Foreign Country* (1985), 66. **3.** Mary Schoeser and Celia Rufey, *English and American Textiles from 1790 to the Present* (1989), 151. **4.** Christopher Wilk, *Marcel Breuer* (1981), 11. **5.** Friedrich Nietzsche, *The Use and Abuse of History* (1957), 29, 17–20. **6.** Christopher Wilk (ed.), *Modernism 1914–1939* (2006), 236, 233. **7.** Ibid., 217. **8.** Ibid., 210, 230. **9.** Ibid., 227. The V&A exhibition of 2006 and its accompanying catalogue both had a whole section (section 6) devoted simply to the interwar Modernist chair. **10.** Wilk, *Marcel Breuer*, 11; Wilk, *Modernism*, 51. **11.** Penny Sparke, *An Introduction to Design and Culture* (2004), 50; Wilk, *Modernism*, 232. **12.** Wilk, *Modernism*, 233. **13.** See Jonathan Woodman, 'The Modern Movement', in Joanna Banham (ed.), *Encyclopaedia of Interior Design* (1997), vol. 2, 831. **14.** Wilk, *Modernism*, 227. **15.** Wilk, *Marcel Breuer*, 68–9; Christopher Wilk, *Thonet: 150 Years of Furniture* (1980), 99. **16.** Stephen Calloway, *Twentieth-Century Decoration* (1988), 129, 237; Anne Massey, *Interior Decoration in the Twentieth Century* (1990), 90. **17.** Wilk, *Thonet*, 99. **18.** Sparke, *As Long As It's Pink*, 109, 110, 112, 118. **19.** Wilk, *Modernism*, 51, 218. **20.** Calloway, *Twentieth-Centiury Decoration*, 214. **21.** Wilk, *Modernism*, 314. **22.** Christine Boydell, *The Architect of Floors* (1996), 61. **23.** Massey, *Interior Decoration in the Twentieth Century*, 84. **24.** Isabelle Anscombe, *A Woman's Touch* (1984), 131, 167. **25.** Adrian Forty, *Objects of Desire* (1986), 107. **26.** Sparke, *As Long As It's Pink*, 50. **27.** Anne Massey, 'Art Deco', in Banham (ed.), *Encyclopaedia of Interior Design*, 43. **28.** See Paul Greenhalgh, *Ephemeral Vistas* (1988), 164–5. **29.** Massey, in Banham (ed.), 35. **30.** Wilk, *Modernism*, 234. **31.** Schoeser and Rufey, *English and American Textiles – 1790 to the Present* (1982), 172.

Why must we turn away from the truly beautiful just because it is 'old'? Why must we bow low in front of the new, as if it were god, only because it is 'new'?

(V.I. Lenin, 1921)

Opposite. Syrie Maugham's drawing room at 213 King's Road, Chelsea, photographed in colour for *The Studio* in February 1933.

Right. A far cry from the Bauhaus: what the average American homeowner aspired to in 1939 – an illustration from *The American Home* of March 1939.

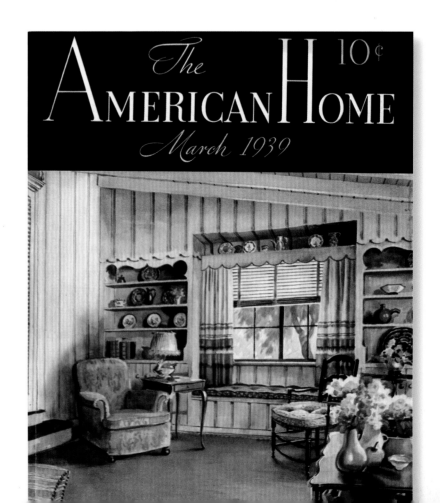

In 1908, in the year that Adolf Loos published his coruscating article declaring war on ornament, the first Daily Mail Ideal Home Exhibition was held in London. The exhibition had little in common with the brazen showcases of national and international industry and enterprise that had prospered in the wake of the Great Exhibition. Its aims were far more modest, and far more realistic: to show homeowners what could be done on a limited budget. New innovations were included, but these generally involved household equipment. The rooms or homes featured generally showed what the consumer wanted – even if those desires were rarely mirrored in the pages of design history: interiors that were welcoming, comfortable, convenient and safe. That could (though not necessarily) mean familiar: thus the 1910 show featured a 'Tudor Village' complete with village green and, the

catalogue opened, 'an atmosphere of old-time peace and quiet'.

To some extent, the Ideal Home Exhibition reflected the customary British tendency to be wary of radicalism and take refuge in a smug, comforting historicism. It is unlikely, for example, that exactly the same sort of show, with its Morrisian emphasis on the past, would have been as successful in Paris or Stockholm. (The exhibitions are still being held annually in London today.) However, it did reflect the sort of house in which most middle- and working-class families wished to, and indeed did, live. Only a tiny fraction of European and American households inhabited Modernist interiors by 1939; most preferred to dispose and decorate their homes – even when those homes were new-build properties, couched in

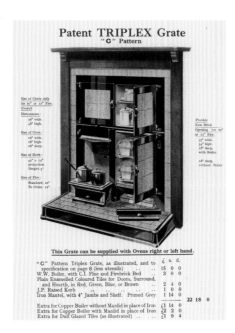

An advertisement for a 'modern' kitchen of 1936, complete with Aga range, from the *Illustrated London News*. Note the 'country' echoes and the Windsor chair.

an unapologetically Modern manner – in the same way as their ancestors had done since the mid-nineteenth century: in a eclectic idiom which valued comfort and expediency over stylistic purity. To most British homeowners, the fact that the first 'Magicoal' electric fire, with an artificial flame simulating a real fire, appeared in the Ideal Homes show of 1920 was probably more important than the recent founding of the Bauhaus in Germany. Unsurprisingly, though, it is the latter event that has been recorded in the histories of interiors, and not the former.

This is not to say that the Ideal Home Exhibitions ignored the consequences of technological advance. By 1926 the 'Tibbenham Tudor House' had half-timbering embedded in

concrete; six years later, a strong Modernist influence was discernible in the 1932 exhibition's 'Minimum Flat', aimed at 'the housewife with a slender purse', and which could allegedly be furnished for less than £100.[1] The 1927 exhibition included soundproof partitions between the newly opened areas 'to avoid conversations in the dining room being overheard in the kitchen' (a problem which the apostles of open-plan, with their vague knowledge of the practical needs of the average family, had never fully grasped).[2]

Helpfully, the concerns of the average householder of the interwar years often coincided with those of the Bauhaus pioneers. As already noted, light, air and hygiene were among Le Corbusier's prime concerns

Inside the 'Type J2 house' of the early 1930s, designed by Peter Wymark for Morrell's Countryside Estates. 'Tudor' leaded lights, a chintz pelmet and Chippendale reproduction furniture coexist happily with an Art Deco fireplace and carpet.

in his iconoclastic manifesto *Vers une architecture* of 1923. They were also key issues for current and would-be homeowners across Europe and America. Bathrooms and kitchens – populated no longer by servants, but by the women of the house – were now promoted to principal status. Sanitation, easy access to natural light and a plentiful air supply, and adequate provision for children (a goal unsurprisingly omitted from Le Corbusier's elevated treatise) were now principal goals of the average householder. Indeed, possession of a good-sized and well-equipped bathroom, rather than an ostentatiously furnished drawing room, became a key status symbol in many Western middle-class homes.

The aftermath of the First World War saw a return to many of the fixtures, fittings and finishes against which both nineteenth-century design reformers and contemporary Modernists had inveighed. The general desire to retreat from the starker and more vicious realities of technological advance was understandable, if disappointing to subsequent historians. Thus marble wallpapers remained very popular, particularly for halls, staircases and corridors; so were flocks, particularly when in shades of deep red or other vivid hues. By 1920 'Regency stripe' patterns and chintz papers were very much in vogue across Europe. These reproduced, on an often very inflated scale, the flowery Chinese-inspired fabric designs which had been so popular for upholstery since the early nineteenth

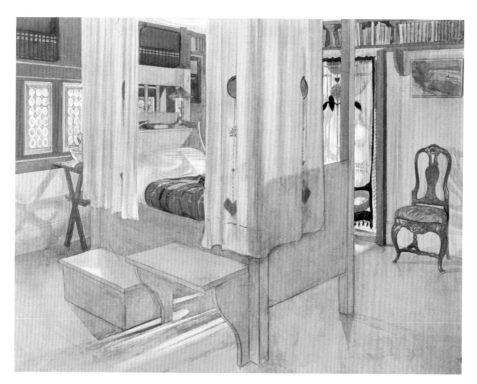

Carl Larsson's own bedroom, published in *At Solsden* in 1910. His colourful furniture and fabrics, set against contexts of off-white and pale tints, proved hugely popular in the West between the wars.

century, and reflected a growing obsession both with historical revivals in general and with the mythologised ideals of the small English country house or Parisian hôtel in particular.

This conscious historicism was both reflected and promoted in the pages of the new country house and home interest magazines, which specialised in creating new interiors using traditionally derived decoration and furnishings. *Country Life*, founded in 1896, started the trend in Britain, creating a market soon enhanced by magazines such as *House and Garden*, *Homes and Gardens* and, in 1922, the more contemporary and deliberately downmarket title *Ideal Home*.

In America, Stickley's pared-down colonialism, unhelpfully labelled the 'Mission Style' for no very good reason (since it was based far more on the colonial forms of the eastern seaboard than on those of the Spanish-owned west), was still very much in vogue after 1918. Homespun checks and plaids littered the American interior. In postwar France, the 'Empire' style was enthusiastically revived. Germany and Austria, economically stricken and militarily humiliated after the treaties of 1919, turned for comfort to the simple Neoclassical truths of Biedermeier.

The designer who most ingeniously synthesised the postwar retreat into revivalism, melding historical motifs with the vibrant Arts and Crafts tradition, the colour experimentation of the Wiener Werkstätte, the rectilinear Art Nouveau of C.R. Mackintosh, Anglo-

Japanese forms, the new interest in folk art, the growing obsession with sanitation and sunlight, and the rising tide of European nationalism, significantly came from one of the neutral nations of the First World War: Sweden. Carl Larsson (1853–1919) produced his hugely influential books *Ett Hem* and *Larssons* (both written with his wife Karin) at the turn of the century, in 1899 and 1902 respectively; and he died soon after the conclusion of the First World War. Yet it was in the postwar world that his astute combination of the new and the old became massively popular. The German edition of the Larssons' plates, published as *Das Haus in der Sonne* in 1910, was a great success in Germany and Austria after 1919, as nations weary of munitions and field grey turned to the colourful examples offered by Larsson's picturesque rural retreat, Lilla Hyttnas (which featured frequently throughout the books), as a design template for a brighter future. Larsson's cheerful, sunny colours, Teutonic simplicity, and suggestions of health and cleanliness seemed to many to reflect what were perceived as 'the light, pretty and unaffected' people and landscape of Sweden.[3] Larsson interiors were invariably painted, in white relieved by strong, clear colours. In a return to practices of the early nineteenth century, all furniture was painted, too.

Larsson borrowed heavily from Arts and Crafts ideals.[4] The resulting synthesis could be adapted to all types of regional or national context. His colourful, fairytale vision paralleled and to some extent even fuelled the growing interest in National Romanticism across Continental Europe. In America, it could be modified into a celebration of regionalism and simplicity in the US – 'material surroundings conducive to plain living and high thinking', as Stickley put it in his periodical *The Craftsman*.[5]

Back in Sweden, Larsson's contemporary idiom became confused with the historic development of Swedish interiors, to the extent that many homeowners – and writers – believed then and now that the Larssons had simply amplified and customised styles of the past. Denise Hagstrømer has noted 'the curious irony that something so brimful of foreign design influences has become an inseparable part of Swedish cultural identity'.[6] The Larssons' coup is thus perhaps the first modern example of the 'reinvention' of heritage in the twentieth century.

Unsurprisingly, the typical post-First World War house was smaller and

Opposite. The freshness and use of bright colour in the surviving interiors of the Larsson home at Sundborn, Sweden, are still very evident today.

Right. 'Stencilling a frieze', from the Swedish *Allers Familj-Journal* of May 1926. The colours are distinctly Larssonian.

Det är både en enkel sak och ett stort nöje att vara sin egen dekorationsmålare. Med de schablo-ner, som finnas i detta nummer, kan man som bevis åstadkomma det vackraste resultat. Dessa schabloner äro nämligen tryckta på för ändamålet avsett satinerat schablongpapper och fram-träda i djup prägel, så att de målade figurerna alltid komma att stå med rena kanter.

meaner than its pre-war ancestors. In Britain, householders dispensed with parlours, opting for the simplified arrangement of a sitting room at the front and (where feasible) a dining room at the rear. Altogether, the typical British home of the 1930s was a far cry from the Corbusian ideal. Floral-patterned wallpapers abutted grained woodwork; vaguely cubist chimney surrounds still bore traces of the past yearning for an inglenook; a suite of comfortably upholstered settee and two chairs was invariably lit by an adjacent standard lamp or centrally placed central opaque glass bowl light on the ceiling; and pride of place in the sitting room was a large wireless set, 'one of the most significant twentieth century additions to the suburban home', whose practical austerity had been deliberately tailored to suit the middle-class household. Familiar motifs appeared wherever

possible: Arts and Crafts and Aesthetic movement symbols such as sailing ships and sunflowers were inserted into the stained glass of suburban front doors, alongside the ubiquitous sunray device that seemed to speak of postwar optimism and a world where the sun had indeed always got his hat on. The typical home 'saw no incongruity in the juxtaposition of rural images with modern equipment', any more than we do now.[7]

For most Western homes, untrammelled, Mediterranean-style Modernism was still a fair way off in 1939. While new 'cubist' and other abstract designs represented the cutting edge of wallpaper design, their use was decidedly limited, and large-scale historicist patterns were all the rage in the 1920 and 1930s. (It was widely held that Brobdingnagian printed flowers increased the apparent size of a room.) Flock and chintz designs were supplemented by other papers that recalled a simpler age − imitative products such as 'tapestry' papers, for example, proved a great success after 1918. In reaction to the lighter colours prevalent at the height of the Arts and Crafts and 'Queen Anne' fashions of the late nineteenth century, designers after the First World War attempted to bring back strident colour to domestic wallpapers and fabrics. In Britain, the Omega Workshops, set up by Bloomsberries Duncan Grant, Vanessa Bell and Roger Fry in 1913, pioneered the use of bright primary and secondary colours in combination with a liberal use of black relief. At the same time, Modernist papers of emphatically cubist

design began to appear. However, innate British conservatism dictated that many of these radical designs should be softened by the additional provision of familiar forms such as sprigs or bunches of flowers, produced in the warm and friendly colours so fashionable worldwide during the 1920s and, especially, the 1930s: browns, oranges and beiges. Even the joinery could be painted brown – generally chocolate or chestnut – although there was also a fad for stripped woodwork, for which historian Stephen Calloway blames the 'handsome carved pine classical drawing room of a house in South Street, Mayfair [London], built shortly after the First World War by architects Wimperis & Simpson'.[8] As Turner and Hoskins remarked of the typical, modest 1930s interior, 'invariably the overall effect would be one of considerable varnished gloom, dimly lit at night by a low-

wattage bulb in a lantern shade'. And all too easily the plethora of browns could result in 'a world of washy porridge beige colour and utter blankness [with] nothing whatever to stimulate the imagination'.[9]

By 1939 Modern Movement carpet designs were certainly available in department stores. However, few were able to afford the inspired but expensive designs of Marion Dorn and her associates. Instead, the public's evident preference for traditional patterns meant that chintzy flower or Georgian-style geometric designs remained the most popular products before the Second World War. It was only in the 1950s, with the introduction of nylon and rayon and the triumph of International Modernism, that carpet design began to change dramatically. Carpets could now be more easily cleaned. In 1909 the first vacuum cleaner went on sale

in the US, having been invented eight years earlier; by 1914 it had appeared in Europe. Bill Bryson has told the story of its unfortunate inventor, J. Murray Spangler: 'Unable to make a success of it, he turned for advice to W.H. Hoover, a local leather-goods maker who knew nothing about electrical appliances but did recognize a business opportunity when it fell in his lap. Before long there were Hoover factories all over the world ... and J. Murray Spangler was forgotten.' Yet labour-saving devices such as the vacuum cleaner, the electric stove (first sold in 1902), the washing machine (1909) and the electric dishwasher (1918) failed, at least during the interwar period, to make any significant savings in the amount of time spent on housework, and accordingly failed to liberate women from their perceived domestic role. Washing machines appear to have

simply encouraged more washes; cookers promoted more frequent and elaborate home-cooked meals.[10] Expensive silk fabrics could now be mimicked at a fraction of the price. 'Artificial silk',

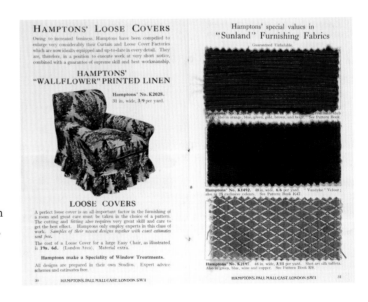

manufactured from the pulp of mulberry leaves, had been manufactured since 1889 at the Besançon factory of Comte Hilaire de Chardonnet. A scientific patent was taken out by two English chemists in 1892; in 1904 Courtaulds bought the product rights for Britain and America; and in 1924 this organic but fake fabric was renamed 'rayon' for an eager new market. After the Wall Street Crash of 1929 and subsequent worldwide depression, the price of natural fibres plummeted, leading to a spate of bankruptcies in the cotton industry, but that of rayon rose. In Britain and America, meanwhile, 'coronation fever' at the time of the coronation of George VI in 1937 led to a great boost for chintz sales.

The 1920s were a time of what Stephen Calloway has called 'confused eclecticism' for the middle-class interior, which often stood 'uncomfortably at the crossroads between vernacular tradition, historic pastiche and ill-digested modernism'.[11] It was, unsurprisingly, a time when confused homeowners with enough money began to call in the professionals. Following in the steps of the American pioneer Elsie de Wolfe, the wealthy Syrie Maugham (formerly Syrie Wellcome, and since 1917 the wife of novelist Somerset Maugham) opened a London home decoration shop in 1922 and, even more enterprisingly, a chain of US stores in 1926. Her decorative designs may have been intended for the rich, but her obsession with white and cream – for which she never tired of inventing new names, such as 'parchment', 'pearl', 'ivory' and 'oyster' – was influential in spreading the interwar taste for pale elegance.

Interwar designers in Britain and America tended to follow the same pattern. Sibyl Colefax (1875–1950) used what fashion designer Cecil Beaton subsequently termed 'off colours': pale almond greens, greys and opaque yellows. Basil Ionides (1884–1950) – who published his theories of interior colour as *Colour and Interior Decoration* in 1926 – preferred pale blues, lilacs, creams and rose pinks.[12] Across the pond, Frank Alvah Parsons (1868–1930), President of the New York School of Applied and Fine Art (subsequently, after 1941, the Parsons School of Design), influenced a generation of Americans with his work *Interior Decoration, Its Principles and Practices* of 1923. In his book plates, and his subsequent designs, he took ideas from Wharton and Codman, and particularly from de Wolfe, and made them available to a wider, middle-class market. His emphasis on practicality, and on achieving a balance between 'period feel' and 'comfort quality' and convenience,

A design for a nursery of the 1920s from R. Goulburn Lovell's extensive portfolio. Lovell was a master watercolourist, and his interiors betray an engaging mix of Larssonian colour, traditional English fabrics and fashionable 'country-style' Arts and Crafts seat furniture.

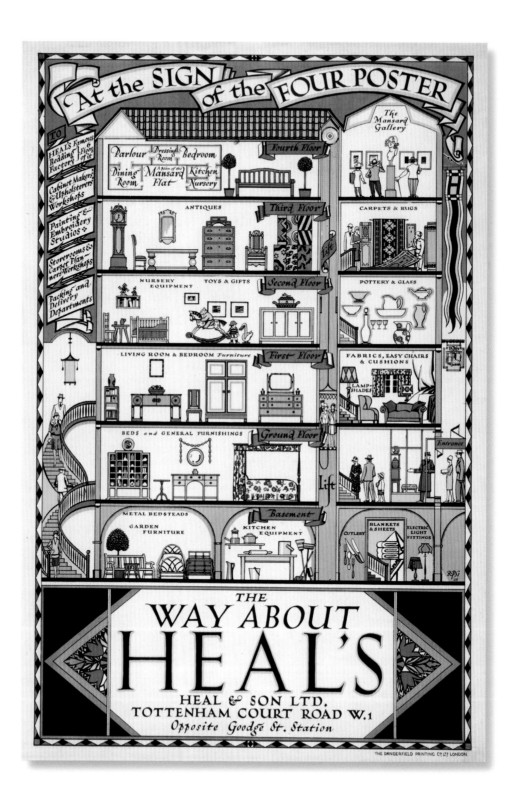

was much admired and imitated.[13]

While the Modernist architects toiled away at their chairs, and the aftermath of the War to End All Wars led uneasily but inexorably towards the debacle of 1939, in average homes the historic revival was in full swing. 'Chippendale', 'Adam' and 'Queen Anne' styles were increasingly popular in interwar Britain and America – and, increasingly, in France and Germany, too. Since the 1880s firms such as Gillows had been championing the designs of Robert Adam, leading to a 1902 reprint of the Adam brothers' seminal *Works in Architecture* volumes of 1773, 1778–9 and 1822. By 1920, post-Adam furniture styles – principally the idiom of Sheraton and Hepplewhite – were also very popular, while a more bizarre approximation of 'Tudor' or 'Jacobean' furniture briefly became all the rage. Tudor was, in Turner and Hoskins's words, 'felt to give a suitably simple, countrified, cottagey effect' evocative of 'an old English past'.

After the First World War, Liberty pioneered the revival of Regency forms, a revival given added interest by the widely publicised 1917 sale of the contents of Thomas Hope's former home, Deepdene. Rival firms subsequently exploited the public enthusiasm for what became known as the 'Georgian style', a vague catch-all denoting either Chippendale and Adam or Regency designers such as Sheraton or Hope. By the 1920s Maple & Company, one of the foremost specialists in period revival furniture, declared that 'Georgian' was 'universally acknowledged [to be] first for beauty, for style, and for the application of both to the purpose of use and comfort'. Maples, Waring and

Gillow (who continued to specialise in 'Chippendale' and 'Sheraton'), and other leading houses vied with each other in producing reproduction pieces for the middle classes during the interwar years. In 1923 *House and Garden* lamented that 'we continue to welter amid a mass of pastiche fakes of every age and country' and called for 'a new Adam to help us out of the mire', while Noel Coward prefaced a surprisingly radical Heal's catalogue of 1930 with the wish that 'the good Thomas Chippendale could be resurrected to broadcast on "Furniture and Decoration"'. In 1931 Christopher Hussey promoted the revival with a batch of articles on Regency homes for the highly traditional periodical *Country Life*. Such invocations neatly linked the stylistic conservatism of British householders during this period with Tory Prime Minister Stanley Baldwin's election-winning slogan of 1935: 'Safety First'.

'Regency Revival' was never particularly serious, particularly when

Opposite. A splendid tube poster for Heal & Son of 1928. While Ambrose Heal championed modern lightwood furniture and Arts and Crafts ideals, his bestsellers remained the sort of historic reproductions pictured here. In this fanciful cross-section, whose title evokes an Elizabethan tradesman rather than a contemporary furniture store, the ambience is distinctly Olde English.

Below. A reception room 'in the Adam style' from *Decorative Draperies and Upholstery* by Edward Thorne, published in New York in 1937.

promoted in tongue-in-cheek manner by Osbert Lancaster (1908-86) in the pages of his gentle satire *Homes Sweet Homes* of 1939. 'Vogue Regency', as Lancaster called it (alternatively christened 'Fourth Empire' by the photographer Angus McBean), could be matched with pieces or treatments couched in any other style ('A Récamier sofa is in no way embarrassed by the close proximity of a rug by Marion Dorn'): 'So long as no attempt is made to follow the fatal will-o'-the-wisp of period accuracy,' he declared, 'Vogue Regency remains as suitable a style as any.'[14]

In France, the Anglo-American fad for Regency Revival was mirrored by a rekindled passion for the Napoleonic era and its 'Empire' styles. During the 1920s the fashion spread for collecting Empire furniture, or at least modern reproductions or approximations, and for reviving the pale colours – green, yellow, lilac, rose and especially white

– typical of the period. And what the British called 'Regency stripe' wallpaper (even though striped papers were prevalent long before the Regency era) soon became common in drawing rooms all over Europe and America.

Outside Britain, France and Germany, the relatively slow pace of European industrialisation meant that traditional, local furniture continued to be made, and bought, until the Second World War. As Penny Sparke has observed, as late as 1947 90 per cent of Italian firms employed fewer than six staff.[15] Contrastingly, in interwar America, the pace of industrialisation had by 1939 outstripped all its European competitors. Yet still 'conservative taste favored solid colors for draperies and upholstery'.[16] Already inspired by the lure of the colonial revival, mixed with the sobriety and taste of the Arts and Crafts movement, Americans turned even more to historical precedents to decorate their homes. Period rooms, real or imagined, were installed in most of North America's major museums. The opening of the American Wing of the Metropolitan Museum in New York in 1924 promoted a growing awareness of the history of America's own decorative arts, spurring a further move towards traditionalism in American interiors. The wing helped fuel admiration for simpler, rustic American furniture, which 'began to be admired by collectors and decorators with the sort of enthusiasm previously reserved for early English pieces or the work of the French ébénistes'.[17]

Even more influential was the example provided by the restoration

Bedroom suite in limed oak, offered by Liberty's of Regent Street in a catalogue of 1935.

Left. The Paris apartment of 'Monsieur B', photographed by Bouchelal for *Ensembles Choisis* and published in 1930.

Below. A beautifully coloured R.Goulburn Lovell design for a 'Georgian style' interwar sitting room. The chimney surround, while impeccably Adamesque, does seem to be rather large for the height of the ceiling.

of the seventeenth- and eighteenth-century remains of the former colonial capital of Virginia, Williamsburg. The idea of restoring Colonial Williamsburg originated with a local cleric, the Rev. W.R.A. Goodwin, who in 1928 persuaded tycoon John D. Rockefeller to finance the project – which he did to the tune of $68 million. Helen Bullock researched and developed the paints; however, the first scientific analysis of those paint traces that remained from the colonial period was only carried out in 1987. After the site's 're-opening' in 1932, 'Williamsburg' colours were developed that actually bore little relationship to genuine eighteenth-century paints. The first paint range went on sale in 1930; the range was expanded in 1951, when new designs (based on eighteenth-century originals) and colourways were added.

The resulting colours and

patterns may not have been academically researched, nor truly 'authentic'. However, this was how colonial homes were perceived by generations of Americans, eager to borrow from history to create interiors that, while they exploited the inspiration of the nation's past, created unashamedly

contemporary interiors that made best use of electricity and gadgets. In the post-war era, the decorating firm of Brunschwig and Fils began to cooperate with the Winterthur Museum in Delaware – an unrivalled repository of historic room recreations – and with the venerable, Boston-based Society for the Preservation of New England Antiquities (SPNEA) to produce everything from historic paints to accurately reproduced furniture. Americans had learned to embrace history while welcoming the future.

1. Deborah Ryan, *The Ideal Homes through the Twentieth Century* (1997), 26–7, 52, 70. 2. Paul Oliver, Ian Davis and Ian Bentley, *Dunroamin* (1981), 91. 3. Stephen Calloway, *Twentieth-Century Decoration* (1988), 60. 4. See Julian Holder, 'Arts & Crafts', in Joanna Banham (ed.), *Encyclopaedia of Interior Design* (1997), vol. 1, 65. 5. Ibid., 66. 6. Denise Hagstromer, 'Carl Larsson', in Banham (ed.), *Encyclopaedia of Interior Design*, vol. 1, 699. 7. Oliver, Davis and Bentley, *Dunroamin*, 179, 181. The popular song 'The Sun Has Got His Hat On' dates from 1929. 8. Calloway, *Twentieth-Century Decoration*, 213. 9. Mark Turner and Lesley Hoskins, *The Silver Studio of Design* (1988), 72; Calloway, *Twentieth-Century Decoration*, 214. 10. Bill Bryson, *Made in America* (1995), 110. Bryson points out that in 1917 Americans spent $175m a year on household electrical appliances; by 1928 'that figure had risen to $2.4 billion'. 11. Calloway, *Twentieth-Century Decoration*, 129. 12. Ibid., 139, 190, 194. 13. Ibid., 168. 14. Mark Pinney, 'Vogue Regency', in Banham (ed.), *Encyclopaedia of Interior Design*, vol. 2, 1348; Calloway, *Twentieth-Century Decoration*, 182. 15. Penny Sparke, *Italian Design* (1988), 99. 16. Jane C. Nylander, *Fabrics for Historic Buildings* (1988), 191. 17. Calloway, *Twentieth-Century Decoration*, 211.

EMBRACING THE MACHINE

The Postwar Interior

Wallpaper! Nobody had talked about wallpaper
for six years, let alone covered their walls with it.
It was an omen of peace.

(Ernest Bevin, 1945)[1]

Opposite. A 1950s American room set. Note the ubiquitous cacti and the emphatically non-Bauhaus fringing on the 'Directory' seat upholstery.

Right. 'Plastic – The Winner of the Half Century!' proclaims *La Vie Pratique* of January 1954. The French housewife featured on the cover looks uncertain about where exactly she should put her plastic broom.

As wartime nations addressed the sort of world they wanted after the war was over, there was a great discussion, particularly in Britain and America, about how the ideal postwar home should look. Much attention was therefore given to the average domestic interior in the postwar years. Designers sought to banish the drab dreariness of wartime's utility colours and forms. (In wartime Europe and America, interiors really had been, literally, drab: the majority of dyes were reserved for military use, while dyes for domestic fabrics had been watered down. Drab, or its grey equivalent, was often all that was available.) Bright mix and match colours – first seen in Russel Wright's multicoloured 'American Modern' tableware range of the 1930s – were an integral part of many modern homes by the 1950s. Bright colours 'were a symbol of the new [postwar] optimism, while the juxtaposition of contrasting colours represented an incitement to jollity and playfulness'.[2]

There were also other important social and aesthetic questions to address. New homes, at least in Europe, were now generally smaller than before, as building materials were difficult to come by and labour was both inconsistently available and expensive. In all but the grandest houses, too, servants no longer existed. So furniture and appliances had to be conveniently located and easy to use and maintain.

Across Europe there was a huge demand for new furniture to replace that lost in bombing. In Britain, the 1941 Utility furniture scheme had introduced an emphasis on good,

simple new design – though much of this was available only to newlyweds or those whose homes had been damaged or destroyed by enemy action – and by 1944 had metamorphosed into the Design Council (or Council of Industrial Design, as it was first named). These initiatives gave a leg up to Modernism; while before the war the Modernist message had sounded strident and inappropriate, in Brave New Europe it was just the thing. And with Britain and the rest of Europe being on the brink of bankruptcy, consumers had no choice anyway: mass-production Modernism was, in the words of one eminent historian, 'imposed on a public with no choice but to buy Utility'. In Marcel Breuer's view there was no need for any 'style' at all; all that was needed was an expression of 'the owner's character'.[3]

Most of these European initiatives put their emphasis on the affordability of new interior design. In France, the Mobilier National et des Manufactures was set up to kick-start a revival in applied art design. A French exhibition of 1947, 'La Résidence Française' – almost the interior's equivalent of Dior's 'New Look' – was sharply criticised 'for having exclusively presented luxury furniture' and thus insulted the victims of the recent war. Le Corbusier's 'Unité d'Habitation' in Marseilles seemed to point to one way forward: with a double-storey living room and balcony for each flat.[4]

Postwar furniture also, like its pre-war predecessors, earned the attention of under-employed (and invariably male) architects. As Penny Sparke has observed of Italian designers of the 1950s, 'they emerged from the war to find a dearth of architectural projects and the possibility of earning a living only from the wealthy northern clients who commissioned them to design the interiors of their private dwellings'.[5]

Back in Britain, many Modernist designers hoped that the strictures of the wartime Utility scheme would survive long after the war. However, many homeowners understandably preferred to return to the familiar, cosy historicism they knew and loved. Heals was one of the few British furniture retailers to champion contemporary furniture – although, as we have seen, this did not preclude Ambrose Heal from offering numerous reproduction lines. However, most retailers preferred to follow Harrods furniture department in offering 'the quality, charm and dignity of a bygone age'.[6] The ambitious exhibition 'Britain Can Make It' of 1946

Below left. Ideal Home of February 1950 features an emphatically Modernist interior, with fully integrated living and dining areas, G-plan furniture (from High Wycombe), task lighting and a simple rug on a dark wooden floor in *The Smaller House & Garden* issue. Wood colours predominate in a quotation from Arts and Crafts tradition and more recent interiors by Frank Lloyd Wright.

Below. Designer Eileen Parker pretending to be at home in the PEL (Practical Equipment Ltd) stand at the British Industry Fair of 1949.

was the Design Council's attempt to foist Modernist aesthetics on to a prostrate and impoverished population, 'at a time when shortages meant that even the most badly designed product would sell'. Its continued embrace of wartime utility came in for much criticism: a Mass Observation survey of the time found that many visitors to the exhibition found the exhibits 'uninspiring'.[7] Once again, though, Britons preferred a comfortable compromise. Gordon Russell (1892–1980) successfully combined modern forms with modern and economic manufacturing methods in a way that was both accessible and affordable. His pale-coloured furniture accorded with the wall colours of the day, his armchairs possess 'the ample and simplified rounded shapes which ... implied comfort to the

conservatively-modern observer', while his undemanding designs 'allowed many people to live comfortably while maintaining their illusion of having avant-garde taste'.[8] The nomenclature of his 1946 ranges – 'Chiltern' and 'Cotswold' – showed Russell's debt to the Arts and Crafts movement, as well as his ability to reassure the market that good design did not necessarily mean ahistorical or incomprehensible.

After the war, the classic tubular steel chairs of the Modern Movement still remained too expensive for most homes. Indeed, the gap actually widened between 'decoration as a luxury activity for an exclusive clientele and commercially manufactured furnishings for the average house'.[9] In America, the firm of Knoll, founded in 1938 and from 1946 run by Hans Knoll and his

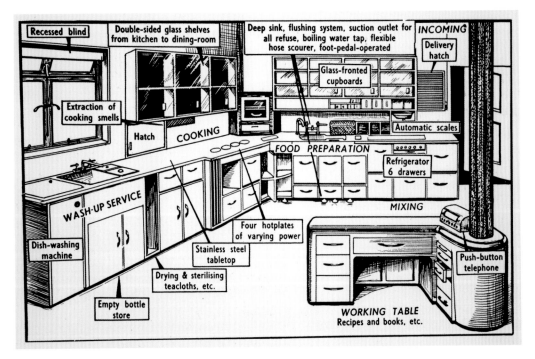

The all-steel 'Kitchen of Tomorrow' shown at the 1949 Ideal Home Exhibition. Its PR blurb made great play of the frosted glass doors and the continuous working surface, 'designed to save time and needless steps from one side of the kitchen to the other'.

Cranbrook-educated wife Florence, dominated the mass-production of contemporary furniture. Their furniture was introduced to Europe via home interest magazines: it reeked of American wealth, and was light years away from pre-war Europe, which for many had meant totalitarianism. Thus for many Modernism was equated with liberal, democratic values.

In Britain, Gomme's 'G-Plan' furniture – 'the quintessential suburban furnishing style' – was launched in 1953 at their High Wycombe factory. The same year, David Hicks (1929–98) daringly reintroduced bold colours into his first interior schemes. The monochrome pre-war austerity of the Bauhaus and the Cranbrook Academy was now overlaid with bright (but not just primary) colours, borrowed in America from the dazzling palettes of the Abstract Expressionist painters.[10]

Thonet's bentwood and steel furniture had been labelled as 'degenerate' by the Nazis after 1933, and most of their factories in the Third Reich had been either closed by 1939 or bombed to destruction after 1942. However, the US branch of the Thonet concern emerged invigorated from the Second World War. Electronically moulded plywood, more durable than the traditional glued forms, had been used to make aircraft – notably Britain's superlative De Havilland Mosquito – after 1941. At the end of the war, Thonet simply adapted this cheap, sturdy and flexible technology for the home, mass-producing what was now called 'bentply' furniture. The first moulded plastic seat for a bentply chair was made in 1946;

the resulting design stayed in production until the 1990s. Inspired by this success, the German Thonet operation, Gebrüder Thonet, eagerly embraced Gerd Lange's new hybrid 'Flex System' neo-bentwood furniture of 1975. Flex chairs, made from wood and plastic and stackable, became Gebrüder Thonet's biggest seller. As the Western world sloughed off its wartime utilitarianism, however, bentwood and its progeny became less popular for domestic use, and became chiefly used for schools and workplaces.

Other by-products of wartime invention began to appear in the home. In the 1950s 'rayon taffeta' shower curtains in America were treated 'with the same mildew and water repellent process used by Textron on jungle hammocks for the South Pacific', while the metallic yarns and prints used before 1945 also enjoyed a vogue in the ensuing decade.[11]

In the 1950s Modernist furniture became mainstream. But it was not the furniture of the Bauhaus pioneers. The large tubular steel and bentwood chairs of the 1920s and 1930s were too big, and still too expensive, for average postwar interiors. Consumers wanted a lighter, pared-down style.

In America, they found it in the work of leading designers such as Charles Eames and Eliel Saarinen, who had honed their skills at America's calmer version of the Bauhaus, Cranbrook Academy of Art – founded in 1932, with Saarinen as its first Director. Eames and Saarinen harnessed new materials and methods of manufacture to what they termed 'organic design'. And, for the first time, they and other cutting-edge

Modernist designers began to take the pursuit of comfort and the desire for display into consideration.

Display was high on the agenda of Eisenhower's newly confident and economically virile America. In 1947 the Japanese-American designer Isamu Noguchi introduced the first practicable and affordable glass-topped table; mass-produced by Herman Miller, it was soon to be a feature of countless Western living rooms. (Noguchi also

invented the first lantern-like paper lampshade.) Ironically, the table's success ultimately prompted one enterprising manufacturer, Cassina, to begin producing its original inspiration, Le Corbusier's adjustable but fragile glass-topped table of 1925. In 1978 Cassina followed this up with Le Corbusier's 1925 design for 'Casiers' storage cabinets. Corbusier's designs were by then revered as design classics, worthy of reproduction. Noguchi's own table was discontinued in 1973, but reintroduced as part of the same 'Modernist Revival' in 1984.

Postwar furniture in the West was also heavily influenced by the design, and/or perceived minimalist aesthetics, of Scandinavia. As one acerbic critic has written, 'In the 1950s virtually all endeavour in the design field can be lumped together in the public eye under the generic term of "Swedish Modern."' In addition, as Penny Sparke has observed, the concept of a unified 'Scandinavian' design ethos 'was less meaningful within the individual countries [of Scandinavia], each of which had its own indigenous traditions and future trajectories'.[12] Nevertheless, it was a useful marketing tool for the British and American markets.

Swedish design in particular exerted a great appeal on North Americans. Sweden, neutral in the Second World War, brought no political baggage to Eisenhower's America, and Scandinavia's Social Democratic tradition could be lauded as eminently egalitarian while definitely non-communist. Scandinavian design of the 1930s dealt with themes popular in the

Left. Two eclectic French interiors of the 1950s, showing a healthy fusion of traditional seating forms with Art Deco and Modernist elements.

postwar West: practicality, flexibility, convenience, hygiene, dignity (if not humour) and ethical responsibility. It was also rooted (unlike American or British Modernism) in the crafts tradition, which provided a good story for its retailers and gave potential customers colourful individual identities to recognise. And it was pragmatic: 'knock-down' furniture – flat-packed by the retailer for self-assembly – was first developed in Scandinavia in the 1950s.[13]

Leading the Scandinavian crusade were the Dane, Arne Jacobsen (1902–71), whose 3100 chair of 1952, Egg chair of 1958 and Swan chair of 1959 reinterpreted the great icons of the 1920s for a more impecunious and cynical age, and the Finn, Alvar Aalto (1898–1976), whose economical bentwood furniture of the 1950s provided benchmarks for postwar seat furniture. Aalto had made his name as a furniture designer in the 1930s at exhibitions in Stockholm and

Looking into the future: the 1960 catalogue for flatpack IKEA furniture.

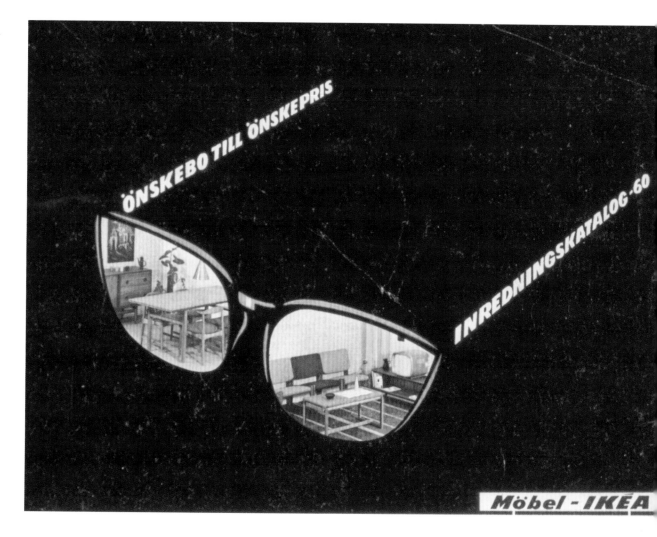

Milan. However, it was in the postwar world that his bentwood designs, watered down for a mass audience, gained widespread popularity. In the US he and his countrymen were helped hugely by the 'Design in Scandinavia' exhibition that toured the country between 1954 and 1957. Thus the industrial aesthetic of America began to absorb the craft aesthetic of Scandinavia.

In postwar America, however, even leading lights of the Modern Movement took care to combine purity of line with the ultimate goal of comfort. Like Aalto, Charles Eames (1907–78) also extended the repertoire of the bentwood chair, adding leather-covered upholstery (which by the 1950s was generally of latex foam) to soften the lines and reintroduce comfort, using the same design principle to add vinyl and foam-padded seats to tubular steel furniture. (Back supports were often lacking, however, leading to accidents for the unwary.) Eliel Saarinen's 'Womb' chair of 1940, with its moulded plastic shell, latex foam upholstery and tubular-steel frame, was manufactured in large numbers by Knoll Associates, and has been called (with unintended irony) 'one of the most comfortable contemporary chairs ever made'.[14]

The key word in postwar American interiors – and, ultimately, in Britain, too – was 'contemporary'. And 'contemporary' now meant open-plan. By the 1950s 'it was now the open-plan modern house rather than the traditional Cape Cod cottage that had caught the popular imagination' in America.[15] As developed by Charles

and Ray Eames and by Eero Saarinen, the open-plan home was promoted as flexible and cheap, and 'the rationale of a room became expansion rather than containment'.[16] With space at a premium in European homes, an open-plan layout provided a sense of airiness. In America, where space was generally not a problem, kitchens and dining rooms were increasingly linked with the living room, with room subdivisions being characterised only by changes in floorcoverings – vinyl tiles for the kitchen area, for example, metamorphosing into a polished wood floor for dining and living area.

Entrance halls were opened up, and rooms introduced at half-floor levels. (The concept of the mezzanine floor was a strikingly new one in domestic contexts.) Le Corbusier had already introduced the idea of a double-height room, to stop small

Opposite. Cane-and metal-framed chairs and a floor-length Venetian blind compete in this colourful 1950s living room.

Right. Le Corbusier's advocacy of double-height rooms is applied to alarming effect in Charles and Ray Eames's own Los Angeles home of 1949. The human scale has been somewhat mislaid here.

floor-plans looking cramped; now his ideas were translated into the average home, with Corb's much-promoted open storage units being used as room dividers in the way he had envisaged. Multifunctional room dividers replaced the traditional sideboard, while 'breakfast bars' appeared in the open-plan kitchen/living room area for the first time.

The Modernists' headlong rush towards open-plan homes ignored one big drawback: the lack of privacy and the permeation of sound. The problem of family noise in open-plan was identified as early as 1961, when *The House and Garden Book of Small Homes* noted how, after 1945, 'open planning was eagerly seized upon as it seemed to provide the joy of long vistas and a really generous feeling of space, even in a small house'; yet it also remarked how 'the problems of noise and distraction that are apt to arise when the various activities of parents and children are accommodated in one space can ... be formidable'. The writer's conclusion was that modern homes should seek to combine some open-planning with 'the self-contained formulas of our forbears'.[17]

The desire to economise on ground plan and maximise internal space led to harmony between the Modernists' zeal for open-plan and the needs of the average family. Kitchens were, where feasible, enlarged and upgraded – though, at the same time, soundly defeminised. In the modern kitchen, 'there was absolutely no room for aesthetic considerations as everything was governed by the laws of efficiency and utility'; the result of this

Left. Case Study House no. 21 by Pierre Koenig in Hollywood Hills, California, of 1956–8.

Below. The Case Study 'Idea House' by architects Riess and Freeman. The Modernist mantra sensitively adapted to liveable domestic proportions.

'masculinisation' of the kitchen was that 'the housewife's tasks were defined now as completely mechanical and rational in nature ... Gone was the communality of the large rural kitchen ... and in its place was the isolation of the efficient "worker-housewife", intent on producing food for the family in the same way as the factory produced standard automobiles'.[18] The introduction of labour-saving devices made the kitchen more of a laboratory or a workshop than a social centre, and its size – at least in Europe – was correspondingly reduced.[19] In America, though, the battery of new kitchen equipment – giant iceboxes, huge dishwashers, waste-disposal units, food mixers, automatic washing machines – was considered a matter of national pride. Significantly, the technological cutting edge of the American kitchen became a focus for debate in the Nixon–Khrushchev exchanges of 1959, which took place in Moscow in a mock-up of a typical American suburban home.[20]

Plastics had been used in the kitchen, and in other principal interiors, for some time. The first true plastic, celluloid, was made as early as 1862; bakelite, a plastic suitable for modelling but not load-bearing, was invented in 1907; plexiglass (the material from which most aircraft cockpit hoods were made in the Second World War) in 1930; and nylon, by Du Pont, in 1938. Breuer's 'laccio' table of 1925 has been cited as the first example of synthetic plastic being incorporated into furniture. But it was the postwar world, eager for new materials and a bright new future, that made the most of its potential. Nylon was marketed as 'Dacron' by Du Pont from

Contemporary furniture, styled for the utmost comfort and so appropriate in the modern home, may be the answer to your furnishing problem. If you are furnishing or refurnishing, why not call in to our Furniture Galleries? Here you can make your choice from the widest possible selection of furniture for every room in the house. You can be sure, too, of getting the finest value at every price level.

Deferred Terms
Harrods simple, convenient scheme enables you to furnish your home so much better—so much easier. The furniture of your choice or a composite order (comprising furniture, curtains, carpets or linens) is delivered on the first payment of 10 per cent. with 12 or 24 months to pay the balance.

Harrods

HARRODS LTD   SLOane 1234   KNIGHTSBRIDGE SW1

18

A refrigerator of 1950 adorns the kitchen at the Rose Seidler House in Wahroonga, Sydney, Australia. This house was designed by architect Harry Seidler for his parents in 1948.

1946. Even though nylon and other early synthetic fabrics did not shape well, were difficult to print, yellowed, and attracted dirt, by the mid-1950s nylon and vinyl-coated fabrics were selling well on both sides of the Atlantic. Knoll spent much of the 1950s promoting new, artificial textiles which had been developed during the war or the ensuing Cold War. In 1950, for example, they unveiled their new 'Knoll Nylon Homespun', and subsequently promoted new fabrics made from 'saran', a resin-based product invented by Dow Chemicals in 1937.

Increasingly, seat furniture began to absorb the symbols of the new, optimistic technological age. Coloured plastic balls, meant to evoke molecular construction and thus bring implications of atomic power and biochemical

advance, were incorporated into chairs as a peculiarly postwar update on the old ball-and-claw motif. In 1960 the Dane Verner Panton produced the first plastic stacking chair from a single glassfibre shell, subsequently mass-produced by Herman Miller. In the same year Panton went one further, and unveiled his 'plastic house' – which did not catch on in quite the way that his stacking chairs did. By 1970, soft furniture filled with tiny polyurethane balls 'epitomised the kind of flexible and formless objects that challenged the static formalism of modernist designs'.[21]

But not every new avenue was productive. In 1951 the British textile giant Courtaulds set up the world's largest synthetic fabric-processing plant; over-capacity in the face of a sluggish

For People like us...

THOMAS WALLIS HOLBORN CIRCUS.

Most consumers were indeed like these customers of the 1960s: looking for modern adaptations of traditional forms. Neither the suspicious-looking man nor the woman who strongly resembles actress Googie Withers, however, can bear to look at the room.

demand for synthetic furnishing fabrics by the early 1970s forced Courtaulds' parent to shed 60 per cent of the synthetic fibres workforce. (British consumers had never taken to synthetic tufted carpets, nor indeed to the latex foam that was so popular with Italian, Swedish and American designers.) By that time, too, the limits of vinyls had been recognised, and they were largely banished to kitchens, shower curtains or commercial use. By the mid-1970s most furnishing fabrics had reverted to printed cottons, still as cheap and durable as when first introduced in the eighteenth century. The rise in oil prices after the 1973 Arab-Israeli War further depressed the market in synthetic fabrics.

But the damage had already been done. In the face of the newfound popularity of synthetic fibres in the 1950s, much of Britain and America's cotton industry collapsed. Over 250 weaving mills closed in Britain between 1954 and 1957, and by 1965 both markets were importing more furnishing fabrics than they made. The post-1973 rise in the price of synthetics merely gave the *coup de grâce* to those firms which had heavily reinvested in plastics. Between 1973 and 1983 65 per cent of the UK's textile labour force was made redundant. The oil crisis of 1973 effectively 'banished plastics to the impersonal hotel or office, or to the garden or patio'.[22]

Fibreglass curtains went the same way as vinyl fabrics. Much touted during the 1960s as a wonder product, fireproof and no ironing needed, in the following decade the anti-synthetic reaction saw its

The 1960s kitchen at 20 Forthlin Road, Liverpool – Paul McCartney's house – with its prominent Belfast ceramic sink.

prompted by the need to accommodate the television set itself, and by the disappearance of the traditional fire. In northern Europe and North America, the convention had long been to make the fireplace the focus of the room, as the principal source of heat. Now, however, seat furniture began to be arranged around the TV. Fireplaces, no longer so crucial to the wellbeing of the family since the introduction of central heating or portable oil or electric heaters, were ignored, boxed in, blocked up or simply erased. This made nonsense of the disposition and proportions of older eighteenth- or nineteenth-century properties, while also ending the throughflow of air, which in turn caused damp to build up inside homes in colder and wetter climes. However, it did allow for a more flexible arrangement of the principal room; in older homes, demolition of the partition between living room and dining room or living room and kitchen was often not far behind. And it brought the colder countries into line with the warmer ones, which had been less reliant on artificial heat sources but were just as entranced by the lure of television.

As central heating systems became far more common in colder countries, radiators became thinner and less obtrusive. When central heating was employed in combination with insulating materials, sales of curtains inevitably declined – while those of Venetian blinds rose. Curtains were needed, however, when large, Modernist 'picture windows' were installed; these required full-length muslin curtains in cotton or rayon (or later, nylon), which

disappearance from the interior. Plastics did survive, however, in the kitchen. By 1960 plastic laminates (particularly Formica, which had first appeared in the 1930s) were widely used for worktops, tables and seating. Vinyl replaced linoleum or asbestos as the preferred material for kitchen floor tiles, while rubberised taffeta and gingham curtains appeared at the windows.

Throughout the Western world, and especially in America, the mass media – including, for the first time, television – was instrumental in communicating 'lifestyle models' to the public at large. Modernism certainly profited by the spread of the home interest media, helping to pass the initiative for redecoration 'from the architect and interior decorator to the consumer, who now exercised a greater degree of choice than ever before'.[23] Perhaps the biggest change to average homes by 1960, however, was

Right. Swedish Modernism at Svapparvaara, Kiruna, of 1961 by architect Ralph Erskine. Wood prevails in the 'living and dining room'.

Below. An advertisement of the late 1950s for Robbiliac paints. Its creams and greys are borrowed from Georgian antecedents, but the reproduction furniture sits very nervously in this unlikely room set. No wonder Derek refuses to come any further than the hideous, undersized window – more Postwar Housebuilder than Georgian Revival.

were often accompanied by fixed 'dress' curtains and pelmet. The chimneypiece, if it survived at all, was often merely used as one of the principal decorative focuses of the room. It could now be sited off-centre; it could, in big countries like the US and Australia, be enlarged to a size not seen since the seventeenth century.

In America, air-conditioning had become widespread during the 1920s and 1930s. Engineer Willis Carrier (1876–1950) had invented an air-conditioning system for a firm of printers in Buffalo, NY, in 1906; having been made redundant in 1918, he created his own company, which by 1930 had offices in Syracuse, NY, and Tokyo, Japan. His success in turn prompted many thousands to emigrate to the southern and western states, and prompted a new interest in what could be done inside the home, as well as outside. By the 1950s air-conditioning had revolutionised the home, enabling architects and designers to ignore the external climate as they wished.

Central heating also helped to bring an end to the admirable and eminently sensible tradition of painting walls. Wood panelling (which the British called 'matchboarding') provided good insulation. And it was now applied unpainted, in modern Scandinavian fashion. This in turn, melded with the influence of the later, pared-down interiors of Frank Lloyd Wright, led to other undecorated materials, from exposed brickwork to bare concrete, being used as wall cladding or wall finishes. As British critic Robert Harling noted, 'the widespread tendency to let the actual

structure of the walls provide the wall finish has arisen from the need to save costs ... and to provide a permanent, easily-maintained surface'.[24]

As part of this revolution in wall finishes, dado and picture rails were finally abandoned, at least in so-called 'modern' homes. However, householders who still preferred a decorated wall (and, in the absence of wall mouldings, there was now a lot of space to cover) increasingly turned back to wallpaper. For a time in the 1950s, wallpaper – whether in traditional guise or with 'contemporary' patterns – enjoyed a substantial revival. The 1951 Festival of Britain saw established wallpaper firms such as Coles and Sanderson making a big effort to break with tradition, and selling abstract papers designed by Guy Irwin and Eduardo Paolozzi. In 1956 Wall Paper Manufacturers Ltd (a combine which had amalgamated all the principal British wallpaper makers as far back as 1899) exhibited a bold new collection of papers from different designers under the collective, if rather irrelevant, name 'Palladio'. Meanwhile, French manufacturers were pioneering 'profile vinyl' papers that incorporated woven threads. By 1973 the venerable French firm of Zuber was inviting leading contemporary designers to lend their talents to wallpaper, and metallic wallpapers were being sold as a spin-off from NASA's research into protective coverings for space travel.

Floors, meanwhile, were changing even more radically. Most new trends in floor materials or decoration were towards the utilitarian: consumers sought flooring that was simple to install, easy to clean and hardwearing. Cheap new woods were now available, as were cork or vinyl tiles and tough new sealants. In the final victory of the nineteenth-century design reformers, carpets were replaced by rugs, as in America and Scandinavia the fashion spread for scattering simply patterned rugs on a polished wood floor. Linoleum fought back against plastics, but could never compete on price. Today lino is only manufactured in Europe, and is generally only made in marbled or solid colours.

By the 1960s a new generation of designers was trying anew to do away with internal partitions and turning to adaptable, multipurpose furniture. The demand for synthetic fibres – which had, as we have seen, never matched the ambitious expectations of the 1950s – was declining, while the advent of the duvet had killed off the blanket and bedcover industry.

In the face of such gloomy tidings, some designers inevitably turned to a more austere minimalism. In 1970 John Prizeman declared that designers were now 'interested in the honest expression of functional materials'. By this, he gushed, 'We are now rediscovering our emotional requirements'. Prizeman championed classless, stateless, anonymous 'international design' as the 'new solution' to social conflict. White was invariably recommended for domestic as well as commercial interiors: white 'cleans a room visually' and creates a 'wonderful calm space'. Most revealingly, this approach put the wife very much in her place. A white kitchen 'is the kind of kitchen that invites tidiness', while a blank sewing room 'is the housewife's own office'. More practically, he pointed out that simple white fittings 'give scope for changing décor over the years', assuming that 'colour is restricted to the accessories'.

Prizeman also noted that 'new synthetic materials have revolutionised furniture': 'new resilient two-way stretch materials have produced a new generation of upholstered furniture designs with shapes hardly possible to cover with traditional materials'. Synthetics offered the consumer 'unique colours', new textures and long life. Synthetic fibres had, moreover, 'made carpeting practicable in bathrooms, kitchens and other ... places'.[26]

The furnishing fabric industry had, meanwhile, been transformed. During the 1950s screen printing was mechanised, and metal mesh printing replaced silkscreen. (Many traditional cylinder printers had been relieved of their cylinders during the war, and never went back to their old methods, or indeed to their old trade at all.) The result was dramatic: screen printing, 'in conjunction with the enthusiasm for vinyl fabrics and un-upholstered plastic, wood or metal furniture, resulted in the most dramatic change interiors over the next twenty-five years: the virtual disappearance, in many homes, of non-printed fabrics'.[27]

By 1970 bright, Day-Glo colours were all in vogue. The successful moon landing of 1969 had introduced a space-age theme back into decoration. Wall hangings were popular – possibly as sound insulation in recently 'streamlined' homes. It was the era of the vinyl pouffe, acrylic velvets – such as the infamous 'Dralon' range, made by Bayer of Germany – and textured wallpaper. It was the age of plasticated tackiness.

The 1970s was also the golden age of Do-It-Yourself. The rising cost of professional labour in the postwar years encouraged homeowners to do their own repair and refurbishment work. (In Scott Oram's opinion, the most significant cause of the fad for DIY was the introduction in 1945 of the lightweight, portable electric drill.) Other factors also helped what soon became known as the Do-It-Yourself tendency to grow. Improved technology led to reduced working hours, allowing more time for home improvement. DIY was not class or gender specific: it was an occupation in which men and women could both involve themselves.

Originating in the US in the 1950s, DIY remained a largely Anglo-American phenomenon. (French householders tended, wisely, to leave well alone.) As *Practical Householder* put it in 1956, DIY was seen as 'an expression of the ingenuity, enterprise and self-reliance of the individual'. In Britain, the confusingly titled *Texas Homecare* (originally a firm founded in 1911 to make wooden fireplaces) opened its first DIY outlets in 1954, and its first warehouse in 1972; by 1990 it had over 200 outlets. In the media, DIY guru Barry Bucknell exhorted two generations of British homeowners to box in their ghastly old fireplaces and unnecessary staircase balusters, and fit suspended ceilings to hide embarrassingly old-fashioned Georgian or Victorian ceiling mouldings. Fortunately, the recommendations of Bucknell and his contemporaries – whose message was repackaged during the 1990s by TV home makeover shows, and by DIY's canonisation as the subject of Tim Allen's highly successful comedy *Home*

Improvement – always bore cost in mind. As early as 1957, *Do It Yourself* magazine was suggesting that flush doors fitted with hardboard panels would give 'the whole house a sleek well groomed appearance', and do away with the 'out of date panelled door [that] tends to provide a series of dust-collecting ledges that are a nuisance to the busy housewife'.[28] The boxing-in of 'ugly' features and the suspension of new polystyrene ceilings was a cheap but ultimately reversible solution; in the event, the avoidance of costly wholesale demolition saved many a historic feature.

Aside from helping in DIY projects, though, what exactly was the place of women in all this? As Penny Sparke has noted, Elsie de Wolfe's long and successful career had 'aided the emergence of independently-minded women wanting to take charge of their own interior worlds'. But to many architects and designers in the brave, new postwar world, women were, as we have seen, often seen as a threat, liable to drag the Trojan horse of traditional ornament into the midst of the Modernist camp. As early as 1944, the designer T.H. Robsjohn-Gibbings, in an article glibly entitled 'Goodbye Mr Chippendale', squarely blamed de Wolfe and her monstrous regiment for any backsliding in postwar design: 'if it was the Chicago World's Fair that held American architecture back fifty years, it was [Elsie de Wolfe] who did the same for American furniture design'.[29]

In the 1950s, the female-dominated trade of interior decoration was submerged by the male profession of 'interior design', which looked more

British TV's Barry Bucknell (1912–2003), who was responsible for helping popularise the DIY craze in the 1960s. His television series of the 1950s *Do It Yourself* attracted nearly seven million viewers, and was followed by *Bucknell's House* in 1962.

to the more lucrative markets of retail and office design than to the demands of the humble home. As Anne Massey has pointed out, in the Museum of Modern Art's 1947 exhibition 'Modern Rooms of the Last Fifty Years' all the room sets were designed by architects, and were mostly of privately commissioned homes or exhibition sets.[30]

Postwar Modernism was predominantly functional and masculine, and guided not by female interior decorators or homemakers but male professionals. Fashion – and humour – had no place in the serious world of standardised design. As Hugh Casson (who can himself be blamed for introducing the term 'interior architect' while teaching at the Royal College of Art during the 1950s) wrote in 1967, 'many architects refuse to believe that such a thing as interior design exists at all. Some place it on a par with the art of the milliner or pastry cook'.[31] As interior design became more professionalised, so women became marginalised. In 1953 the Incorporated Institute of British Decorators added 'and Interior Designers' to their title; in 1976 they dropped the word 'Decorator' entirely.

The 1960s also saw the promotion of 'name' designers rather than the products of anonymous corporations. As Americans and Western Europeans travelled more, the use of foreign scenes and motifs in fabrics and wallpapers increased, together with clichés such as 'café-style' metal furniture and gingham tablecloths.

The retailer who best exploited these trends was Terence Conran. Conran's Habitat store was being planned in 1963 as a retail outlet not just for furniture but for a wide range of home goods. The white-walled and tiled interior was deliberately simple and 'stark to the point of eccentricity by the standards of the day'.[32] His use of light-coloured natural woods was in huge contrast to the majority of 'teak-finish' furniture then available. And his 'Modernism lite' formula proved a huge success: Habitat Mail Order was launched in 1969, and outlets in Paris and New York opened in 1973 and 1977.[33] Conran was never a slave to Modernism, or any other style, and always kept abreast of trends: he understood just how much 'Design' consumers could tolerate. By the mid-1970s, for example, Habitat was selling Victoriana, and by the 1980s it was adopting a pseudo-Provençal air. Eclecticism was fashionable again.

Opposite. East Germany's bizarre take on the 1970s: historical references sit uneasily in a bleak Modernist box spotted with undersized pictures. The whole is fractured rather than harmonised by the use of dazzling titanium white.

1. Shortly after VE Day in 1945, the journalist Tom Pocock was sent to cover a Savoy lunch at which Labour minister Ernest Bevin addressed the Institute of Wallpaper Manufacturers with these words. See Maureen Waller, *London 1945* (2004), 290. 2. Lesley Jackson, 'Mix and Match Colour Schemes', in Joanna Banham (ed.), *Encyclopaedia of Interior Design* (1997), vol. 2, 824. 3. Anne Massey, *Interior Design of the Twentieth Century* (1990), 159. 4. Anne Bony, *Furniture and Interiors of the 1940s* (2003), 32; Massey, *Interior Design of the Twentieth Century*, 151. 5. Penny Sparke, *Italian Design* (1988), 11. 6. Penny Sparke, 'The Furniture Retailer as Taste-Maker, in Penny Sparke (ed.), *Did Britain Make It? British Design in Context 1946–86* (1986), 132. 7. Mary Schoeser, '"Good Design and Good Business": A Survey of the Changes in the British Textile Industry 1946–86', in Sparke, *Did Britain Make It?*, 71; Massey, *Interior Design of the Twentieth Century*, 160. 8. Stephen Calloway, *Twentieth-Century Decoration* (1988), 226. 9. Ibid., 286. 10. Ibid., 288, 327. 11. Mary Schoeser and Celia Rufey, *English and American Textiles from 1790 to the Present* (1989), 202, 204. 12. Sparke, *Did Britain Make It?*, 201. 13. Lesley Jackson, *Contemporary* (1994), 157. 14. Cherie and Kenneth Fehrman, *Postwar Interior Design 1945–60* (1987), 24. 15. Jackson, *Contemporary*, 73. 16. Ibid.; Penny Sparke, *As Long As It's Pink – The Sexual Politics of Taste* (1995), 177. 17. Quoted in Jackson, *Contemporary*, 91. 18. Sparke, *As Long As It's Pink*, 85–6. 19. See Jackson, *Contemporary*, 128, 133. 20. Ibid., 134. 21. Penny Sparke, *An Introduction to Design and Culture* (2004), 119. 22. Schoeser and Rufey, *English and American Textiles from 1790 to the Present*, 204, 213; Susan Hoyal, 'Plastics', in Banham (ed.), *Encyclopaedia of Interior Design*, vol. 2, 974. 23. Massey, *Interior Design of the Twentieth Century*, 163. 24. Quoted in Jackson, *Contemporary*, 108. 25. John Prizeman, *Interiors of European Homes* (1970), 12, 24, 55–6, 60, 66. 26. Ibid., 85–6. 27. Schoeser and Rufey, *English and American Textiles from 1790 to the Present*, 206. 28. Scott Oram, 'DIY', in Banham (ed.), *Encyclopaedia of Interior Design*, vol. 1, 381. 29. Penny Sparke, *Elsie de Wolfe* (2005), 23. 30. Massey, *Interior Design of the Twentieth Century*, 148. 31. Ibid., 161. 32. Barty Philips, *Conran and the Habitat Story* (1984), 28, 119. 33. Craig Allen, 'Conran', in Banham (ed.), *Encyclopaedia of Interior Design*, vol. 1, 305.

Manderley bore witness to our presence. The little heap of library books marked ready to return, and the discarded copy of *The Times*. Ash-trays, with a stub of cigarette; cushions, with the imprint of our heads upon them, lolling in the chairs; the charred embers of our log fires still smouldering against the morning.

(Daphne du Maurier, *Rebecca*, 1938)

Opposite. The look of the Sixties: traditional furniture in a bright modern setting at the Vanna Venturi House of 1964 in Philadelphia, USA, by architect Robert Venturi for his mother.

Right. Postwar Modernism domesticised: 'Eames' seat furniture sits uncomfortably amongst deep-buttoned revivalist sofas in a Habitat catalogue of the early 1970s. The appearance of the model – complete with obligatory tanktop, flares and moustache – gives an unmistakable clue as to the period.

Despite what the Modern Movement preached and the design press was keen to infer, historical styles were still massively popular in countless postwar homes. Already by the mid-1950s many European and American consumers were turning back from the utilitarian designs produced during and after the war in favour of historic reproductions. The British Council of Industrial Design was horrified, citing a 'betrayal of their ideals'. Journalist Dorothy Meade blamed the gullible working classes and high-pressure salesmanship, 'seen at its worst in new, isolated housing estates where families depend mainly on mail order catalogues and traveling salesmen for their choice of furnishings'. Designer Gordon Russell blamed women: whether they were unduly influenced by male salesmen or their mothers, or whether men were buying repro items to impress them, 'well-designed contemporary furniture does not get much of a look-in'.[1]

In Britain and America – and, to some extent, continental Europe – it was the Georgian styles of eighteenth-century England to which more conservative homeowners resolutely clung. Modernist designers, too, were not averse to praising the homes of Georgian Britain, based as they were on a rigid system of mathematical proportion which anticipated the inflexible prescriptions of the Modernists themselves.

Historic revivals or adaptations proved a lifeline for traditional decorating firms. From 1958 Sandersons, who had taken over the bankrupt Morris & Company in 1940, began to sell Morris wallpaper designs – adapted for machine printing (which must have had Morris turning in his grave) – to exploit the growing interest in Victorian revival. This prompted other long-established firms, or their heirs, to raid their own archives for historic designs they could adapt. In 1955 Manchester's Colour, Design and Style Centre found itself exhibiting traditional chintzes; the Victoria and Albert Museum's exhibition on cotton printing of 1960 gave the chintz revival another shot in the arm.

Unsurprisingly, the further away such revivalism got from the Modernist aesthetic, the more conceptions or reinventions of the Georgian era were inextricably linked with notions of class and gender. The principal arbiters of 'taste' in fashionable interiors of the eighteenth century were, as in 1945, stereotypically male. The advice of that doyenne of early interior decorators, Elsie de Wolfe, that in order to reach the nirvana of 'Good Taste' and thus secure and demonstrate our social status, 'we

Windsor chairs and chintz curtains humanise a 'contemporary' interior of the mid-1950s. Eclecticism triumphs over dogma.

are better safe if we take our problems to male architects',[2] applied just as much to the creation or adaptation of 'Georgian' rooms in the second half of the twentieth century as it did to de Wolfe's elegant Edwardian interiors.

The typically romanticised view of a stable, unchanging Georgian society, in which everyone knew their place and waited to receive advice on design and ornament from the enlightened few (who were themselves either aristocrats or dependent on aristocratic patronage), had little foundation in fact. But it does perhaps explain why 'Georgian taste' became the bedrock for the hugely successful 'Country House Style' – that curiously antiseptic homage to 'the age of chintz'[3] – which became so prevalent in larger British and American homes during the postwar era. Apologists for this style have been quick to

acknowledge the class-based appeal of a notional aesthetic which originates from 'the romantic longing for the ennobling [Georgian] past', and which aims at 'creating a level of comfort suggested by long-established ownership'. The adoption of a class-charged aesthetic in order to help reinvent or clothe modern suburban homes, however, is on the face of it a less obvious progression. Even in these contexts 'Georgian' taste invariably signals social aspiration and a desire for exclusivity. Yet it did not 'really represent the English Country House'; rather it was 'a reinterpretation of something which was itself a fabrication'.[4]

Much of the success of the Country House Style can be traced to the postwar influence of one particular, transatlantic decorating firm: Colefax and Fowler. Lady Sibyl Colefax turned to decoration at the age of fifty-five out of financial necessity, in the wake of the 1929 Stock Market crash. In 1933 she began to decorate for her aristocratic friends; the following year she founded Colefax and Company. Using Robert Adam's bravura, synthesised Neoclassicism and the confident colours and rectilinear forms of the Regency era as her touchstones, she had made a significant impact by the end of the 1930s. In 1938 she hired decorator John Fowler as her partner; however, after the Second World War she retired and gratefully sold her business to Lady Astor's niece, Nancy Lancaster.

Lancaster (1897–1994) was a wealthy Virginian who had settled in England in 1915 and bought the interior decoration firm from Lady Colefax in the late 1940s. Her eclectic yet fundamentally Georgian style was perfected at Ditchley,

Oxfordshire, her home from 1933 to 1947. Here the emphasis was firmly on comfort: soft furnishings predominated. It was the weight given to comfort and convenience that ensured the style's popularity in both North America and Northern Europe.

The third member of this revivalist Holy Trinity, John Fowler (1906–77), developed his personal approach to interiors while working at London's Peter Jones department store from 1931. During the ensuing decade he firmly eschewed the contemporary palette of browns and creams ('those porridge tones that were so much in favour'), popularised toile de Jouy furnishing fabrics, and – perhaps less helpfully – initiated a lifelong obsession with Marie Antoinette.[5] John Fowler's restorations of National Trust properties

Sibyl Colefax's luxurious, unashamedly revivalist drawing room in Lord North Street, London, in a photo taken just after the Second World War.

during the 1960s were certainly not archaeological: 'underpinned by a knowledge of the past but not in thrall to it', his schemes have recently been welcomed as 'the victory of imagination over scholarship' (as if this was a battle that needed to be won).[6] As museologist Tim Knox has noted, Fowler's paint redecoration schemes 'may well have made them look far more presentable, but did nothing for their individuality or family atmosphere'. Relying on paint scrapes rather than scientific sections in attempting to determine the nature of historic colour schemes, his historical evocations were often simply wrong. In addition, his practice of applying thin glazes to painted walls was inappropriate for historic finishes, and belongs more to the world of furniture. As eminent paint historian Patrick Baty has written, Fowler's colour choices were 'based on whimsy and taste alone … not on historical precedent'.[7] Fowler always avowed that he was a decorator, not a historian. However, his schemes were used by the Trust, and by many others, to imply historical pedigree and authenticity.

In using furnishing fabrics, Fowler followed very much in the footsteps of Elsie de Wolfe. He was a great advocate of chintz, and his use of the fabric in great houses during the 1950s and 1960s in turn helped to spark its general revival during the 1970s. His use of decorating techniques to create an artificially 'distressed' look for wall finishes also helped engender (posthumously, in his case) the paint effect revolution of the 1980s. His fabric-based style was defined by

A Walpamur (Wallpaper Manufacturers' Company) paint advertisement from the 1950s, showing a distinctly Mediterranean interior combining traditional features

his enthusiasm for old English styles – notably Regency and, later, Baroque – and he cheerfully mixed 'large-scale floral designs with sprig patterns, checks and stripes' and hung 'generously swagged pelmets … from exaggeratedly large poles'.[8]

Colefax and Fowler's practice expanded rapidly on the east coast of America in the 1950s. Here their lush interiors deliberately omitted the faded fabrics and wishy-washy colours of old English interiors, and always accommodated the latest technology. American clients demanded a more polished look for their homes that spoke more clearly of conspicuous consumption, necessitating 'a level of finish and sparkle that [was] much more studied than in Britain'. As historian Claire Brisby has noted, 'The novelty of Colefax and Fowler's approach lay in their ability to enhance period features'.[9]

By the end of the 1980s Colefax and Fowler stood at the pinnacle of success. The company had floated on the London Stock Exchange, opened offices in New York, Paris and Sydney, and bought emerging rivals such as the decorating business of Jane Churchill and Kingcome sofas. More importantly for the middle-class interior, their promotion of watered-down Georgian motifs, colours and forms, cleverly adapted to twentieth-century taste and technology, meant that during

the 1980s chintz and sprig designs were now widely available from firms which in 1945 would have not dared to contemplate reworking the decorative styles of the eighteenth century.

The 'Georgian style' that Colefax and Fowler promoted was quintessentially English. 'Georgian' as a label instantly conjured up a world which is not only aristocratic and patriarchal, but was fundamentally English – rather than holistically British. This surely accounts for the huge success of the English Country House decorative style. Drawn primarily from eighteenth-century inspirations, the 'innate taste and flair' which it allegedly embodies – extracted from 'lifestyle qualities ... rather than visual characteristics' – created an appealing (if largely mythical) world of chintz,

John Fowler in the 1960s: the Drawing Room of a London apartment.

An overtly historicist American room set by Brunschwig and Fils of the mid-1980s. The desire to display as many 'colonial' floral and striped patterns as possible has perhaps made the room a little unreadable.

swags and bows, all rooted in ill-defined, Austenesque nostalgia. The Georgian period as evoked by Colefax and Fowler, Laura Ashley and their rivals was – and is – characterised by the presumptions of immutable taste, of certainty, of social immobility, and of apparent simplicity. The resulting synthesis of old and new was comfortable, unthreatening, and just sufficiently academic so as to reassure consumers as to its 'authenticity'.

The transatlantic appeal of this aesthetic was always particularly strong – largely since, as one scholar has recently noted, 'this fabricated ideal of Englishness was ... inherently American', a 'romantic longing for an ennobling past'.[10] Louise Ward has noted the difference between genuine, cluttered English country houses and 'the carefully orchestrated look' created by Colefax and Fowler: the former 'suggests a life lived spontaneously', the latter was artfully created to appeal to a

North American audience which did not care for faded beauty. As the aspirational magazine *World of Interiors* noted in 1988, 'True clutter is very different from those artfully arranged tablescapes ... aimed to give an instant lived-in look'. The result was 'the English Country House as it might have been but never was'.[11] David Lowenthal has suggested that this Brigadoon-like preference for the new and the utilitarian, even when applied to historical styles, fits well with the American psyche: 'Americans seem reluctant to allow anything to decay: old things are acceptable only as long as they remain visibly and functionally fit.' [12]

This Americanised 'English Country House' look was in turn exported back to Europe, where it greatly encouraged the manufacturers of middle-range and mass-market goods towards 'Georgian', 'Victorian' and 'Edwardian' styles. During the 1980s 'the understated appearance of

time-worn elegance' in traditionally decorated homes was replaced by 'a more polished version in which characteristic objects and decorative treatments were accentuated'. In this fictional England, there was no place for dog hairs, frayed borders or faded colours; what was sought was a reflection of lifestyle and social aspiration, 'an overall mood that [was] informed and relaxed'.[13]

The firm that successfully reinterpreted, for a worldwide audience, the grand, historically sourced decorative schemes devised by the heirs of Elsie de Wolfe was Laura Ashley. Bernard and Laura Ashley (1925–85) established a company selling silkscreen-printed fabrics in 1953. (Originally named Ashley Mountney, husband Bernard soon realised its wares would be more marketable using just his wife's full married name.) Clothes came later, in 1966; six years after that they introduced wallpapers, using the small-scale, historic designs previously used for dress fabrics. In 1969 the Ashleys opened their first London shop, and in 1974 a similar store in Paris. Inspired by Laura Ashley's success, countless imitators also set up shop in Britain, France and North America during the 1970s.

Laura Ashley's rustic designs were based loosely on Liberty patterns, on Colefax and Fowler's bowdlerised Georgian adaptations, on the ever-popular French 'toile' copperplate patterns, and on folk sources such as patchwork quilts. The result was a homely, vaguely historical cottage style that evoked times past but did not mirror them. Very few of its designs, for example, were genuine historic

Above. French Country House style: Neoclassical mouldings, *'ancien régime'* chairs and toile de jouy fabrics adorn what is still an unmistakably late twentieth-century interior in Normandy.

Below. A Laura Ashley interior at the height of the retro boom of the Thatcher-Reagan years. The wallpaper design is remodelled after a design by the legendary late eighteenth-century French master paper-maker, Réveillon.

reproductions; this more academic trade was left to the niche manufacturers. Laura Ashley colours evoked the old vegetable dyes used by the Georgians and revived by William Morris. Their names – muddy blues and dusty pinks – suggested an idyllic, pre-industrial countryside.

In 1987 the authors of *Laura Ashley* Style acknowledged that 'it was ... the lifestyle qualities of this enduring decorative tradition, rather than its visual characteristics, that were presented to the consumer'.[14] The firm's winning synthesis of lifestyle qualities, historical allusion and down-to-earth practicality certainly powered the Country House style so prevalent in the West from the mid-1970s. In the US, too, the Laura Ashley/English Country House Style 'look' intermingled with a renewed interest in American regional vernacular and that perennial favourite, Stickley's 'Mission Style'. By the mid-1970s a more historically minded American market abandoned the big, bold fabric motifs of the 1960s in favour of small-scale historic designs. The export of English reproduction chintzes to America was thriving as firms such as New York's Brunschwig and Fils began to specialise in archive reproductions of fabrics and wallpapers. Festoon curtains made from bold Georgian chintzes became de rigueur astride even the most unlikely of windows by the middle 1980s.

Buoyed by success, Laura Ashley's range of fabrics was expanded. In 1980 the firm launched its 'Decorator Collection', based partly on motifs from Réveillon wallpapers, toiles de Jouy and other eighteenth-century papers and fabrics. 'Not only did the prints become

more sophisticated, [but] interiors were also created based on contemporary [i.e. eighteenth-century] sources' – although these prints or fabrics were invariably recoloured for the modern market. However, the company ultimately overreached itself. The introduction of new product ranges such as kitchenware and door fittings, particularly after Laura Ashley's sudden death in 1985, diluted the illusion of artisan craftsmanship, and the 1990s proved a difficult time for the ambitious chain. In 1998 it was rescued by the conglomerate MUI Asia, who now aim 'to focus on modernising the brand whilst remaining true to Laura Ashley's brand values'.[15]

The Georgian era was not the only historic period to be raided for revivalist inspiration. The 'Regency Revival' of postwar Britain – 'one of the first styles to be reduced to the level of a series of visual key symbols' – had given way to a Victorian Revival by the 1960s.[16] In 1958 the Victorian Society was founded in Britain to campaign for the preservation of Victorian architecture and interiors, and 'Victoriana' became all the rage in Britain and America, with genuine nineteenth-century patterns often being adapted in size and colour to suit the blowsy and garish preferences of the 1960s.

Art Nouveau underwent a revival in Europe after the Aubrey Beardsley exhibition at the Victoria and Albert Museum in London, much to Liberty's delight. Yet the ersatz Victoriana preferred by homeowners of the 1980s was not necessarily to the taste of historians. Looking back from the vantage point of the late 1980s, Charlotte Gere

Left. The Arts and Crafts inspiration of these 'Mission Style' pieces is very evident in this contemporary furniture by American designers Strictly Wood Furniture Company.

Opposite. Historic Lyon silk patterns on offer in a Paris showroom in 2005. The 1980s' passion for heritage approximations has metamorphosed into an interest in genuinely academic authenticity.

observed that 'The recreated Victorian interior favoured today ... usually consists of a rather tasteless version of a middle-class urban scheme, all voluminous drapery, bobble edgings and crowded, over-stuffed furniture, garnished with some coarse pottery ornaments and stuffed birds in a glass case', while also noting that 'The brilliance of the original [Victorian] colours revealed by recent research have [sic] come as a not altogether pleasant surprise to many admirers of the period'.[17]

The turning-point for historicism, when average homeowners began to turn away from the waning certainties of Modernism to the reassurance of past idioms, came in the mid-1970s. Many factors have been suggested for the loss of confidence in Modernist design. In Britain, the collapse of the Ronan Point flats in 1968 'tragically signalled the failure of the industrialized, formula-designed house'.[18] In America, the 1972 demolition of the postwar Pruitt-Igoe housing project in St

Louis, Missouri, was similarly seen as a harbinger of doom for the utopian ideals of the Modern Movement.

Prompted by the faltering pace of Modernism, a new interest in architectural conservation spread across the West. In Britain, France and America in the late 1960s and early 1970s, the rescue from demolition and subsequent refurbishment of key historic urban landmarks – notably the massive railway termini of St Pancras, Orsay and Grand Central[19] – fuelled public involvement in conservation and prompted a general reappraisal of the worth of historic buildings. Events such as the highly influential 1974 exhibition at London's Victoria and Albert Museum, 'The Destruction of the English Country House', curated by the formidable trio of Roy Strong, John Harris and Marcus Binney, also helped to spread the growing appeal of the Country House

Style, as well as the development of the conservation movement.

The Postmodernism of the 1980s sought to harness this new interest in historicism. Postmodern designers rejected the monochrome interiors of Modernism for subtle secondary colours, ignored since the Second World War in favour of more strident, assertive primary hues. Ice cream tones were preferred inside and out. So-called 'Shaker' colours and 'Shaker' furniture were suddenly in vogue – despite the slender historic basis for most of these designs.

The popularity of the 'Shaker' style encapsulates the innate contradictions of so many interiors of the 1980s and 1990s, as manufacturers cheerfully exploited a term which was highly evocative of simple craft, and which resonated with Arts and Crafts idealism. The English mystic Anna Lee had left Britain's shores in 1774 to found

Genuinely old or recently recreated? Historically inspired 'Shaker style colour palette' finishes – 'London Stone and Old White' – in a kitchen set of the 1990s (left); and the real thing (right): a kitchen interior from Hancock Shaker Village in Massachusetts.

her version of Quakerism in what were still (just) then the American colonies. The furnishings that were subsequently made for her Shaker communities (which by 1860 boasted over 6,000 members) were subsequently governed by the Shakers' all-embracing Millennial Laws of 1823. The Shaker mantra, 'A place for everything and everything in its place', was hugely popular in an era which tried to convince itself that its fundamental materialism was only a veneer. It also exploited the public's hankering for a more Eastlakeian austerity. The Millennial Laws, 'invented to meet the needs of cleanliness and order', helpfully declared that 'Beadings, mouldings and cornices, which are merely for fancy, may not be made by believers'. The Shaker Revival sought to exploit this moral, minimalist ethic for a more confused age, 'ironically manufacturing the very forms that the rise of industrial America had eradicated'.[20]

The simplicity and standardisation of Shaker furniture was highly appealing to the postwar world: an aesthetic 'that substituted function and simple beauty for applied ornamentation and historical references'[21] would always be attractive to a materialistic society which yearned for the over-simplified certainties of the Arts and Crafts and Modern movements. In the hands of the mass-manufacturers, however, most of the Shakers' noble ideals were predictably lost. The promotion of 'Shaker' paint colours in the 1980s had little base in Shaker practice: the genuine Shaker communities of the eighteenth and

nineteenth centuries had largely used only white paint in their interiors, relieved by beige or natural wood, and had used paint as sparingly as possible. Meanwhile, the number of genuine Shakers in America now barely reached double figures.

In Britain and America in the 1980s, design conservatives looked to the Georgian age for inspiration and reassurance. The furniture of David Linley and the decorative treatments of Timney Fowler, for example, were both based on Neoclassical imagery. Postmodernism gave the eighteenth century a new respectability, albeit in a very mangled and ironic guise. The 1980s saw the phoenix-like revival of the fortunes of interior decorators, the reappearance of 'traditional' paints (although often with little genuine relationship to eighteenth-century products), and the newfound popularity

Georgian homage: an austerely tasteful 'Palladian style' design by David Linley of the mid-1980s.

Left: A classic Timney Fowler interior of the 1980s. The work of this British firm, which specialised in adapting Neoclassical motifs and reproducing them in a limited palette, grounded in black and white, was hugely successful in France and the US.

Opposite. Historical references – and a Chesterfield sofa – dominate this Milan apartment of the 1990s by Italian designer Barnaba Fornasetti.

of finishes meant to evoke old treatments or methods of application, such as marbling, stencilling and rag-rolling. Even though many of the results said more about the 'me' decade than about

the Georgian period they were trying to evoke, the message was clear: homeowners had lost faith in the machine ethic and were trying to turn the clock back to a more dependable and comforting age.

1. Penny Sparke, *As Long As It's Pink – The Sexual Politics of Taste* (1995), 192–3. 2. Elsie de Wolfe, *The House in Good Taste* (1913), 6. 3. Ibid, 94. Penny Sparke has noted that de Wolfe 'was among the first practitioners in the modern era to understand the close relationship between taste and social status' (Penny Sparke, *An Introduction to Design and Culture* [2004], 64). 4. Chester Jones, *Colefax and Fowler* (1989), 215, 217; Louise Ward, 'Chintz, Swags and Bows: The Myth of English Country House Style 1930–90', in Susie McKellar and Penny Sparke (eds.), *Interior Design and Identity* (2004), 95. 5. Jones, *Colefax and Fowler*, 216, 18, 21 6. Ward, 'Chintz, Swags and Bows', 98; Jones, *Colefax and Fowler*, 29. 7. Tim Knox and Patrick Baty in Helen Hughes (ed.), *John Fowler* (2005), 18, 35. 8. Claire Brisby, 'Colefax & Fowler', in Joanna Banham (ed.), *Encyclopaedia of Interior Design* (1997), vol. 1, 297. 9. Jones, *Colefax and Fowler*, 216–17; Brisby, 'Colefax & Fowler', 297. 10. Ward, 'Chintz, Swags and Bows', 110, 215. 11. Ibid., 102, 104, 108, 110. 12. David Lowenthal, *The Past is a Foreign Country* (1985), 145. 13. Stephen Calloway, *Twentieth-Century Decoration* (1988), 364; Ward, 'Chintz, Swags and Bows', 105; Jones, *Colefax and Fowler*, 112. 14. Ward, 'Chintz, Swags and Bows', 107. 15. Clare Taylor, 'Laura Ashley', in Banham (ed.), *Encyclopaedia of Interior Design*, vol. 1, 172. 16. Calloway, *Twentieth-Century Decoration*, 322. 17. Charlotte Gere, *Nineteenth-Century Decoration* (1989), 40, 45. 18. Paul Oliver, Ian Davis and Ian Bentley, *Dunroamin* (1981), 21. 19. See Steven Parissien, *Station to Station* (1997). 20. Gere, *Nineteenth-Century Decoration*, 128; David Sokol, 'Shaker Design', in Banham (ed.), *Encyclopaedia of Interior Design*, vol. 2, 1157. 21. Sokol, 'Shaker Design', 1159.

We all expect a great deal from our decoration these days, as though it really is going to make us better people.

(Kevin McCloud, 2007)

Opposite. Bathroom in an eco-designed family house in Munich by Gassner & Zarecky Architects (2001). Hidden, under-floor pipework.

Right. The triumph of convenience consumerism: IKEA flatpack furniture. This is the 2007 'GORM' range, intended 'to create storage areas and optimize space'.

The dilution of the Modernist ethic in the West in the 1970s laid the foundations for the cheerful eclecticism of the last two decades of the twentieth century. In many ways the design parameters of the 1980s recalled those of the 1830s: an increasingly confident and wealthy middle class, bent on conspicuous consumption and ostentatious displays of status and success; a rejection of stylistic dogma and prescription; and the assumption of a magpie-like attitude to disposing and decorating the home, a strategy which would have horrified the design purists of thirty years before.

The result was homes which combined elements of every style and idiom. Wooden-faced 'country' or 'Shaker' kitchen units, whose stylistic origins lay in the back-to-basics mentality of the Design Reformers of the nineteenth century, were juxtaposed with unapologetically functional cookers and ever-larger refrigerators. (In many middle-class Western homes by the 1990s, the degree of sophistication or aspiration of the household could be judged not by the ostentation of the living room nor the type of car in the driveway but by the size and functionality of the refrigerator.) In living rooms, floors of old, bare wooden boards in the Arts and Crafts manner supported banks of flat-pack shelving, hi-tech audio-visual technology and arrays of seat furniture which merrily juxtaposed Modernist icons of the 1920s with unapologetically comfortable, well-upholstered sofas whose design and purpose harked back to the deep-buttoned forms of the 1850s. Upstairs, bathrooms finished in impeccably functional ceramic, steel and glass led into bedrooms which looked

Simple, comfortable eclecticism: 'Shaker-style' kitchen units and vaguely revivalist wooden chairs adorn an English kitchen of the turn of the twenty-first century.

as it they had been master-planned by William Morris himself, with brass or iron beds, pine furniture, rugs, bare boards and chintz fabrics. The principal difference between the bedroom of the 1980s and that of the 1880s is that, at least in Europe, the former has been decreasing in size as the average family has got smaller.

Fiercely defending what they perceived as the moral high ground, the high priests of the Modern Movement had by the early 1980s enthusiastically swapped concrete and wood for steel and glass. In contrast to the Modernist gurus of the 1920s, designers now sought to celebrate technology by using a range of standard, industrially produced parts to celebrate the achievements of technology. Taking their cue from the generation of 'Hi-Tech' architects led by Renzo Piano (b.1937), Richard

Rogers (b.1933) and Norman Foster (b.1935), interior designers found their salvation in the clean lines of cold steel and structural glass. However, this design approach was, owing to its high build cost, largely limited to commercial uses. Far more appealing in terms of the everyday home was the emerging philosophy of the Postmodern movement. In 1966 the American architect Robert Venturi (b.1925) first enunciated his revolutionary design theories in his book *Complexity and Contradiction in Architecture*. He discarded the Modernists' apparent rejection of historical styles and issued a call for stylistic tolerance and plurality, an approach which, he convincingly argued, put human beings, rather than the ethic of the machine, back at the heart of interior design. Venturi and his followers happily combined Modernist idioms and

By 1990 many householders were happy to juxtapose hi-tech minimalism in their bathrooms with something more cheerfully eclectic in the principal public rooms. The New York bathroom on the left is by Hariri & Hariri Architects; the chairs on the right are Venturi's celebrated, tongue-in-cheek 'Chippendale' design of 1985.

forms with those of the eighteenth and nineteenth centuries. Venturi's famous 'Chippendale' chair, designed for Knoll in New York and first produced in 1978, fused the plywood technology of Thonet, the springtime palettes of Larsson and the Neoclassical inspiration of Adam and Chippendale to produce a design that was both lighthearted and stoutly functional. In a similar vein, since 1990 Frank Gehry (b.1929) has been making bentwood furniture for the Knoll Group, starting with the immensely strong yet remarkably comfortable 'Powerplay chair' and other designs based on Thonet's timeless material, laminated wood.[1]

Postmodernism was about celebrating the seemingly contradictory, melding the past with the present and

synthesizing humour with function. Its lessons were imbibed by neo-Modernists such as the Milan-based 'Memphis' group of designers: from 1981 these Italian designers, led by Ettore Sottsass (b.1917), began to eschew the stern, unbending machine ethic of the Modernist tradition in favour of playfulness, eclecticism and cheerful colour. References to Ancient Rome jostled with knowing nods to Le Corbusier and Breuer and blithe homage to the precepts of the Arts and Crafts pioneers. Philippe Starck (b.1949) used the basic materials of Modernist furniture – metal, glass and plastic – to create unexpected effects and forms which, like those of the Memphis group, gleefully compounded whimsy and historical scholarship to create strikingly original objects. Although best known as an industrial designer, Starck's highly successful commercial interiors exerted a strong influence on the decorators and designers of the 1990s.

The eclectic historicism of Postmodernism led inexorably to the intellectual bravura of Deconstructivism. By 1990 leading designers, inspired by the Deconstructivist agenda of Philip Johnson and Mark Wigley's groundbreaking 1988 exhibition of the same name at the Museum of Modern Art in New York, Israeli designer Ron Arad (b.1951) – who deliberately uses salvaged materials, together with prescient images of decay and collapse, to construct his furniture and sculpture – and the work of American architects Peter Eisenmann (b.1932) and Frank Gehry, were breaking familiar interior elements into their component parts in order to stress

Left. Superman cheerfully guards these inviting, primary-coloured chairs from Sottsass's 'Eastside Lounge' collection of the late 1990s for Knoll Studio. Mind your head when standing up, though.

Right. Sottsass's commercially influenced 'Mandarin' chairs.

Below. Neoclassical elegance permeates Philip Johnson's New York apartment.

their unique role and meaning. While opportunities to apply this philosophy to the average home were initially minimal, a decade later the incorporation of whimsically deconstructed storage units or suites of seat furniture were becoming increasingly common in even the most modest of interiors.

So, as we proceed further into the twenty-first century, what is the next trend in Western interior design? Gazing into the crystal ball is always fun, but any magisterial judgements made as a result are always liable to date very quickly. However, there are a number of exciting developments that can be discerned in current interiors, which give us both hope and direction for the future.

Perhaps the most interesting feature of Western interiors today is the increasing trend towards celebrating a cheerful and confident eclecticism. As the grip of Modernism has weakened, so the average interior has become more diverse and, most importantly, more inclusive. The democratisation of taste that mass-production brings has encouraged householders to have more diverse approaches to the challenges of everyday interiors. These have, as a result, also become less gendered – a development which may return us, in some sense, to the status quo of the 1850s.

Modern eclecticism is inevitably allied – as everything now is – to the technological triumphalism of hi-tech design, which has erased traditional barriers between architecture and   . design and fostered a more accessible and unashamedly commercial approach to furniture and fittings. It is also indissolubly linked with the media.

Fêted by television and the press, the designer or decorator has become a hero and, in some cases, a household word. Auction houses have played their part, too, in celebrating the cult of the named designer. Designer labels, sometimes of bewildering provenance, are used to sell house fittings, wall finishes and ceramics as well as clothes and perfumes. Emboldened by the flood of information available via the internet and the television, householders have become bolder and more independent – and less willing to be told what is right and what is good for them. They have also become less guilty about indulging in conspicuous consumption and display. It is surely no coincidence that the last decades of the twentieth century witnessed the wholesale removal of net curtains from middle-class windows, not merely because nets tended to attract dust, but also because they obstructed the contents of the home from admiring view.

The ascetic, minimalist straitjacket of the Modern movement has seemingly been discarded. As Stephen Calloway has noted, 'the heroic years of the Modern movement [now] have a certain period charm'.[2] As Calloway predicted, early, domestic Modernism is now viewed as just one of many styles of the preceding century, its classic tubular steel chairs being reproduced for home use just as Chippendale and Sheraton designs were after 1862. Wit, humour and, reassuringly, even romance have been allowed back into the interior; these developments have in turn enabled ornament to resurface once more. The individual who perhaps best epitomises

Unashamedly contemporary sofas confront each other across the tastefully restrained cream-and-beige living room of a Rococo-style Parisian apartment by Andrée Putman. The precepts of Elsie de Wolff are still going strong after almost a century.

this encouraging trend is the French designer Andrée Putman (b.1925), whose lavish interiors readily combine Rococo boiseries, postmodern seat furniture and hi-tech lighting.

Some developments, though, have been firmly ahistorical. By 2000 flat-pack furniture dominated the economy end of the market, exemplified by the worldwide success of the Swedish chain IKEA (which in 1993 acquired Habitat). Many of IKEA's bestselling products are, interestingly, actually borrowed from Danish postwar designs, such as the adjustable shelving originally introduced by Danes Grethe Meyer and Borge Mogensen as 'Boliogens Byggeshabe' in 1954, and the now-ubiquitous pleated paper lampshade, first devised for the Danish firm Klint in 1947.

Surely the most blatant expression of the new freedom to dispose interiors with more individual confidence has been that homes are beginning to embrace colour for the first time since the crisis of manufacture in the mid-nineteenth century. This does not just mean the primary colours to which the Modernists were converted in the 1950s, nor the DayGlo hues beloved of the 1960s and 1970s. Modern decorating colours can be complex secondary or tertiary hues, based not just on technological potential but, significantly, also on historical precedent. This interest in historic colour schemes dates from the reinvention of Colonial Williamsburg, Virginia, in the 1920s, but has been given a gloss of spurious authenticity as present-day homeowners seek to validate their 'heritage' kitchens. Even unambiguously modern kitchens and bathrooms now make use of allegedly traditional colours, which after all were originally developed to blend with and adapt to the local lighting and climate conditions, rather than with brightly lit, anonymous showroom sets.

Yet while the parameters of 'historic' colours can certainly serve as a very useful guide to decorating possibilities, the genuinely historic article is almost impossible to recapture. The enormous changes in lighting technology, wall construction, paint composition and the methods of paint manufacture (it is, for example, impossible to recreate the uneven surface and texture of Georgian paints with today's consistent products) make

it extremely difficult to recapture the effect of, say, lead-based paints on poorly lit historic interiors. And there is still a lot of misleading marketing concerning the pedigree of 'heritage' colours and wall finishes. British design guru Kevin McCloud, for example, has labelled the 'Shaker' colours, so beloved of contemporary furniture and kitchen designers, 'the colours of theatrical fakery and of instant heritage'. Instead, McCloud simply exhorts us to use the right period colour 'that doesn't make your house look like a museum'.[3] He recommends brown, 'the most common colour on the planet', even though modern colour models have little place for browns ('or their murky relatives'),[4] and to many older individuals brown is still inextricably associated with the

Modern Historical: the use of Farrow and Ball's 'off white no. 3' gives this well-proportioned home a decidedly Victorian look.

middle decades of the twentieth century.

Today, the benefits and perils of globalisation affect the suppliers for average interiors just as much as other areas of everyday life. In Britain in the mid-1980s, at the apex of Margaret Thatcher's Tory revolution, the once-proud descendants of Morris & Company and Wallpaper Manufacturers Limited were sold to American buyers. In 1992 Habitat was bought by a Dutch corporation; six years later, as we have seen, Laura Ashley was purchased by a South-east Asian concern. By 2000 the tide had turned only in terms of branding imagery, as numerous multinationals all over the world pretended to be regional or historical concerns, clothing their products in formerly discarded brand names or fabricated heritage.

Interior design is now big business. Even international fashion retail chain Zara has entered the home furnishing market. This does not, of course, necessarily mean more choice: as Adrian Forty has noted, 'However much people may wish to pursue an entirely original treatment in their interiors, they invariably find themselves constrained by the market'.[5]

Thankfully, the modern-day homeowner has been made far more aware of green issues than was the case even twenty years ago. Ecological interest in interior design is not new, and can theoretically be traced back at least to Stewart Brand's *Whole Earth Catalogue* of 1968. Green design emerged in Germany in the 1970s, while the 1990s saw a rise in interest in recyclable and sustainable interiors. In 1989 Habitat stopped selling furniture made from tropical hardwoods; other furniture retailers soon followed suit, with the IKEA chain boasting that it used only environmentally friendly materials throughout.

As global warming becomes increasingly apparent, the alarm bells have begun to ring for our home environment. By 2000 even relatively modest homes were becoming increasingly reliant on artificial lighting and heating, air conditioning and unsustainable building materials. It is obvious that we cannot continue to persist with the same lifestyles that we have enjoyed since the days of cheap, seemingly inexhaustible energy. But in many ways the problem we are faced with is merely the same paradox that interior designers, architects and householders have been grappling with since the industrial revolution came to maturity: how to reinterpret and harness machine-made goods in a way that benefits the individual – attaining our goals of comfort, convenience and display – without irrevocably damaging the planet.

Modernism conquered the planet after 1945 by using expensive, energy-hungry air-conditioning and heating systems to create glass-and-steel boxes which were able to blithely ignore the world's vastly disparate climates. With fossil fuels disappearing, this will simply not be possible in the medium-term future. In which case we need to look to new ways – or possibly adapt and update traditional methods – of constructing homes that are light on embodied energy and finite resources but heavy on comfort and expediency.

Towards the Eco House: the front cover of ZARA's home catalogue for autumn/winter 2007. Ecological concerns have now reached the average home.

Opposite and below.
BedZed (Beddington Zero
Energy Development)
at Wallington, Surrey,
completed in 2002 by
Bill Dunster Architects for
the Peabody Trust. This
was at the time the UK's
largest carbon-neutral
eco-community, and
indeed the first of its kind
in this country. It included
provision for solar
power, reduced energy
consumption and the
recycling of waste water.

At the same time, we also need to remind ourselves that our homes are not infinitely capable of change. While, for example, the issue of heat loss has rightly won considerable attention from governments across the world – although a 2006 survey found that Victorian and even Tudor interiors were far more efficient at retaining heat than those built since 1945[6] – relatively little notice has been paid to the vast increase in moisture levels in the average post-war home, caused by the provision of more (and bigger) bathrooms, more showering and the increased use of kettles, and by the disappearance of the chimneypiece and the effective sealing of windows and door openings. There is no longer the healthy throughflow of air that existed when homes had active fires and sash or casement windows. Moisture has, therefore, nowhere to go, and the result is serious internal damp and structural decay.

Green design is now becoming accepted as a necessary, indeed unavoidable, prerequisite even of mass-produced interiors. The need to employ sustainable and recyclable materials, constructional and decorative elements of a low embodied energy, and to maximise natural light, integrate airflow, embrace rain harvesting, prioritise heat retention and incorporate locally produced renewable power sources are issues which are beginning to dominate the agendas of housebuilders, interior designers and homeowners alike.

Left and opposite. The Way Ahead? Marty Häuser's eclectic, practical and ecologically friendly Ruedlinger House in St Gallen, Switzerland. The timber is sustainably sourced and the (prefabricated) house incorporates thermal insulation and rainwater collection, to help operate the utilities.

Our goal over the next few decades must be to reconcile pressing ecological imperatives with the continuing quest for interiors which are attractive, comfortable, aesthetically pleasing and, crucially, fun and consistently enjoyable, yet appropriately utilitarian and technologically responsive – a mission which design historian Penny Sparke has calmly characterised as the search for 'a more human, more comfortable approach to decorating [our] private spaces'.[7] We must exploit the benefits of mass-production, and not be cowed by them or, even less helpfully, dismiss them out of hand. The interplay of craftsmanship and industry has provided us with the ability to make choices; we just need the confidence to do it our way.

1. Peter Lizon, 'Bentwood', in Joanna Banham (ed.), *Encyclopaedia of Interior Design* (1997), vol. 1, 132. **2.** Stephen Calloway, *Twentieth Century Decoration* (1988), 360. **3.** Kevin McCloud, *Choosing Colours* (2003), 18. **4.** Ibid., 33; Kevin McCloud, *The Complete Decorator* (1996), 256. **5.** Adrian Forty, *Objects of Desire* (1986), 118. **6.** British Gas survey, October 2006. The widely reported study found that, in leakage per hour, square metre of floorspace and cubic metre of gas, Tudor and Victorian houses scored 10.1, 1960s homes 15.1, the 1980s between 12 and 40.1, and 1990s houses between 12 and 23.6. The poor showing of post-war buildings was attributed to poor materials and poor workmanship offsetting tighter modern building regulations. **7.** Penny Sparke, *Elsie de Wolfe* (2005), 23.

Anscombe, Isabelle, *A Woman's Touch: Women in Design from 1860 to the Present Day* (Virago, 1984)

Ayres, James, *Domestic Interiors – The British Tradition 1500–1850* (Yale University Press, 2003)

Ball, Victoria Kloss, *Architecture and Interior Design* (John Wiley, 1980)

Banham, Joanna (ed.), *The Encyclopaedia of Interior Design* (Fitzroy Dearborn, 1997)

Banham, Joanna, Sally Porter and Julia McDonald, *Victorian Interior Design* (Cassell, 1990)

Beard, Geoffrey, *The National Trust Book of the English House Interior – Craftsmen and Interior Decoration in England 1660–1820* (John Bartholomew, 1981)

Birren, Faber, *Colour for Interiors* (Whitney [1963])

Blakemore, Robbie C., *A History of Interior Design and Furniture* (Van Nostrand Reinhold, 1997)

Bristow, Ian, *Architectural Colour in British Interiors 1615–1840* (Yale University Press for the Paul Mellon Centre, 1996)

Bristow, Ian, *Interior House-Painting Colours and Technology 1615–1840* (Yale University Press for the Paul Mellon Centre, 1996)

Bony, Anne, *Furniture and Interiors of the 1940s* (Flammarion, 2003)

Boydell, Christine, *The Architect of Floors* (Schoeser, 1996)

Calloway, Stephen, *Twentieth-Century Decoration* (Rizzoli, 1988)

Calloway, Stephen (ed.), *The Elements of Style* (Mitchell Beazley, 1996)

Clabburn, Pamela, *The National Trust Book of Furnishing Textiles* (Viking, 1988)

Cooper, Jeremy, *Victorian and Edwardian Furniture and Interiors* (Thames & Hudson, 1987)

Cornforth, John, *Early Georgian Interiors* (Yale University Press for the Paul Mellon Centre, 2005)

The Crystal Palace Exhibition Illustrated Catalogue (The Art-Journal, 1851; reprinted Dover, 1970)

Eastlake, Charles, *Hints on Household Taste* (Longmans, Green & Co, 1868; reprinted Dover, 1969)

Entwisle, E. A., *The Book of Wallpaper* (Kingsmead, 1970)

Fairclough, Oliver, and Emmeline Leary, *Textiles by William Morris and Morris and Co 1861–1940* (Thames & Hudson, 1981)

Fehrman, Cherie and Kenneth, *Postwar Interior Design 1945–60* (Van Nostrand Reinhold, 1987)

Forty, Adrian, *Objects of Desire* (Thames & Hudson, 1986)

Gere, Charlotte, *Nineteenth-Century Decoration* (Weidenfeld & Nicolson, 1989)

Gere, Charlotte, with Lesley Hoskins, *The House Beautiful* (Lund Humphries, 2000)

Girouard, Mark, *Sweetness and Light* (Oxford University Press, 1990)

Goodnow, Ruby Ross, *The Honest House* (The Century Company, 1914)

Greenhalgh, Paul, *Ephemeral Vistas* (Manchester University Press, 1988)

Hoskins, Lesley (ed.), *The Papered Wall* (Thames & Hudson, 1994)

Hughes, Helen (ed.), *John Fowler – The Invention of the Country House Style* (Donhead, 2005)

Jackson, Lesley, *Contemporary* (Phaidon, 1994)

Jacobsen, Dawn, *Chinoiserie* (Phaidon, 1993)

Jennings, Jan, and Herbert Gottfried, *American Vernacular Interior Architecture 1870–1940* (Iowa University Press, 1993)

Jervis, Simon, *High Victorian Decoration* (Boydell Press, 1983)

Jones, Chester, *Colefax and Fowler* (Barrie & Jenkins, 1989)

Jones, Owen, *The Grammar of Ornament* (Day & Son, 1856; reprinted Dorling Kindersley, 2001)

Long, Helen, *The Edwardian House* (Manchester University Press, 1993)

Massey, Anne, *Interior Design of the Twentieth Century* (Thames & Hudson, 1990)

Mayhew, Edgar de N., and Minor Mayers, *A Documentary History of American Interiors* (Charles Scribner's Sons, 1980)

McCloud, Kevin, *Choosing Colours* (Quadrille, 2003)

McCloud, Kevin, *The Complete Decorator* (Ebury Press, 1996)

McCorquodale, Charles, *The History of Interior Decoration* (Phaidon, 1983)

McFadden, D.E. (ed.), *Scandinavian Modern Design 1880–1980* (Abrams, 1983)

McKellar, Susie, and Penny Sparke (eds.), *Interior Design and Identity* (Manchester University Press, 2004)

Menz, Christopher, *Morris and Co* (Art Gallery of S. Australia, [2003])

Montgomery, Florence, *Printed Textiles: English and American Cottons and Linens 1700–1850* (Viking, 1970)

Moss, Roger, *Lighting for Historic Buildings* (The Preservation Press, 1988)

Moss, Roger, *Paint in America: The Colors of Historic Buildings* (The Preservation Press/John Wiley, 1994)

Muthesius, Hermann, *The English House* (Berlin, 1904–5; trans. and repr. BSP, 1987)

Newton, Charles, *Victorian Designs for the Home* (V&A Publications, 1999)

Nylander, Jane C., *Fabrics for Historic Buildings* (The Preservation Press, 1990)

Nylander, Richard C., *Wallpapers for Historic Buildings* (The Preservation Press, 1992)

Oliver, Paul, Ian Davis and Ian Bentley, *Dunroamin* (Pimlico, 1994)

Peirce, Donald C., and Hope Alsway, *American Interiors* (Universe, 1975)

Phillips, Barty, *Conran and the Habitat Story* (Weidenfeld & Nicolson, 1984)

Pile, John F., *Colour in Interior Design* (McGraw-Hill, 1997)

Pile, John F., *A History of Interior Design* (John Wiley, 2000)

Praz, Mario, *An Illustrated History of Interior Decoration* (Thames & Hudson, 1964)

Prizeman, John, *Interiors of European Homes* (Queen Anne Press, 1970)

Rosenstiel, Helen von, and Gail Casey Winkler, *Floor Coverings for Historic Buildings* (The Preservation Press, 1988)

Ryan, Deborah, *The Ideal Home through the Twentieth Century* (Hazar, 1997)

Saumarez Smith, Charles, *Eighteenth Century Decoration* (Weidenfeld & Nicolson, 1993)

Saumarez Smith, Charles, *The Rise of Design* (Pimlico, 2000)

Savage, George, *A Concise History of Interior Decoration* (Thames & Hudson, 1966)

Schoeser, Mary, and Celia Rufey, *English and American Textiles from 1790 to the Present* (Thames & Hudson, 1989)

Service, Alastair, *Edwardian Interiors* (Barrie & Jenkins, 1982)

Smith, Ray C., *Interior Design in Twentieth Century America* (Harper & Row, 1987)

Sparke, Penny, *As Long As It's Pink – The Sexual Politics of Taste* (HarperCollins, 1995)

Sparke, Penny, *Elsie de Wolfe* (Abrams, 2005)

Sparke, Penny, *An Introduction to Design and Culture* (2nd edn, Routledge, 2004)

Sparke, Penny, *Italian Design* (Thames & Hudson, 1988)

Sparke, Penny (ed.), *Did Britain Make It? British Design in Context 1946–86* (The Design Council, 1986)

Sparke, Penny, and Brenda Martin, *Women's Places* (Routledge, 2002)

Tate, Allen, and C. Ray Smith, *Interior Design in the Twentieth Century* (Harper & Row, 1986)

Teynac, Françoise et al., *Wallpaper – a history* (Thames & Hudson, 1982)

Thornton, Peter, *Authentic Décor* (Weidenfeld & Nicolson, 1984)

Thornton, Peter, *Form and Decoration: Innovation in the Decorative Arts* (Weidenfeld & Nicolson, 1998)

Turner, Mark, and Lesley Hoskins, *The Silver Studio of Design* (Webb & Bower, 1988)

Wharton, Edith, and Ogden Codman, *The Decoration of Houses* (1902; repr. 1978)

Whitehead, John, *The French Interior in the Eighteenth Century* (Laurence King, 1992)

Wilk, Christopher, *Marcel Breuer* (Architectural Press, 1981)

Wilk, Christopher, *Thonet: 150 Years of Furniture* (Barrons, 1980)

Wilk, Christopher (ed.), *Modernism* (V&A Publications, 2006)

Wolfe, Elsie de, *The House in Good Taste* (The Century Company, 1913)

Images in this book are reproduced for the purposes of illustrating critical discussion and review. Whilst reasonable efforts have been made to trace the copyright holders, the publisher offers to rectify any inadvertent omissions in future printings.

AKG Images (78, 81, 111, 182b, 188, 195); AKG Images/Bildarchiv Monheim (62, 108); AKG Images/Kunstsammlungen Böttcherst (50t); AKG Images/Archives CDA/St-Genès (79, 276); photo AKG Images/CDA/Guillemot [© ADAGP, Paris and DACS, London 2007] (246); AKG Images/Electa (61); AKG Images/Erich Lessing (59, 95, 147); AKG Images/Cordia Schlegelmilc (109); AKG Images/Straube (261, 265)

The American Museum in Britain (Bath, UK) (25l, 40t, 40b)

By kind permission of Laura Ashley Ltd (274b, 275b)

© BBC Photo Library (263)

Bildarchiv Monheim (2, 48, 50b, 52)

Bridgeman Art Library, London (193); Private Collection/Bridgeman Art Library, London (57, 92, 135); Private Collection/Archives Charmet/Bridgeman Art Library, London (245); Brooklyn Museum of Art/Bridgeman Art Library, London (39); Private Collection, The Stapleton Collection/Bridgeman Art Library, London (199t)

Brunschwig & Fils, Inc. (273, 275t)

© Richard Bryant/ARCAID (70, 72, 85, 171, 232, 256, 278r); photo © Richard Bryant/ARCAID [© DACS 2007] (180)

Martin Charles (6, 23, 25r, 30, 33, 36, 41, 42, 66, 152, 154, 183)

Chicago Historical Museum (129b)

© Langdon Clay/ESTO/VIEW (71t)

Colefax & Fowler (270, 272)

© Peter Cook/VIEW (284); photo ©Peter Cook/VIEW [© FLC/ADAGP, Paris and DACS, London 2007] (214t)

© Stéphane Couturier/ARTEDIA/VIEW (287t)

© Crown copyright: NMR (17b)

© Richard Davies (287b)

© Richard Einzig/ARCAID (259t)

Mary Evans Picture Library (16, 17t, 115, 117, 119t, 120, 128b, 162t, 167, 173, 192b, 204, 208, 209, 222b, 228b, 229, 233, 234); Mary Evans Picture Library [© ADAGP, Paris and DACS, London 2007] (222t); Mary Evans Picture Library/Weimar Archive (202)

© Farrow & Ball (278l, 291)

Getty Images/Bridgeman Art Library (29)

© Dennis Gilbert/VIEW (13, 295)

© GuyHervais.com (281)

© Copyright Habitat Ltd (267)

Courtesy Marty Häuser, St Gallen, Switzerland (296, 297)

Photo © Karin Hessmann/ARTUR/VIEW [© DACS 2007] (206, 214b)

Courtesy of Historic New England (7, 89, 101t, 177, 191t)

The Historical Society of Pennsylvania/Centennial Collection (127)

© Angelo Hornak Photo Library (38, 44, 68, 71b, 73, 225)

Courtesy of Inditex (293)

© Copyright Inter IKEA Systems B.V (1, 251, 283)

Courtesy Ian Bavington Jones (67, 166)

Knoll, Inc. (286, 288tl, 288tr)

Photo © Reiner Lautwein/ARTUR/VIEW [© DACS 2007] (176)

© Di Lewis/Red Cover (274t)

© Liberty Plc (161, 240)

© John Edward Linden/ARCAID (254t)

By kind permission of LINLEY (279)

© Raf Makda/VIEW (285l, 294)

Museum of London, Picture Library (228t, 259b)

National Trust Photographic Library/Dennis Gilbert/Bridgeman Art Library, London (258)

© NTPL/Andreas von Einsiedel (22, 24l, 26b, 51l, 160); © NTPL/Geoffrey Frosh (165); © NTPL/John Hammond (192–3t); © NTPL/Nadia Mackenzie (163, 194r); © NTPL/Ian Shaw (21); © NTPL/Rupert Truman (19)

Pallant House Gallery, Chichester, UK (24r, 27)

© Derek Parker/Merchant's House, Marlborough, Wilts (26t)

© Sabrina Rothe/ARTUR/VIEW (282)

Photo SAM, Arkitekturmuseet Archive, Stockholm (210)

Karl Shultz, The Swedish Museum of Architecture Archive, Stockholm (211)

© Deidi von Schaewen (4, 290)

Stapleton Collection, London (3tr, 3bl, 9, 15, 20t, 20b, 31, 32, 34, 35, 43, 45, 46, 49, 51t, 53t, 53b, 54t, 54b, 55, 56, 58, 63, 65, 74, 75, 76, 77, 80, 82, 83, 86, 87, 88, 90, 91t, 91b, 93t, 93b, 96, 97, 98, 99, 100, 101b, 102, 103, 104, 106, 107, 110, 112, 113, 114, 116, 118, 119b, 121, 122, 123, 124, 126, 128t, 131, 133, 134, 136, 138, 139t, 139b, 140, 141, 142, 143l, 143r, 144, 145, 148, 149, 151t, 151b, 153, 155, 156, 158, 159t, 159tr, 159bl, 159br, 160t, 162b, 164, 168, 169l, 169r, 170, 172, 175, 178, 179, 182t, 184, 185, 186, 189, 190, 191b, 194l, 196l, 196r, 197, 198t, 198b, 199b, 200 201, 203, 205, 207, 212, 213, 215t, 215b, 216l, 216r, 217l, 217r, 218, 219, 220t, 221b, 226, 230, 231, 235, 236t, 236b, 237, 238, 239, 241t, 241b, 243, 244, 247l, 247r, 248, 250t, 250b, 252, 255t, 255b, 257, 268, 269, 271); Stapleton Collection, London/Doubleday, Doran & Co. Inc. (227); photo Stapleton Collection, London [© Estate of Duncan Grant / licensed by DACS 2007] (220b)

© Ezra Stoller/ESTO (69, 254b)

© Tim Street-Porter/ESTO/VIEW (253)

Courtesy the Strictly Wood Furniture Co., USA (277)

© Tate, London 2007 (132)

Timney Fowler, Sue Timney Ltd, London, W10 5SA. Tel. +44 (0)20 8969 5000 (280)

Topfoto/Roger-Viollet Collection (129t, 181, 221t, 224)

© Albert Vecerka/ESTO/VIEW (288b)

Courtesy Venturi, Scott Brown and Associates, Inc./Rollin LaFrance (266)

Wadsworth Atheneum Museum of Art, Hartford CT., Gift of the Atlantic Refining Company (18)

Wallace Collection, London/Bridgeman Art Library, London (14)

Matt Wargo for VSBA/credit design to Venturi, Scott Brown and Associates, Inc (House in Glen Cove, Long Island NY, 1985) (285r)

Winterthur Museum & Country Estate, Delaware (47)

ACKNOWLEDGEMENTS

I would like to thank all those who were involved in the production of this book, particularly Roger Sears, the godfather of the work, with whom I have talked about this project for many years; the astonishingly efficient and always delightful Sophia Gibb; Philip and Liz de Bay of the Stapleton Collection; copy editor Annie Lee; the enviably talented David Pocknell and his design team of Christopher Bell and Will Pocknell; and our splendid project editor, Johanna Stephenson.

I would also like, once again, to thank the Director and staff of Yale University's inestimable Paul Mellon Centre for Studies in British Art, London, for their help, courtesy and consistently warm welcome.

Last, but not least, I would like to jointly dedicate this work to Professor Mowl and Dr Stewart, whose help, advice and support over the years have been inspirational and invaluable.

Dr Steven Parissien
Oxford, 2007

Published in 2009 by
Laurence King Publishing Ltd
361–373 City Road
London EC1V 1LR
Tel: +44 (0)20 7841 6900
Fax: +44 (0)20 7841 6910
e-mail: enquiries@laurenceking.co.uk

Text © Steven Parissien 2009

This book was produced by
Laurence King Publishing Ltd

A catalogue record for this book is available from the British Library.

ISBN-13 : 978-1-85669-538-1

Design: Pocknell Studio
Editorial project management: Johanna Stephenson
Picture research: Sophia Gibb

Printed in China

Page 1: The IKEA Årstic table lamp, 2007
Page 2: Bedroom at Château de Talcy, France
Page 3: Chandelier designed by Le Bouteiller, 1830s (above); chair designed by Marcel Breuer for Isokon of London, 1936 (below)
Page 4: House interior in San Sebastian designed by Andrée Putman

DATE			